T0320314

# CRITICAL PERSPECTIVES ON
# RURAL CHANGE

Volume 4

# LABOUR AND LOCALITY

# LABOUR AND LOCALITY

## Uneven Development and the Rural Labour Process

Edited by
**TERRY MARSDEN,**
**PHILIP LOWE**
**AND**
**SARAH WHATMORE**

Routledge
Taylor & Francis Group

LONDON AND NEW YORK

First published in 1992 by David Fulton Publishers Ltd.

This edition first published in 2023
by Routledge
4 Park Square, Milton Park, Abingdon, Oxon OX14 4RN

and by Routledge
605 Third Avenue, New York, NY 10158

*Routledge is an imprint of the Taylor & Francis Group, an informa business*

*British Library Cataloguing in Publication Data*
A catalogue record for this book is available from the British Library

ISBN: 978-1-032-49781-5 (Set)
ISBN: 978-1-032-49619-1 (Volume 4) (hbk)
ISBN: 978-1-032-49704-4 (Volume 4) (pbk)
ISBN: 978-1-003-39508-9 (Volume 4) (ebk)

DOI: 10.4324/9781003395089

**Publisher's Note**
The publisher has gone to great lengths to ensure the quality of this reprint but points out that some imperfections in the original copies may be apparent.

**Disclaimer**
The publisher has made every effort to trace copyright holders and would welcome correspondence from those they have been unable to trace.

CRITICAL PERSPECTIVES
☐☐☐☐ ON ☐☐☐☐
RURAL CHANGE SERIES

# LABOUR AND LOCALITY

## UNEVEN DEVELOPMENT AND THE RURAL LABOUR PROCESS

EDITED BY

TERRY MARSDEN
PHILIP LOWE
SARAH WHATMORE

**David Fulton Publishers**
London

David Fulton Publishers Ltd
2 Barbon Close, London WC1N 3JX

First published in Great Britain by
David Fulton Publishers, 1992

Note: The right of the authors to be identified as the authors of this work has
been asserted by them in accordance with the Copyright, Designs and Patents Act
1988.

Copyright © David Fulton Publishers Ltd

*British Library Cataloguing in Publication Data*

A catalogue record for this book is available from the British Library

ISBN 1-85346-182-2

Typeset by Chapterhouse, Formby L37 3PX
Printed in Great Britain by Biddles Ltd., Guildford.

# Contents

# Contributors

Reidar Almås     Centre for Rural Research
The University of Trondheim
N-7055 Dragvoll
Norway

Miren Etxezarreta   Departament d'Economia Aplicada
Edifici B
Universitat Autonoma de Barcelona
08193 Bellaterra (Barcelona) Spain

Jonathon Murdoch   Rural Studies Research Centre
University College London
26, Bedford Way
London WC1H 0AP
United Kingdom

Lars Olof Persson   Expert Group on Regional and Urban Studies
(eru)
Ministry of Labour
S-103 33 Stockholm
Sweden

Max Pfeffer     Cook College
Department of Human Ecology
The State University of New Jersey,
RUTGERS
New Brunswick
New Jersey
08903 USA

Jan Douwe Van der Ploeg Department of Rural Sociology and
Development
The Agricultural University
Wageningen
The Netherlands

PREFACE

# Critical Perspectives on Rural Change Series

This series aims to promote the international dissemination and debate of current empirical and theoretical research relevant to rural areas in advanced societies. Rural areas, their residents and agencies face considerable change and uncertainty. The balance between production, consumption and conservation is being adjusted as economic activities are relocated and primary production is transformed. Similarly the values placed upon rural living and landscape are altering. Local and external political forces structure choices within rural areas, not only for those concerned with agriculture, but also with regard to rural development, general ecnomic and social policy, and regional fiscal arrangements. To understand contemporary rural change, therefore, demands a critical and holistic perspective able to transcend traditional disciplinary boundaries and to encompass different spatial and institutional levels of analysis. The series is intended to contribute to the development of such a perspective, and the volumes are designed to attract a wide audience associated with international comparative research. Each provides a review of current research within its subject.

Terry Marsden
Philip Lowe
Sarah Whatmore
Hull 1992

INTRODUCTION

# Labour and Locality: Emerging Research Issues

*Terry Marsden, Philip Lowe and Sarah Whatmore*

## Introduction

In previous volumes of the series we have assembled theoretical and empirical analyses linking international processes of restructuring to the more locally specific nature of rural and agrarian change. The focus upon rural society and space provides a perspective on wider processes of change. In most advanced economies in the late twentieth century the notions, ideologies and actions shaping rural areas are central to the direction of national development and to the maintenance of social cohesion within and between regions (see European Commission, 1991a, b). Rural change whilst distinctive, is also variably integrated into the current political and economic tendencies governing nation-state development.

The nature of both the levels of integration *and* distinctiveness apparent in rural society are particularly expressed when we consider labour processes. Researchers have tended to characterise rural and particularly agricultural labour as highly exploitable, more deferential, less collectivised and unionised and more 'flexible' than its urban and industrial counterparts. The changing demands of an essentially urban conditioned agribusiness and food industry, and a heightened capitalistic sensitivity to the identification of cheap and flexible labour pools, are now tending both to transform distinctive rural labour processes and to integrate them more directly into the vagaries of national and international competition and trade.

The growing literature on rural labour suggests new sets of problems and possibilities. There has been the progressive diminution and casualisation of hired agricultural labour; and the growing dependence of the family farmers and workers who remain on the continual adoption of externally generated technologies, all designed to reduce to a minimum the very social conditions and work practices that historically farming has reproduced. Overlaying these tendencies, the uneven urban–rural shift in manufacturing and services has provided a higher level of diversified employment for some rural areas (Cheshire and Hay, 1989). Here the waning agrarian deferential 'dialectic' rubs shoulder with new entrepreneurial and professional labour which is spatially and socially mobile and expresses novel demands and cultures in rural localities.

Contemporary analyses of rural labour suggest significant and indeed, developing levels of employment insecurity, poor working conditions, high levels of exploitation and inadequate social infrastructure. Indeed, in a highly mobile international framework, both the potentially lower unit costs of rural labour and its perceived hard working qualities are suggested as powerful influences on the rural relocation of manufacturing and service industries (see Summers *et al.*, 1990). Moreover, more desirable rural living conditions, together with firms' attempts to reduce their fixed labour costs, are beginning to evolve a variety of forms of home working – the new putting out system – in some rural localities in North America and Europe, involving not only assembly work but also the so-called 'out sourcing' of professional and administrative services (see Pennington and Westover, 1989; Gringeri, 1990). Although there may be novel features in these practices – for example, the extensive use of telecommunications – they reproduce many of the traditional employment relationships of the rural artisan; including the nominal freedom of being freelance and some discretion in the organisation of work. This is set, though, in the wider context of intensive exploitation and dependency. Indeed, similar relationships prevail in much of modern farming (Hall, 1990). The equivalence of these separate labour processes suggests that rural deprivation is unlikely to disappear, but will adopt novel forms in new contexts, and still be compounded by problems of physical isolation and remoteness (Falk and Lyson, 1990; Summers *et al.*, 1990; Freshwater and Ehrenschaft, 1990; Etxezarreta, Chapter 2 in this volume). Whilst then, in aggregate terms, many rural areas have experienced economic buoyancy over the last decade, leading some commentators to speak enthusiastically of a 'rural renaissance', many of the labour processes contained in these areas are now more dependent and vulnerable, particularly given the greater volatility of the more deregulated economies and markets to which they are more closely bound.

The search for ever more flexible labour and working conditions is a key factor behind industrial decentralisation but is also associated with technical changes and a restructuring of capital. The strategies of the more highly mobile and innovative multi-plant enterprises often rely on the use of both low-skilled local workers and exogenous expertise. Industrial firms in developed countries must search for new ways to compete with the low wage sectors and corridors in the Third World. The intense pressure to reduce labour costs, and to create and exploit new markets, has led to an increase in informal and casualised economic activity. Piore and Sabel (1984) argue that 'flexible specialisation' is an important aid to industrial capital productivity and is thus shaping international economic competition. Under these social conditions, workers have to adapt rapidly to constant innovation. The existence of a 'flexible', multi-skilled as well as unskilled labour force, and the particular social conditions that can stimulate these, can give an industry the ability to adjust to the frequent changes required by small batch production and rapid shifts in consumer demand without the need for extensive recruitment and retraining. The benefits of any increased skills and autonomy that may result are likely to affect only a small minority of white-collar workers, with the workforce as a whole experiencing segmentation, and a larger proportion of blue-collar workers entering down-graded, deskilled jobs in a secondary labour sector. There is some evidence to suggest that such dualistic labour processes may be more pronounced in rural areas, but both the causes for this and its policy relevance have yet to be fully assessed (see Errington, 1990). New technologies allow some workers to accumulate greater skill but require of others a deskilling. This disaggregates the labour process into basic components that can be dispersed amongst a variety of types of worker (e.g. part-time female, homeworkers, full-time male, pluriactive workers). As a result, the production process can gain both a spatial mobility and increased dispersion, at the same time atomising and making the workforce more dependent. Thus, even in the most advanced economies, this makes rural local areas increasingly vulnerable targets for rapid change in the supply, demand, quality and social organisation of work. Alongside the growth of casual employment, the effect is to give a new twist to the old notion of rural areas as labour reserves.

Many writers point to the low levels of unionisation as being an important factor in attracting new high-tech and service industries to rural areas (Sassen-Koob, 1986). Also the development of informal and casual working practices can be a way of reducing production costs associated with taxation, social insurance and the maintenance of health and safety standards (Pahl, 1984). Studies in the contrasting contexts of Less Developed Countries (LDCs) and North America (Fernandez and Kelly, 1983; Castells and Portes, 1986) have identified important economic and social consequences of the trends towards increased flexible specialisation and informal employment, including decentralisation of the workforce and of production, increased capital productivity, decreased labour costs, and a diffusion of firms' economic and political risks. It may also diversify the nature of labour demand, attracting former domestic labour (Little, 1990). Whilst often bringing a welcome diversity to the employment opportunities within particular localities, this fragmentation of labour contributes to the growth of contracting and sub-contracting, and tends to undermine the social cohesion and rights of full-time workers.

In this introduction to the volume we wish to set out a number of key issues currently treated rather separately, but which together begin to provide a framework for the critical and comparative study of rural labour processes. These debates need to go beyond the perceived success, failure or sustainability of the varied labour processes themselves. The contributors to the volume depart considerably from traditional studies of rural labour in several respects. First, whilst the tendency amongst researchers has been to delineate rural labour categories according to either sector or type (largely due to the constraints associated with the official statistical definitions), the contributors here draw on a range of empirical evidence to convey the integrative, if diverse, nature of rural labour processes, exploring how workers themselves make sense of and attempt to orchestrate the often competing labour demands they face. Implicit here is the point that, with the end of the Fordist period, we are witnessing a return to the organising of work around more pluriactive rather than Taylorist conditions (see Friedland and Pugliese, 1989; Fuller, 1991). Thus the material conditions of work embody new sets of time and space relationships. It also confers different degrees of control/dependency upon workers in their different *working contexts*. These processes extend beyond agricultural diversification to a whole range of rural activities associated with the production and consumption of rural-based resources. The 'post-Fordist' stage of economic reorganisation is not, therefore, leaving rural work untouched. Rather, it is rendering many of the conventional categories and boundaries of rural labour redundant, with an increasing emphasis upon flexible time and activity patterns; more casual and freelance work; more varied leisure patterns; an erosion of the separateness of domestic and formal labour; and variable 'hire and fire' vulnerability.

Second, and inextricably linked to this general point, concerns a renewed focus on the *local embeddedness* of labour processes. We are now beginning to identify not such mechanistically driven spatial *divisions* of labour (Massey, 1984) in and across rural regions, but rather revised ways in which the locality (as social space) succinctly impinges on and *combines labour processes* (see Persson, Chapter 3). Rural work, we would contend, whether in the field or the factory, is now becoming more locally differentiated, and this is coming about through external pressures and changing local conditions. The nature of local and regional working practices can contribute to both industrial and local identities and thus can reinforce elements of particular social change or continuity (see Villa and Almås, Chapter 5; Smith, Chapter 6; Murdoch, Chapter 7). Moreover, sets of local social conditions (as we shall see from the contributions) can give rural workers *action space* or room for manoeuvre within which local strategies and styles of social action can emerge, compete with each other, and be sustained.

Of course, local and regional conditions have always played a role, albeit a largely unrecognised one. But now we can identify significant changes in the spatial requirements and sensitivity of the productive forces that exploit rural labour which run counter to the processes of concentration and specialisation. First, we are now seeing a decline in the uniform policies supporting agricultural intensification, allowing for greater rural diversification, and spatial differentiation (from below, as well as from above). Both food-based and other manufacturing and service-oriented firms are also becoming more highly sensitised and specific about where and under what social conditions they wish to introduce and sustain production. In addition, the growth of consumption functions in many rural areas – such as residence, recreation, tourism – is acting to heighten new local economic developments (e.g. small businesses, craft working, niche markets). This is further breaking down the seeming uniformity of previous rural markets and their 'horizontal support measures' (see Persson, Chapter 3). These trends do not deny the significance of other processes, either new or reconstructed, that are transcendant (e.g. see below concerning neo-conservatism); nevertheless they do provide for new sets of relationships which combine local and labour identities and in more aggregate terms, *rural cultures*.

Probably the clearest illustration of the pivotal links emerging between labour and locality stems from the sociology of development debates concerning the processes of differential commoditisation (see Van der Ploeg, 1990; Marsden, 1991). Whilst it is now generally accepted that unilinear assumptions concerning capitalist rural development are mistaken, it is also clear that there is a local dimension to the social and economic construction of both use and exchange (market) values. Indeed, they arise out of the combinations of labour and local conditions. Thus the rural labour process is crucial in continuously re-defining both its own use and exchange value, and those conferred on the *objects* of that labour. For instance, the local craft production of wooden chairs or glassware may serve a national and international commoditised market, but consumer demand is initiated and reinforced by the fact that the produce derives from local labour processes based on a whole range of historically derived use values. In a consumption-oriented age, consumers are increasingly attracted by locally derived *and worked* products.

As a result many of the corporate interests procuring, processing and providing these marketised goods need to continuously reconstruct their *localness*. The products now explicitly need to reflect the application of local labour and skills. In this sense we can now begin to see parallels and complementarities between both *niche* and *mass* market production. Supermarket chains have to increasingly identify that their fresh fruit and vegetables are grown *somewhere* by *some* people. Locally oriented niche production no longer contradicts internationalised mass processing and consumption. As a result, the local distinctiveness of labour processes based on the production of locally derived products (for either niche or mass markets) becomes more significant to the broader processes of uneven capitalist development. Whilst, for corporate capital, the localness of labour and production takes on new meaning; in turn, for rural workers, the continual reconstruction of the use and exchange values of local labour may tend to secure or underline the sustainability of the combinations of economic activities occurring in their localities.

There are obviously considerable temporal and spatial lags built into these emerging tendencies. The maintenance of a state-supported technologically intensive food system has done a considerable amount to reduce, rather than enhance, the attachment of labour to particular places, regulating labour mobility and the progressive casualisation of the workforce (Van der Ploeg,

Chapter 1; Etxezarreta, Chapter 2). Technological developments can overcome the obstacles and differentiation of space, routinise and compartmentalise the numerically reduced workforce, and produce significant supply gaps of trained personnel. In these processes, locality becomes something of a residual factor along with human labour itself. Capital penetration attempts to relegate and transform locality, land and labour. We need to appreciate, therefore, that there are divergent and lagged processes operating in the rural areas of advanced societies. The vertical links emphasised by integration into national and international commodity systems collide and cross cut the horizontal links generated by diversification within the local and regional economy. These competing tendencies raise particular questions as to how we should theorise and investigate the labour process. The contributions here are examples of ongoing research undertaking this task from a variety of different and emergent theoretical stances.

**Deregulating labour: dependent rural space, dependent rural labour**

Of critical significance to the well-being of rural areas are the revised methods by which states regulate labour. This is a key factor determining the quality and diversity of rural labour processes. The mass production–consumption model was predicated on a Keynesian mode of state regulation variably designed to protect collectivised rights of workers and to promote public programmes so as to maintain the quantity of jobs, political legitimacy and security of work. A version of this model was applied to rural society, first through the development of the archetypical agricultural and regional support programmes developed both nationally and internationally across the advanced economies. Second, there developed a policy concern for the protection of the distinctiveness and maintenance of rural life. The policy objective of equalising farm and industrial wages was a central pillar of this mode of rural regulation of employment and work, universally adopted but never achieved. It pervaded most policy discourse until the 1980s (von Meyer, 1990).

As most of the chapters in this volume illuminate, the breakup of these models of state regulation is having a pervasive and uneven influence on the conditions and organisation of labour in rural areas. In many nation states (most notably US, UK, Canada, Spain) the rise of neo-conservative ideology has been particularly targeted towards the deregulation of labour, promoting more flexibility and a reduction in collectivised rights. This has been encompassed by specific rural policies that stress the deregulated growth of rural small businesses, freedom from planning controls, decentralised decision making, long distance commuting and speculative development. Under this approach rural areas and rural work represent a potential opportunity for entrepreneurial and corporate capital (Boucher *et al.*, 1991). Rural resources, including labour, need only to be unlocked from their previous ossified regulatory structures in order to generate new incomes and profits. We can see here a close parallel between the neo-conservative ideology and the growing corporate interest in selecting particular rural locations to site new plants. Rural areas need unlocking from their bucolic and cushioned agrarian past. Both through a macro-oriented policy of removing labour legislation, and through the construction of specific rural-based marketised policies, rural labour has been confronted with a transformation in conditions. Under these auspices rural areas represent sociological 'greenfields' conveniently socially apart from the urban industrial conflict. Such notions have (as Persson, Chapter 3 identifies) coincided with increased urban and exurban mobility. Under this ideology the European agricultural common market – the prototype transnational and structural compromise – is an embarrassing legacy, the reform of which is an urgent matter.

Within Europe, for instance, this political ideology has gained considerable ground, being assisted by the twin negatives of increasing surpluses and environmental costs of CAP, on the one hand, and the broader fiscal and budgetary crises of particular nation-states on the other. In addition, reducing the barriers of either commodity-based or labour-based protectionism meant a logical withdrawal of support from both regional and rural development. Rural or regional imbalances, either in the quality of labour or in the production of goods, were inevitably a frictional consequence of capitalist development, encouraged rather than ameliorated by Keynesian state intervention. A consequence of this was to assume an increased need for the mobility of labour and capital, bringing about more 'efficient' uses and combinations of rural resources. As some of the essays indicate here, it is not clear what the full consequences of these neo-conservative perspectives are likely to be for rural labour beyond reducing the security of employment for paid employees and tending towards the increasing (international as well as national) migration of 'cheap' labour to particular employment nodes (see Etxezarreta, Chapter 2; Pfeffer, Chapter 4). They also suggest a redefinition of dependent rural and regional space, that is, a changing social and political balance between centre and peripheral areas. Both at the macro-political and economic level, and with regard to specific regional and rural policy, the tenets of neo-conservative thinking have gained considerable ground in northwestern Europe and North America. Its social effects are summarised by Reid for the rural United States. He argues:

> deregulation exposed most industries to freer competition, further subjected the rural economy to the pressures of the market place. The result has presumably been to emphasise the natural competitive disadvantage of rural location. Foreign competition, especially in manufactured goods rose during the 1980s reflecting the diminished ability of rural manufacturers to compete in world markets on the basis of low land and labour costs. As a consequence, stiff job losses occurred in heavily import-penetrated industries. The shift in labour demand toward more highly educated workers has been concentrated almost entirely in metropolitan areas, leading to a widening

urban–rural income differential and out migration of the best educated rural youth (1990, p. 125).

Nevertheless, the growing economic and political integration of much of the advanced world should not belie the considerable existence of *divergent and competing ideological strands*. Interestingly, these are becoming noticeable in the rural sphere, particularly as the post-war agricultural productivist food order begins to lose hegemony. In the UK and the US, notions of rural development and rural welfare are largely conceived of in terms of their productivist opportunities – providing a 'green' playing field where uneven labour deregulation encourages uneven inward capital investment. In this context, the abandonment or partial reform of the agricultural support systems provides a further justification for the removal of the principles of guaranteed social and regional incomes, and the attempts to ameliorate regional imbalance. The political power of images of an archaic and backward peasantry absorbing large amounts of public investment provides a powerful reinforcement to remove *other* elements of social welfare and economic planning from the rural sphere. This is expressing itself at an international political level, and whilst rarely explicitly referring to the status and position of labour, as such, this is directly implicated in the discourse.

More broadly, of course, whilst increasing integration and growing European trade reaches new levels, the considerable resistance about the social 'underwriting' of this by common worker rights and welfare infrastructure means that valuations in the cost and spatiality of labour are still likely to substantially diverge. Indeed, it is the uneven spatial *social valuation* of labour which is likely to become a major factor in the international relocation of capital and investment. For instance, as Lipietz has recently argued:

> on the one hand West Germany, the Netherlands and Northern Italy have adapted a strategy for increased competitiveness based upon the skills and 'negotiated involvement' of their workers. On the other hand, Britain, Spain, France and Southern Italy are playing the card of low wages and 'flexible' labour contracts. In these conditions, the negotiation of higher wages and for shorter working time – the counterpart of workers involvement in the first group of countries – is limited by the competition of the second group. Hence the endless battle between regions for the lowest labour cost by unit of product, resulting both in the EC's global surpluses and in high internal unemployment. (1990)

Integrated capital and product markets, not least in the corporate food sector, together with a reorientation of CAP, are thus developing upon the basis of significant social variations in the state-regulated and constructed cost and quality of labour. These variations look set to continue to act as important stimuli of uneven inward investment and competition, technological change and capital accumulation. Moreover, the ideological struggles between neo-conservatism and welfarism are likely to be fought out in the different comparative and competitive realities of the regional and local markets for labour in Europe. Hence, whilst the existence of hired labour may have been progressively numerically reduced through technological change, the particular social organisation and conferred *value* placed on existing rural workers still represents a key factor in sustaining mobile capital accumulation and investment.

Within much of mainland Europe, however, we can still identify the mainstream of a strong, if adjusted, rural welfarism founded now on the need to protect a vibrant rural sector through encouragement of diversification and non-agricultural employment. These were very much the sentiments of the debate initiated by the European Commission's *Future of Rural Society* published in 1988. Nevertheless, such positions, calling for enhanced structural and regional budgets so as to encourage both *integrated* rural development and 'increased' *indigenous* rural resource use, sit uncomfortably astride an acute contradiction constructed by the broader deregulatory raft of economic and political change. That is, how can rural welfare and development policies designed to *protect* and promote the 'development' of rural communities operate when the whole thrust of European market integration is based on the free flow of corporate capital, implying increased regional and national competition in order to exploit low labour costs? Drawing boundaries around rural regions whilst politically and socially expedient becomes economically at best illogical and at worst isolationist and unsustainable, given the penetration and growing legitimacy of neo-conservative thinking. A doubling of the EC's structural fund is likely to do little to reduce regional disparities (von Meyer, 1990). From the perspective of specific rural labour processes, the harmonisation and integration of the European and broader global economy is likely to bring forth more inter-regional conflict over capital investment rather than less, higher levels of competition between regions and sectors for skilled labour, and the likelihood of rejuvenated dualities in the labour markets between low or no-skill immobile work and high-skill mobile employment (see Etxezarreta, Chapter 2). New rounds of commoditisation are likely to become more highly differentiated as this competition is spatially and socially expressed. For instance, as agricultural markets become less regulated, food and agribusiness firms are becoming more highly sensitised to both production and consumption niches, producing new demands and opportunities for certain localities and labour. Regional, national and, indeed, internationally derived social policies (such as the EC's social charter) will be difficult to construct and implement. Even where they have been more universally applied (e.g. Scandinavia, see Persson, Chapter 3) to significantly distinctive rural regions, they are now facing crises in their legitimacy.

At a broad level these changes in the political regulation of the rural economy, taken together with the economic restructuring of the manufacturing, services and agricultural sectors suggest a renewed significance in the centrality of rural labour processes. As the contributions to this volume will illuminate, sociologically this needs to place a renewed emphasis upon the *variable and historically derived social relations of production*. These relations are now subject to somewhat diverging economic and regulatory trends both through the reorientation of sectoral and national policy and the related restructuring of the markets. As Marx suggests:

> No producer, whether industrial or agricultural when considered by himself alone, produces value or commodities. His product becomes a value and a commodity only in the context of definite social inter relations. (1974, pp. 638–9)

It is, therefore, to the very reorganisation of these social relations of production that both corporate restructuring and revised state regulation are directed. Moreover, it is increasingly through the social reorganisation of labour relations that spatial comparative advantages and disadvantages reappear in the context of higher levels of mobility and integration of capital markets. Thus, as Van der Ploeg argues:

> the social relations of production . . . are that set of specific relations that constitutes the labour and production process (i.e. giving the labour process its concrete form) and that defines the distribution of produced wealth . . . . Relations between farm enterprises, markets and market agencies shape the labour process to an important degree, either because they allow (farmers) 'freedom' to exercise control over labour objects and the means of production, or because they directly condition, prescribe and sanction the organisation of labour and production. (1990, p. 278)

It is in these ways that an emergent spatial comparative analysis of labour processes and organisation can begin. The contemporary period, through both the economic restructuring of capital and the deregulatory surges of the state, brings forth new contradictory sets of relationships between the social organisation of labour and its spatial unevenness. This is more than simply recognising the existence of differentiation (Newby, 1989).

Arguing that labour and the ways in which it is locally embedded and socially organised provides a critical set of conjunctions for the understanding of comparative rural change. More so than in the immediate post-war past, the sets of organising principles arranging labour and locality become a source for competitive spatial variation; and this conditions the degree to which rural areas are *integrated* or *peripheralised* within the international capitalist economy. In this context, changes in macro-socio-economic policy (for instance, a reduction in workers' rights) can often be much more significant in affecting labour processes than specific sectoral rural or agricultural policies. It is this realisation which is stimulating researchers to accommodate the salience of the macro economy and policy into their specific sectoral analyses (Pfeffer, Etxezarreta, Persson, this volume; Freshwater and Ehrenschaft, 1990). Cheap and deregulated rural labour regions (conjunctions of dependent labour and dependent space) increasingly *need* to be created and sustained *alongside* growth areas where labour costs are high and demand is increasing. Regional and local differentiation increasingly takes a further twist in the mobile capitalist world, such that the regional and local conditions for certain types of labour organisation can be developed and sustained. The changing sociopolitical ideologies are then further applied to society in order to legitimate these new social labour conditions.

## From labour-market areas to local labour processes

How are these concerns influencing social scientific debate and what conceptual tools do we require to deal with them? As Summers *et al.* (1990) argue, in their extensive review of rural labour market work, research conducted on rural labour traditionally fits into, first, attempts to define the labour market as referring to the social relations between buyers and sellers of labour. More effectively, second, researchers use as their focus *labour-market areas*, i.e. the localities in which the multiplicity of market relationships occur. Within any geographical area or administrative unit there may be a whole range of labour markets operating. These combine, and we would argue, are *socially organised* to produce a major structuring mechanism for the locality (see also Bradley, 1985). It is this latter definition which more appropriately, if not completely, reflects the contributions assembled in this volume. Despite a voluminous literature on the sociometric analyses of rural labour markets (particularly in North America) we suggest that insufficient attention has been paid to examining the quality of labour processes through the application of sociological concepts. In addition, and stemming from a different set of origins, one can begin to see a focus upon locality-based rural research (see Marsden and Murdoch, 1990; Labao, 1990; Fitzsimmons, 1990). This has, however, failed so far to incorporate the changing significance of labour processes within social conceptions of locality from within the rural sphere.

The contributions attempt here, taking national and local case studies, to begin to bridge this important gap between existing literatures on rural labour and locality. Local and regional working conditions represent variable exploitable social space whereby the interactions between labour and land help to construct local identities and cultures. These, in turn, will affect the likely propensity for further change and exogenous influence. Localised labour processes have the abilities to mould and reorganise national and internationalised forces of change to variable degrees. They perform an *active role* in sustaining levels of uneven economic and social development between one region and another.

The contributions vary according to their scale of analysis and perspective. The first three contributions (Van der Ploeg, Etxezarreta and Persson) take a national and international scale of analysis, identifying some of the key forces operating in the changing labour markets in advanced capitalist societies. All the contributions outline the emergence of new conceptual debates concerning the processes affecting rural labour and working practices in rural societies. Van der Ploeg starts by identifying the specific interrelations between agriculture and locality. The processes of technological development in agriculture and the food system have led to the production of a range of disconnections and dislocations between farm labour, the locality and the rest of the food system. The supranational processes leading to increasing farm capitalisation and technological adoption have tended to reduce the spatial particularity of 'locality' and space. These have been far from unilinear or uniform processes. They have led to an uneven process of disconnection. Nevertheless, revised and new localised knowledge systems are both required by agribusiness and by the emergent form of farm production, which is attempting to develop more ecologically sustainable systems. Van der Ploeg, following his earlier work, addresses the need to explore the links and contradictions here between empirical diversity and the social organisation and reorganisation of agricultural labour. This is an inherently *social process* based on the development of a range of *crafts*. These need to locally link to broader market mechanisms which are also socially organised. He brings forth empirical evidence from the Netherlands to support his theoretical propositions. Differential commoditisation leads to succinct levels of diversity becoming socially engrained in local conditions. Here, cultural conditions play a role in providing a basis for social construction and labour coordination. The pending ecological crises implicit within the productivist mode of agricultural regulation is bringing forth a renewed emphasis on the 'art de la localité', and the role of local labour as a potential force for social and political change.

The next pair of contributors, in their different ways, take up many of the themes Van der Ploeg identifies. They contrast, however, in the effects these hold due to the considerably different stages of development being experienced in the two regions under consideration; (i.e. Spain, Etxezarreta; Scandinavia, Persson). In addition, in comparing these contributions we can begin to see how the radically contrasting regulatory histories of the nation-states has impinged upon their development logics. For Etxezarreta, who identifies the key features in the transformation of the labour process in the contemporary period, the speed of technological and capital penetration is bringing forth quite radical shifts in rural labour conditions. She examines the new forms of uneven development and differentiation being established, showing how agricultural labour is becoming more highly integrated and dependent on other sectors at the local, regional and national levels. Here, the pressures to revise the productivist agricultural development model are severely limited, as are any realisable moves towards more sustainable rural diversification strategies. In particular, as with Pfeffer's chapter, we see the processes of casualisation developing alongside the increasing mobility and professionalisation of a minority group of agricultural workers. In this context it is difficult to resist some of the evolutionary developmental assumptions which so bedevilled the sociology of development throughout the 1970s. Etxezarreta turns many of Van der Ploeg's propositions about agricultural productivism into a stark empirical reality. The capitalisation of agricultural sectors and the absorption of the former north European agricultural development 'model' is producing homogenisation and convergence. Under these conditions local social control declines. Localities become socially disconnected.

Persson (Chapter 3) presents us with a more positive if somewhat vulnerable Scandinavian portrait. His analysis demonstrates the post-war welfarist and ruralist 'track' associated with rural and regional development, applied as it was, somewhat bluntly, to the vast sparsely populated areas of northern Sweden and Norway. His analysis of the position of rural labour holds both an evolutionary logic – emerging from an emphasis on the rural–urban continuum, through specifically spatially defined rural labour markets, to the realisation of what he terms the *arena society*. These development models played a tangible role in the derivation and implementation of regional and rural policy in Sweden after the war. More recently, with increased levels of mobility experienced by many, particularly in the more 'urbanised rural areas'; and the growing expectation by rural residents for a diversity of rural goods and services, higher levels of local distinctiveness and exploitation of rural resources are now apparent. Rural labour markets are shown to have disproportionately benefited (often unintentionally) from general national welfare and social programmes, rather than as a result of the more direct regional and rural forms of policy. This is of particular concern given the deregulatory perspectives held by the current national government and the more 'individualist' values expressed by a growing proportion of rural residents. Whilst the 'arena' society advances then, it brings with it a range of contradictions which even the more neo-conservative sections of the national polity have difficulty in overcoming. 'Post-materialism' runs parallel with reductions in the universality of policies which had previously increased the quality of labour markets through education and training. Whilst fewer households are dependent on the traditional staple rural resources, they make new demands in a more segmental and detached way (see also Mormont, 1990). As a consequence, the traditional functions of local labour markets are losing their significance just at the time that state planning and policy based on collectivism and solidarity is shedding ideological support. Persson's contribution analyses how these parallel sociopolitical trends are affecting rural labour.

Whilst the first three chapters are written from different national experiences and vantage points, they also set a broad conceptual context for the remaining contributions. Van der Ploeg and Etxezarreta concentrate their attentions mainly on the commoditisation and transformation of agricultural labour; Persson points to the non-agrarian, and indeed, non-rural policies as a key to the contemporary development of rural areas. The following four contributions have been selected to exhibit current theoretically informed empirical case studies. In doing so they also apply a range of theoretical tools in focusing on labour processes. As with the first three, they outline a range of national regulatory contexts and focus upon the ways workers' conditions of existence and reproduction are locally and regionally embedded; sometimes in spite of, and sometimes because of, the more internationalised global interconnections and processes.

The position of rural labour under the more deregulated context of the United States, is currently the subject of considerable attention. Pfeffer conducts a dynamic analysis of the incorporation of Cambodian migrants into day-haul work on the fringes of Philadelphia. He pays particular attention to the ways in which both the increased levels of poverty experienced by inner-city blacks and Cambodians resulting from the decline of manufacturing, intersected with the Reagan administration's placing of both restrictions on earnings of women receiving welfare aid to families with dependent children; and the process of formalisation through registration of migrant and seasonal workers (that is, the Migrant and Seasonal Agricultural Worker Protection Act (MSPA) 1983). Pfeffer demonstrates how the class differentiation of the incoming migrants influences the social reconstitution of this ethnic group once it is absorbed into the inner urban residential and rural labour context. Some of the more educated and entrepreneurial Cambodians have experienced social mobility, such that they can act as 'social buffers', providing labour market access to other Cambodians with fewer skills. Structural changes in the urban economy and the class-based, as opposed to culturally based, social differences are relevant in understanding the nature of these multi-ethnic labour market changes. This supports Wilson's (1987) claims concerning the remaking of America's underclass through economic restructuring and class recomposition of inner-city neighbourhoods. Pfeffer's novel empirical analysis also demonstrates the dangers of constructing too spatially rigid definitions of rural labour markets. They are, rather, linked directly to the fluid recomposition of the broader economy.

Villa and Almås's theoretical standpoint is somewhat different. They apply a Scandinavian 'life-mode analysis' to one rural community in Western Norway. Life-mode analysis has been constructed, partly out of a dissatisfaction with the economistic assumptions associated with many of the petty commodity production debates, and the lack of consideration given to the cultural significance of the locality. For Højrup (1983), mode of production and ideology creates the new concept of *life modes*. These provide a basis for integrating the social analysis of labour *with* locality. In considering a range of qualitative evidence, the authors argue that an adapted life-mode analysis can assist in explaining the behaviour of the working class in Stordal. It helps to unify what is often regarded as a duality in much of the literature. That is, that small-scale farmers as petty commodity producers can also be centrally attached to furniture firms as wage earners. An agrarian history, and close social ties, makes the local cultural context essential in understanding the maintenance of a more diversified, pluriactive Chayanovian logic. The analysis goes some way in identifying and explaining why high levels of worker exploitation are socially sustained in these rural communities. Nevertheless, as Persson (Chapter 3) argues, there are severe questions surrounding the local maintenance of these diversified and flexible labour processes, given the growing effects of international comparative advantage operating under conditions of diminished social and regional welfare programmes. These *could* severely test the locally constructed life modes and the delicately organised labour processes identified in this chapter. The arguments also link directly to Van der Ploeg's notions of disconnections between localities. Stordal is a case where local distinctiveness has been socially constructed and maintained in the context of broad post-war state support for encouraging investment in isolated rural communities. New, more competitive interconnections between the locality and the rest of society could make it much more vulnerable.

Taking somewhat larger spatial points of reference, the final pair of contributions focus more specifically on the nature of rural – in these cases agricultural – labour processes, seeing them as a central element in the production and maintenance of regional identity and culture. Along with Villa and Almås, they raise some important questions concerning the contradictory tendencies currently evident in Europe. That is, how can the increasing emphasis on the maintenance (and, indeed, in the context of Eastern Europe, re-emergence) of cultural and regional identity be sustained during a period of what, Van der Ploeg and Etxezarreta identify as internationalised processes of convergence and social homogenisation? That is, how is the 'art de la localité' to be constructed now? These parallel tendencies are a central axis of enquiry and debate for the contributions to this volume.

Smith provides a historically grounded account of crofting in the Scottish Highlands. This particular labour form, born out of past rounds of externalisation and restructuring, gives the region its distinctive social form. More recently, it provides a major source of social identity for the pluriactive crofters: many of whom are now urban-incomers. Crofting is experiencing new, more complex forms of diversity, raising some central questions concerning its theoretical understanding. Whilst they define *themselves* as crofters through the *holding of land*, as with their counterparts on Stordal, they are engaged in a large variety of economic relationships, only one aspect of which being defined as agricultural production. On the one hand, there is a deepening of the process of reproduction through commoditisation, as more family labour relates to this new diversity of market relationships. On the other, these commodified links provide a basis for a distinctive way of life. Agreeing with Van der Ploeg and Almås, Smith argues that these complex forms cannot simply be seen as the outcome of the 'logic of capital', or indeed, the tendency to see petty commodity production as functional for capital. These labour processes have their own values and meanings, partly based on past rounds of uneven restructuring and partly on the dynamic centre–periphery interactions. This leads to a form of *sustained marginalisation* based on distinctive social relations of production and a dominant central state.

In this context we must remind ourselves that space is far more than a convenient backdrop on to which social action is superimposed. Rather, as Murdoch argues in the final chapter, space is a socially active context which stimulates individual, local and regional identities. Murdoch adopts this theme with reference to the ways in which the nascent Farmers Union of

Wales attempted to represent the predominantly small farmers in the principality. Murdoch provides a sociological analysis of how a peripheral region and its farmers become institutionalised within central state polity and society. Here he applies Paasi's (1991) provoking framework, focusing on the development of territorial, symbolic and institutional *shapes* of regions. His chapter provides a useful purpose in linking, in a socially and politically dynamic way, local and regional identities and cultures to central state action. He shows how regional and local negotiation and 'room for manoeuvre' develop despite the centralising tendencies of the state.

Both Smith's and Murdoch's contributions explore the social and political mechanisms by which centralised state mechanisms based in a dominant region (England) fosters regional dependencies and cultures around distinctive forms of agricultural and diversified labour. Radical changes in the nature of this central state can ultimately influence such sustained marginalisation.

These final contributions together suggest a set of new vulnerabilities and questions concerning the nature and value of rural labour processes. This focus leads to a consideration of different rural development 'logics' operating over time and space. The direction and geography of these is uncertain, but the role of the social organisation of local labour is central to their degree of 'success', legitimacy and sustainability.

## References

Boucher, S., Flynn, A. and Lowe, P. (1991) 'The politics of rural enterprise: a British case study', Ch. 7 in S. Whatmore, P. Lowe and T. K. Marsden (eds) *Rural Enterprise: shifting perspectives on small scale production*, Critical Perspectives on Rural Change Vol. 3. Fulton, London.

Bradley, T. (1985) 'Reworking the quiet revolution: industrial and labour market restructuring in village England', *Sociologia Ruralis* 25, pp. 40–59.

Castells, M. and Portes A. (1986) 'World underneath: the origins, dynamism and effects of the informal economy', Conference on the comparative study of the informal sector. Hampers Ferry, West Virginia.

Cheshire, P. and Hay, D. (1989) *Urban Problems in Europe*. Blackwell, Oxford.

Errington, A. (1990) 'Investigating rural employment in England', *Journal of Rural Studies* 6, 1, pp. 67–84.

European Commission (1988) *The Future of Rural Society*. Supplement 4 to the bulletin of the European Communities.

European Commission (1991a) *The Future of Rural Areas*. Europe 2000 documentation.

European Commission (1991b) *The Development and Future of the CAP*. Reflections paper to the Commission, EC Documentation Commission.

Falk, W. W. and Lyson, T. A. (1988) *High Tech, Low Tech, No Tech: Recent Industrial and Occupational Change in the South* State University of New York Press.

Fernandez and Kelly, M. P. (1983) *For we are Sold, I and my People: women and industry in Mexico's frontier*. State University of New York Press.

Fitzsimmons, M. (1990) 'The social and environmental relations of US agricultural regions', in P. Lowe, T.K. Marsden and S. Whatmore (eds) *Technological Change and the Rural Environment, Critical Perspectives on Rural Change* Vol. 2. Fulton, London.

Freshwater, D. and Ehrenschaft, P. (1990) 'Direct and indirect rural development policy in a neo-conservative North America', Chapter 6 in M. Tracy (ed.) *Rural Policy Issues*. The Arkleton Trust, Aberdeenshire, Scotland.

Friedland, W. and Pugliese, E. (1989) 'Class formation and decomposition in modern capitalist agriculture: comparative perspectives', *Sociologia Ruralis* 14, pp. 86–92.

Fuller (1991) (ed.) 'Pluriactivity in Europe', *Journal of Rural Studies* 6, No. 4, Special issue.

Gringeri, C. (1990) 'The nuts and bolts of subsidised development: industrial homework in its rural mid western communities', PhD thesis, University of Wisconsin, Madison.

Hall, R. (1990) Poultry project update, *Ruffling Feathers*. Southern Exposure, Institute for Southern Studies, Durham, North Carolina.

HMSO, House of Lords Committee on the European Community (1990) *The Future of Rural Society*.

Højrup, T. (1983) *Det glemke folk* Livsformer og cenbaldirigering. Institut for europaeisk folklivsforskning/statens byggeforskningsinstitut, Hørsholm.

Labao, L. (1990) *Locality and Inequality: farm and industry structure and socio-economic conditions*. SUNY, New York.

Lipietz, A. (1990) 'The debt problem, European integration and the new phase of world crisis', *New Left Review* pp. 37–51.

Little, J.K. (1990) 'Women's employment in the food system. Chapter 6 in T.K. Marsden and J.K. Little (eds) *Political, Social and Economic Perspectives on the International Food System*. Gower, Aldershot.

Marsden, T.K. and Murdoch, J. (1990) 'Restructuring rurality: key areas for development in assessing rural change', *Working Paper 4*. ESRC Countryside Change Initiative, University of Newcastle.

Marsden, T.K. (1991) 'Theoretical issues in the continuity of petty commodity production', Chapter 1 in S. Whatmore *et al. Rural Enterprise: shifting perspectives on small-scale production*, Critical Perspectives on Rural Change, Vol. 3. Fulton, London.

Marx (1974) *Capital* Vols 1 and 3. Progress Publishers, Moscow.

Massey, D. (1984) *Spatial Divisions of Labour: social structures and the geography of production*. Macmillan, London.

Mormont, M. (1990) 'Who is rural? or how to be rural, towards a sociology of the rural', Chapter 1 Marsden *et al.* (eds) *Rural Restructuring: global processes and their responses*, Critical Perspectives on Rural Change, Vol. 1. Fulton, London.

Newby, H. (1989) 'Restructuring rural labour markets', Chapter 2 in G. Summers *et al. Agriculture and Beyond: rural economic development*. University of Wisconsin, Madison, USA.

Pahl, R. (1984) *Divisions of Labour*. Blackwell, Oxford.

Pennington, S. and Westover, B. (1989) *Homework*. Macmillan, London.

Piore, M. and Sabel, C. F. (1984) *The Second Industrial Divide*. Basic Books, New York.

Portes, A., Benton, L. and Castells, M. (1989) (eds) *The Informal Economy: studies in advanced and less developed countries*. Johns Hopkins University Press, Baltimore.

Reid, J. N. (1990) 'Economic change in the rural US: a search for explanations', Chapter 8 in M. Tracy (ed.) *Rural Policy Issues*. The Arkleton Trust, Aberdeenshire, Scotland.

Robins, K. (1989) 'Global Times', *Marxism Today* pp. 20–7.

Sassen-Koob, S. (1986) 'The dynamics of growth in post-industrial New York City', paper presented at the workshop at the Dual City, New York.

Summers, G., Horton, F. and Gringeri, C. (1990) 'Rural labour and market changes in the United States', Chapter 5 in T. K. Marsden, P. Lowe and S. Whatmore (eds) *Rural Restructuring: global processes and their responses*, Critical Perspectives on Rural Change Vol. 1. Fulton, London.

Van der Ploeg, J. D. (1990) *Labour, Markets and Agricultural Production*. Westview Special Studies in Agriculture Science and Policy. Boulder, Colorado.

Von Meyer, H. (1990) 'From agricultural to rural policy in the EC', Chapter 3 in M. Tracy (ed.) *Rural Policy Issues*. The Arkleton Trust, Aberdeenshire, Scotland.

CHAPTER 1

# The Reconstitution of Locality: Technology and Labour in Modern Agriculture

*Jan Douwe Van der Ploeg*

## Introduction: locality and heterogeneity

Throughout history, agriculture has developed a highly diverse mosaic: its spatial expansion added new forms, and time rendered it, as it were, more colourful. The interlinking of the separate pieces produced no confluence into grey or green, but articulated instead the contrasts. As Van den Akker, a farmer turned chronicler noted, 'agriculture [was] like an archipelago' (1967, p. 138). It was composed of many, many islands, or farming systems, each linked with others but containing contemporaneously its own identity, that is, viewed comparatively, its own locality.[1] As Van den Akker's chronicle makes clear, this locally bound specificity was not due to relative isolation. On the contrary, it was through travelling, through story-telling, through communication and interchange, that specificity was reproduced and, above all, increased. Locality, was thus not to be seen as a space-bound residual, but as locally produced specificity. And this was not only the case for stubborn Friesians such as Van den Akker. It applied to Englishmen as well. As another chronicler, Robertson Scott recorded:

> Every year that I live in the country, and every year that I know more of what the people who work the land of the United Kingdom are doing, I realise more fully the profound agricultural truth underlying the remark of a skilled Dutch farmer to an English landowner ... 'If you should come to Holland to farm, you would imitate me, but if I were to go to farm in England I would imitate you' (1912, p. ix).

19

Indirectly, this quote also refers to the patterns underlying the diversity, that is, to the centrality of labour processes and to the localised set of conditions in which these were embedded, and finally to the social mechanisms through which the specificity of labour processes and therefore of agriculture as a whole was reproduced. Every location acquired, maintained and enlarged (through, among other things, the exchanges mentioned), its own cultural repertoire: its own norms and criteria that together established the local notion of 'good farming' (Graham Brade-Birks, 1950, p. xvi). The founding father of Dutch agrarian sociology, Hofstee, analysed and defined this specific unity of cultural repertoire and localised practices as 'styles of farming' (1948, 1985). The 'art of farming' (an expression that goes back to Columella, the well-known Roman agronomist), as Hofstee made clear, consisted of (a) the creation of adequate, that is, specific responses to local conditions, limitations and possibilities and (b) the social reproduction of these 'responses' and the social relations of production that they implied. That was how locality was produced and reproduced.

It is important for the scope of the argument I want to develop here, to stress again that locality is not to be understood as a result of 'isolation', but rather the contrary. Von Thunen stressed the differential impact of generalised commodity relations, and in like manner, Hofstee underlined the differential impact of politico-economic systems. He argues, for example, that it was the generalised nature of feudalism that encouraged specific reactions in the periphery, i.e. the emergence of new cultural repertoires in which 'farming freedom' constituted the central axis (see also Slicher Van Bath, 1978, p. 71).

Central to the argument here, is that locality, and hence the nature of heterogeneity as a central feature of agriculture, have been and are deeply affected by the current process of technological development. Labour processes are increasingly reshaped through uniform and standardised procedures. Consequently, locality and heterogeneity would seem to be bound to disappear. I will not enter into a phenomenology of this process. The most immediate expressions of this tendency are well known: the 'outdated' character of the quoted chronicles being just one of the many indications of the global (although far from complete) 'monotonisation' of agriculture. The mosaic appears to be disappearing. The once impressive range of local breeds such as the *la rossa reggiana, the rijnsburger blaarkop,* the *chianina,* have given way to the now dominant position of American Holsteinblood. The same goes for architecture. Inside the cowshed, it is hardly possible any more to establish whether one is in *Bavaria, Emilia Romagna,* or *Friesland.*

However, it is possible for unifying tendencies at one level to go together with differentiation at other levels. This leads to my second argument that the centralising and homogenising implications of technological development in agriculture are countered by a completely new set of responses. Since agricultural sectors, such as those composed of thousands if not millions of simple commodity producers, are not, as argued by Newby (1980) 'passive receivers of innovations emanating in towns and industry' and since technological development is not just a neutral 'route towards progress', differential reactions will and do emerge. Hence, locality and heterogeneity are reconstituted, not as the mere repetition of former expressions. They re-emerge as a repertoire of new, strategic responses to the now dominant tendencies and relations containing an undeniable 'blueprint' for standard-isation.

## Technological development and the production of disconnections

Potentially, science-based technology[2] entails the far-reaching homogenisation of agriculture. This will be demonstrated here on three levels that look at both the practice and theory of technological development as well as at the outcome of recent planning studies considering the spatial distribution of tomorrow's agriculture.

The development of science-based technology materialises as the growing dislocation or independence of the different processes of production from those factors that initially composed its locality and diversity: that is, agriculture is increasingly *disconnected* from those structuring elements that initially introduced specificity into it.

There is, in the first place, the well recognised disconnection of agricultural processes of production from land, nature and ecology. Natural growth factors such as soil, soil fertility, rain, nutrient supplies, temperature and the availability of light, are no longer the object of detailed regulation through and within the labour process. Labour objects, and the raw materials[3] for constructing the required instruments are no longer derived from local ecosystems,[4] but are instead produced and delivered by agribusiness. Local 'nature', as it were, is increasingly being replaced by a completely new set of artificially created 'growth factors'.[5] Hence, agriculture is disconnected from the local ecosystem. The glasshouses used in horticulture, and the intensive, computer-controlled, breeding of cattle and poultry, are the most familiar examples of this tendency. Another, equally well-known, although less far-reaching example is represented by the Green Revoluton model (cf. Bernstein, 1990; and Oasa, 1981). It is important to note, however, that such scientifically constructed disconnections are not limited to the examples mentioned.

The irony is that this type of disconnectedness is especially accelerated by the environmental 'fall-out' already produced by the 'modernised' agrarian sectors. This is the case in Dutch dairy farming for example, where the production of roughage from meadowland is increasingly affected by both acid rain and by the depositing of all kinds of toxic elements such as heavy metals, dioxines, etc. This implies lower yields as well as lower quality levels, and induces particular health hazards into the end product.[6] One of the potential technological answers to this type of problem is the introduction of glasshouses for grass-production (RPD, 1986). This would allow the discon-nection of this particular process of production from the (deteriorating) natural growth factors.

The systematically produced separation of agricultural production and environmental conditions permits a sharply increased 'mobility' of agricultural activities. Specific conditions no longer matter. As several case studies now demonstrate, this type of disconnectedness is indeed being used increasingly as a means to shift and abruptly reallocate agricultural activities. Fruits and vegetables for instance can now be grown in deserts (see for instance Gonzales, 1991). The required growth factors can be constructed artificially and consequently can literally be applied everywhere. It would seem that the absence of any traces whatsoever of history, society, and especially of farmers, even turns out to be a comparative advantage within the framework of these new technological models.

A second type of disconnectedness emerging from recent technological trends is to be encountered within the labour process itself. The agricultural labour process constitutes a complex but carefully integrated unity of an impressive number of tasks and subtasks.[7] Whilst historically, progress in farming and the emancipation of farmers often coincided with the further expansion of the range of tasks and subtasks that together composed the concrete labour process (cf. Bieleman, 1987; Hofstee, 1985; and Van Zanden, 1985), technological development nowadays follows the route of continuous externalisation. An increasing number of tasks and subtasks are delegated to external institutions, after which the produced or processed goods and/or services are obtained through specific markets (Van der Ploeg, 1990a). This type of disconnectedness, which substitutes the 'integrated' character of farming for an increased division of labour, partly coincides with the first type of disconnectedness. This is especially the case for specific tasks, such as the reproduction of soil fertility and the reproduction of labour objects such as animals and plant material. But the process of externalisation[8] goes far beyond the management of 'natural growth factors' as such. It also concerns the management and reproduction of 'economic' factors, such as the formation and mobilisation of capital; the socialisation of the labour force, the mobilisation and (re)distribution of land, the mobilisation and allocation of required inputs, the development of adequate knowledge and techniques and, in particular, the reproduction of the *social relations* that regulate the specific forms for the production and reproduction of the factors and required non-factor inputs. The formation of capital, for instance, is disconnected from the creation of savings, from production within the labour process itself,[9] and from the typical social arrangements (including gender relations)[10] that guaranteed the reproduction of several forms of endogenous capital formation. The formation of capital is now crucially linked with and dependent upon capital markets and the agencies operating in them.[11] The same goes for the socialisation of the required labour force and the mobilisation and (re)distribution of land: the once decisive and highly diverse local settings in which these processes took place have been to a large extent replaced by generalised commodity relations. The interrelation with science-based technology is evident. It more often than not presupposes, and therefore requires, a decisive step across the boundaries inherent to these local settings. The introduction for instance of the *ligboxenstal* (loose box stall or shed) required investments that went far beyond the *local* possibilities for capital formation (and especially beyond the implied 'social calendar').[12] Hence, a pattern of farming has emerged that is crucially dependent on the *generalised* relations reigning in capital markets. The same is true for the development of required know-how and the division of labour within the farm. All such aspects have had to be reordered so as to fit in with the new technological scheme, and this has more often than not implied – also for these 'additional aspects – an increasing dependency on external, more generalised relations.

There is an important methodological observation to be linked to this discussion. The actual (although far from 'complete') submission of agriculture to agribusiness, and to capital in a general sense, would be unthinkable if not accompanied or preceded by a contemporary (or prior) disconnection of farming activities from the local sets of social relations of production. These regulate the mobilisation, allocation and reproduction of land, labour, capital and required non-factor inputs.

The separation from their local settings and arenas of these processes of reproduction, mobilisation and allocation (a separation that entails an equally far-reaching impact towards homogenisation, i.e. towards the 'liquidation' of locality), cannot be attributed in a unilinear way to an 'unfolding logic of capital', as is sometimes hypothesised. Although homogenisation is an empirical phenomenon no one can deny, neither can we neglect the fact that it only emerges when the process of disconnecting agriculture from local settings is articulated with, and is actively *interlinked* to, the global projects of agribusiness groups and other market-agencies operating at a supra-local level. This consideration is especially important if diversity is to be understood as the outcome of the combined but uneven process of disconnection and interlinking. I will return to this point below.

A third type of disconnectedness concerns the relation between the labour process and the required labour force. Until recently, the qualities embodied in the labour force (obtained sometimes through painful socialisation and/or through long experience)[13] were crucial for the degree to which specific labour processes could be developed further. *Craftmanship* was indispensable for 'good farming' and also for the ongoing development of the process of production.[14] Today, however, it is not only the quantity, but also the quality of labour that is becoming increasingly superfluous. Quality is expropriated. The case of automation (cf. Frouws and Van der Ploeg, 1988) represents a clear and widespread example of this new type of systematically produced disconnectedness, in which the nullification of the *'art de la localité'* and the labour force as a vehicle for this specific type of knowledge, goes together with an abrupt strengthening of external 'production regimes' (Burawoy, 1985).

A fourth type of disconnectedness that is also strongly interwoven with the increasing scientification of agriculture – that is, the continuous reorganisation of labour and development processes according to the designs elaborated in agricultural sciences and 'introduced into' agriculture or 'mediated' by agribusiness groups through the propagation of new technological models – concerns changes in the social organisation of time and space. As Mendras (1970, pp. 47–75), among others, has made quite clear, the social organisation of time and space was initially highly inter-woven with the (local) labour process itself. The mutual coordination of 'natural' growth cycles as entailed in the local ecosystem as well as the coordination of 'natural' rhythms with 'social calendars' as entailed in the prevailing social relations of production, gave rise to an impressive variety of 'agrarian calendars' (cf. Bourdieu, 1982, p. 97). The same can be said for the perception and organisation of space. Work was the 'measure' for time and space; the 'localised' conceptualisation of space and time then became the 'carrier' for the reproduction of specific, i.e. local labour processes. Such specific interconnections evidently become nullified. Time, space and labour become increasingly disconnected. Again, it is new technology (entailing, as Mendras pointed out, an 'industrialisation' of work, space and time) and its interrelated linking to 'universal markets', that produce this specific type of disconnection. The current organisation of time and space is increasingly 'pre-coded' by technological designs;[15] the organisation of the labour process (and consequently of the required social relations) is 'derived', being a mere function of the externally established parameters for organising time and space. This turn-over in the interrelations between labour, time and space (between 'work, time and the land', as Mendras would put it) not only occurs at the ideological level and/or within the laboratories in which the R&D of new technologies is organised. It is omnipresent and very obvious within farming practice also. It quite often implies that labour input, and as a consequence relations within the family (between generations and sexes) are to be reorganised so as to fit in with the technological current models. This is a radical and often dramatic 'turn-around' of what was until recently at least, the 'centrality' of the family. The consequences go further. Specific cattle-breeding systems, such as those related to the Romagnolo and Chianina cattle, for example, are increasingly put under pressure (if not to say marginalised), by other breeding systems produced by applied science, which present different time-horizons. Thus, the impact of the process of scientification goes far beyond its immediate (and consciously selected) scope. Once the feed/meat conversion rate and the intercalving and fattening period have been 'improved', that is shortened for the most 'suitable' breeds (through whatever kind of intervention, manipulation and/or reorganisa-tion), the shortened time-horizon immediately affects other breeding systems through the change in the degree of competitiveness. What follows from this, more often than not (the exceptions will be discussed later), is the need to 'align' these other systems with the 'improved' one. If not, a quick and abrupt marginalisation might be the outcome. In synthesis, when the (local) labour process loses its centrality (through the design and implementation of new technologies aiming at its reorganisation), the social organisation of time and space will also lose its specificity. Labour, time and space will increasingly be defined by generalised institutional and politico-economic networks, introducing as it were 'general' schemes that only allow for specificity as a 'comparative advantage' or a 'hindrance'.

A fifth type of disconnectedness is to be located in the increasing separation of agricultural processes of production from the specificity of the produced end-products. Agricultural production increasingly became identical to just one element of a much longer chain – a chain that comprises both trading and industry on the input side as well as trading and transformation on the output side of the farms. In farming, the raw materials obtained on the 'input-side' are converted into semi-processed products for further industrial transformation. That is, farming is no longer oriented to the production of specific consumer goods, be it a specific cheese, variety of potato or whatever. Consequently, specific conditions that relate to ecology, to timing, to craftmanship, etc., are becoming, if not completely irrelevant, at least less so. For instance, once a particular kind of milk, produced when cows first entered the meadows in spring and which contained specific types of caseine, was needed to produce a particular kind of cheese (the so-called *graskaas* or grass cheese). Now it can be made regardless of the kind of milk, or origin, or specific elaboration. The production of specificity is, in this case, replaced by engineering along the industrial chain. Through all kind of interventions and additions, the required ingredients and qualities are 'constructed' (Reynders, 1990).

A sixth type of disconnectedness, already anticipated above, concerns the disappearance of the family (in terms of the previously embedded gender and generational relations, its specific history and specific projects for the future) as the gravitational centre of the farm enterprise and its development. There are still farming families, but as the central point of reference for the definition of the direction, rhythm and tempo of the farm development process, its timing and the selection of required mechanisms, the family has disappeared. These parameters are now defined, directly or indirectly, by prevailing technological models, that barely allow for adaptations. It is now, rather, the family that is to be 'adapted' to a process of production that is externally defined.[16]

It is through the creation and diffusion of these disconnections discussed here that farming as social practice became increasingly (although not everywhere with the same rhythm) disengaged from:

(1)  nature and ecology;
(2)  the once integrated and autonomous structure of the labour process;
(3)  the quality of the labour force;
(4)  a specific social organisation of time and space;
(5)  its links with the elaboration of specific qualities as contained in specific end products;
(6)  the family as an organising principle.

Consequently, locality, to an increasing degree, has been abolished; the mosaic is, as it were, evaporating.

Science and technological development played a dominant role in this remodelling of agriculture. Although it is not possible here to enter into the details,[17] it should be noted that the leverage function of science and technology is *not* the outcome of a unilinear, continuous and autonomous development of science and technology as such. Both contain in their recent history (the 1930s and 1950s are especially crucial periods in this respect) important moments of *rupture*. Agrarian sciences developed from *agronomy* (which typically focused on heterogeneity, on local knowledge systems, etc.) into the current *technological sciences* that embark into designs of how agriculture *ought* to be reorganised. Consequently, a large array of malleable techniques gave way to increasingly exclusive technological systems made up of mutually dependent and interlinked innovations. This connects with an equally important shift in the inter-relations between the supply and demand of technologies.[18] Whereas initially demand (as evolving from current practices in agriculture) guided supply, it is now the latter that has its own momentum. It guides, legitimises or de-legitimises demand. It is through the supply of technologies that farmers' behaviour, including the required demand for technology, is defined.

A clear illustration of the impact of the disconnections produced can be derived from current planning studies on 'optimal land use' within the EC.[19] The synergistic effect of the technological changes indicated above would, according to these studies, lead to the superfluousness of at least 70 per cent of the agricultural area now under cultivation. Agriculture would be reallocated and concentrated in the main deltas of Europe, i.e. those areas offering the best conditions for the submission of agriculture to agribusiness. This is not to suggest that such a perspective will come true, but to indicate that it is increasingly presented as a political claim.[20] Simultaneously, such a claim demonstrates that the quite specific[21] process of technological development is in no way neutral. It entails the far-reaching submission of agriculture to capital. A proper analysis of future development trends, however, should not just consider one side of the equation. Apart from science, technology and capital, the position of farmers and their interests, perspectives and responses must also be considered.

### The reconstitution of locality

Generalised knowledge as offered by applied science and standardised technologies supplied by agribusiness, both require new forms of local knowledge for their application. As a result, new specific knowledge systems, of a strictly localised character emerge. These not only concern, in different situations, the application of general rules, procedures and artefacts, they also entail specific responses on how to resolve the particular problems that emerge from such an application. These latter kind of problems cover a considerable range of empirical phenomena. I will mention just some of them.

Increasingly, the integration of segmented pieces of scientific knowledge[22] gives rise to a range of immediate and far from microscopic problems.[23] Farmers are also faced with unevenness in the process of technology development: investment in the newest technologies at moment $t = 1$, might quite well imply a dysfunction at moment $t = 2$ (cf. Benvenuti, 1991). Thirdly, one could point to yet another level of complication; the 'unadaptedness' of generalised rules and uniform technologies that are designed from a particular horizon of relevance which defines and delimits the parameters considered to be strategic for indicating 'success' or 'failure' (cf. Staudenmaier, 1985, p. 47). Normally, so-called 'optimal conditions' which allow for a 'rational agriculture' are considered to constitute such a horizon of relevance. It almost goes without saying that agriculture as differentiated praxis, contains a myriad of 'diverging', 'suboptimal' and/or 'marginal' conditions. These are seen as 'deviations' from the optimum as assumed in the project of science and technological development. This is more relevant since technological development in today's agriculture is no longer to be understood as simple delivery of artefacts containing increasing degrees of 'efficiency'. Although the new 'artefacts' are represented as being simple objects that carry an inherent superiority (cf. 'miracle seeds', 'improved varieties', etc.), their application usually requires a profound and far-reaching restructuration of the labour process and of the interrelations between farming and outside agencies. One of the central assumptions of design processes is the continuous process of *externalisation* (cf. Van der Ploeg, 1990b, pp. 18–21), that is, the delivery of standardised growth factors that entail an incorporated productivity from external agencies to the farms. In the practice of farming this implies an increase (sometimes an abrupt one) in the degree of commoditisation. That is, the balance of autonomy/dependency vis-à-vis the markets will be deeply affected by the application of new technologies.

These problems all require specific responses. We have been trying to study such responses through a new approach to heterogeneity as an ominipresent empirical phenomenon. In this approach, heterogeneity is not conceptualised as an archaic remnant, but tackled as possibly containing and expressing a certain range of strategic responses to the dilemmas outlined above. Farmers have to relate their farming activity in specific ways to the market, both on the output as well as the input side. Equally, farmers have to define their position vis-à-vis the dominant supply of technologies. Theoretically, this allows for the conceptualisation of a certain 'space for manoeuvre': farmers might relate their farming activities in different ways to markets and technology.[24] Also on theoretical grounds, one might assume that these differential positions are not strictly individual nor atomistic. They are inherently social. Mutual comparison, specific networks for communication, the interchange of new solutions and insights, the ongoing debates on what is to be considered as 'good farming', etc., have always been part and parcel of farming. Through comparison, intercommunication, negotiation, distancing or rapprochement, specific and differentiated responses emerge as socially constructed. This is particularly so where a specific historic repertoire of different experiences in relation to markets and technology is part of the game (cf. Van der Ploeg *et al.*, 1992).

The linking of the farm enterprise to markets and technological development has, during the recent decades, been the object of continuous prescription and sanctioning. A wide range of 'political apparatuses' exist (Burawoy, 1985) in the form of a 'technico-administrative task environment' (Benvenuti, 1991). This is a quasi organisation from which prescriptions of the required 'behaviour' as well as accompanying 'social definitions' of, for example 'the good enterpreneur', the 'supporting wife' has evolved. It involves a huge 'intelligentsia' (Rambaud, 1983) related to primary production and the actors concerned. It is remarkable, especially in retrospect, to see how much the agrarian sciences aligned themselves with this specific agenda. One of the consequences, among others, is that along with specific knowledge, also specific fields of institutionally created ignorance are created within the domain of science. This applies, for instance, to the *empirical ways and mechanisms* through which farms are linked to markets and technological development. In neo-classical agrarian economics and much of mainstream development economics, farming is understood as representing essentially a function of production. Projection of the prevailing market and price relations on this function then determines the 'optimum' (Saccomandi, 1991). Within this framework the actual degree of commoditisation, the *empirical complex of interrelations with the markets*, is considered to be irrelevant. Whether, for example, labour is mobilised through the labour market or through non-commodity relations, is irrelevant for the required calculations. The same is true for capital, for land and for all the major inputs. In the calculations of the 'good' entrepreneur, such production factors and non-factor inputs are seen as being mobilised through the corresponding markets; consequently, they are to be considered as commodities, that is, whatever their specificity (including their specific social value), it is only their price as established by the 'universal market' (Polanyi, 1957) that matters. Hence, one understands that at the level of the 'political apparatuses' involved, the farmers who calculate differently or who actively distance their farming business in one way or another from the markets, quickly become labelled as 'bad entrepreneurs', or 'anti-economic men'. In its turn, agrarian economics also reifed such images. Exactly the same happens concerning the interrelations between farming and the development of technology. Suffice it to recall the once dominant categories developed within the diffusion of innovation tradition and later within extension science.

Recent research demonstrates that there is considerable variability in the empirical degrees of commoditisation, that is in the actual interrelations between farms and the different markets. Through new theoretical developments (e.g. the application of neo-institutional economics to agriculture, notably by Saccomandi (1991), and the so-called 'commoditisation debate' (cf. Long et al., 1986; and Long and Van der Ploeg, 1988) it also became possible to represent this empirical diversity as a theoretically meaningful phenomenon. New research studies (see for instance Roep et al., 1990) clearly demonstrate that the position of farming vis-à-vis the markets and technological development is the outcome of goal-oriented strategies, actively managed and adapted by the actors themselves. The implication speaks for itself: heterogeneity is not to be considered as an archaic remnant of the past, nor as a kind of casual outcome of the interaction between different 'initial' conditions at farm enterprise level and general processes, such as increased market-dependency and technological development.

Markets and technology contain a specific distribution of potentialities and restrictions (a 'specificity' increasingly moulded by the 'production apparatuses' involved). This specific distribution and the consequences implied, increasingly provoke different responses. They are countered with specific 'projects', that not only entail specific linkages to markets and technology, but also specific modules for the organisation of the farm labour and the farm development process.

Let me illustrate this with Roep's study on styles of dairy farming on the eastern sandy soils of the Netherlands (Roep *et al.*, 1990). Using an elegant, albeit somewhat complicated methodology, several styles of farming were identified. Folk-concepts were initially used to identify each of these styles. Subsequently, each style of farming was related, by farmers, to some of the dimensions that were, in their opinion, crucial to characterising the main differences. In this way, a 'social mapping' (as used earlier by e.g. Bennett, 1981) was elaborated (see Figure 1.1). The same styles of farming were also related, by a sample of farmers (n = 126), to markets and technology as 'structuring principles' (see Figure 1.2).

**Figure 1.1**  Styles of farming as recognised by the dairy farmers

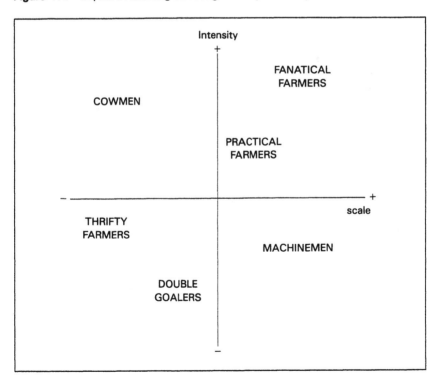

**Figure 1.2** Differential orientations on markets and technology

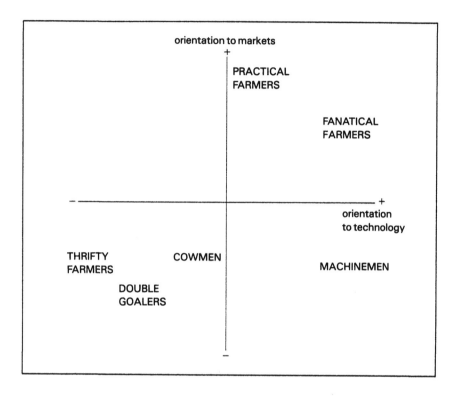

At first we might regard it as somewhat surprising that interrelations between specific, socially constructed entities, i.e. styles of farming, are reproduced on completely different sets of dimensions, such as scale and intensity of the process of production (as in Figure 1.1), and the interlinking between farming and markets and technology (as in Figure 1.2). However, if one starts from the premise that the labour process is central, there is no need for surprise whatsoever.

It is in the labour process that the different domains of farming (e.g. the organisation of specific technico-economic relations with 'outside' agencies, the specific structuration of the processes of production and reproduction, the management of all kinds of social relations *in* and *of* production, etc.) are coordinated and put together into one and the same coherent strategy. That is why one could also introduce the colour of the cows, and/or the specificity of gender relations on the farm as distinguishing dimensions.[25]

The position of farming activities vis-à-vis markets and technology is in no way a neutral issue. Let me illustrate this for the case of technology. Technological artifacts contain specific projects that concern the necessary (or 'optimal') organisation of the farm labour process. This affects in turn the social relations of and in production. Many technologies suppose, and therefore introduce, a specific social division of labour. This includes a division between tasks considered to be crucial, important and decisive, and a range of tasks that, taken together, might be considered to be 'work of a secondary kind' (as defined by De Rooy, 1991). To put it bluntly, milking is 'important', but cleaning the instruments used is 'work of a secondary kind' (or 'invisible work'). These are tasks that can hardly be interchanged, since 'milking as an important job' requires a daily routine, an up-to-date knowledge of the animals, their behaviour, their health, as well as thorough preparation. It also requires a fixed time-schedule. On the other hand, 'additional' activities such as cleaning, or any other activities associated with the notion of 'secondary complementarity', can easily be 'attached' to new technological designs, since they presuppose *gender*, in the sense that it is assumed that women will be available to perform them. A considerable part of today's technologies are indeed, in this respect, *'engendered'*, that is, based on this assumption of the availability of a kind of 'second class of workers'. As De Rooy demonstrates in a beautiful empirical study, gender is reproduced through current technologies. It is striking that wherever women are missing in the farm enterprise, men are obliged to develop new, original solutions.[26] It is also striking that wherever women, for whatever reason, refuse to be reduced to a job or to a social definition of a secondary order, *specific* styles of farming, containing 'deviant' technological paths, emerge.[27]

Another crucial assumption underlying today's technological development is, as argued before, the notion of ongoing *externalisation*. Technology is designed as a function of an increased division of labour between farm enterprise and industry. The latter produce the standardised growth factors that entail 'embodied' productivity. The former acquire these growth factors (be it improved varieties, more productive cattle, nutrients, feed, growth stimulators, etc.), in order to convert them into high productivity levels. The point of course is that such a scheme links farming practice to an uncontrollable set of market relations. To put it in brief: the vanguard farms applying this kind of scheme have to produce 50 per cent or more milk to acquire the same income level per unit of labour force than what scientists call the more 'traditional' farms. But this difference is only the 'tip of the iceberg'. The investment in new technologies mostly presupposes further incorporation into the capital markets. In today's Dutch dairy farming, this implies, in the typical 'vanguard farms', that up to 100.000 guilders per annum are paid out in interest (Klaassens, 1985). This is more or less equal to 1.5 or 2 mean annual incomes per unit of labour force. Consequently, total output (and hence labour productivity with all its implications) will have to compensate for these additional expenses.

Hence, one can see that in the *practice* of farming, the parameters as defined (and judged) by the designers of technology, on their drawing boards and/or in their laboratories, are sometimes judged somewhat differently. In this respect a yet unpublished study of Mok and Tillaert is highly significant. They confronted both farmers and extensionists (to be regarded in this case as typical representatives of the 'political apparatuses' surrounding agriculture) with a set of technical parameters describing the specific processes of production on the farms studied. Both farmers and extensionists evaluated these parameters in terms of 'good', 'medium' and 'bad' performance. Hence a $3 \times 3$ table emerged. The striking result of this approach was that in only 30 per cent of the cases was there any agreement between the two groups. In the remaining 70 per cent, farmers considered the results to be 'good' while extensionists considered them 'bad', or vice versa. The background of this typical difference is illuminating. As Mok and Tillaert demonstrate, 'good' results as defined by extensionists, are seen by farmers to indicate a situation in which stress dominates, or where the risks in the game are too high, or where there is 'no longer time for family life'.

Farming thus requires a careful coordination of different domains. The domain of production, for example, must be coordinated with those concerning the different but interlinked processes of reproduction, or the negotiation and renegotiation of the social relations in which the farm enterprise and the family are embedded. From this it follows that what emerges as 'optimal' in the domain of production, if taken in isolation, might become troublesome or even counterproductive when related to other domains and the interests, perspectives and criteria entailed in those domains. That is, simple commodity production is not based on a separation, but presupposes instead a balance between commodity production as such and the conditions in which it is realised, including different 'non-commodity' relations. This implies necessarily that different positions vis-à-vis dominant technological designs, should be sought and put into effect.

The same reasoning of course can be developed as far as economic relations (i.e. the interlinking between farming and markets) are concerned. This is especially the case, since we are no longer studying the typical 'free market situation'. Interlinkages with 'markets' are structured through specific contracts with particular 'market-agencies'. Interlinking presupposes an articulation with specific projects for domination as designed by agribusiness groups. In short, the situation itself obliges differential responses. That is how different styles of farming emerge.

In Figure 1.2 (on styles of farming on the eastern sandy soils in the Netherlands), differential positions vis-à-vis markets and technology are shown. Each position implies a specific structuration of the farm labour process as well as a specific modelling of the farm development process. A wide range of agronomic and micro-economic differences are described in the research. Styles of farming emerge as socially coherent and multi-dimensional social constructions and are not to be conceptualised as mere derivation, or deduction of prevailing market relations and available technology. The different positions vis-à-vis markets and associated technological developments are socially defined: they are the outcome of strategic reasoning which typically entails continuous anticipation of the possible behaviour of other actors, e.g. agribusiness groups, state-agencies, other farmers, etc; and they are to a considerable degree mediated through (i.e. the product of) mutual comparison, communication and cooperation. Evidently each style contains a specific form and content as far as this communication, comparison and cooperation is concerned.

We can illustrate this with a *pars-pro-toto*, that is, the specific use farmers make of the now widely available computerised systems for farm management support. In dairy farming one of the most widely spread systems is DELAR. This system not only offers the participating farmers a detailed description and analysis of their own management record, it also contains data on (a) previous years; (b) the performance of other farmers as well as; (c) a set of specific criteria produced by applied agrarian sciences on 'optimal' practices. The latter are typically referred to as being the 'norms'. As Table 1.1 demonstrates, each style of farming contains a specific pattern for comparison (which evidently relates to actual practices of communication, cooperation and distancing). For instance, the typical 'cowmen' (those who achieve very high levels of craftmanship and consequently of technical efficiency), are very much concerned with the improvement of their *own* labour process. Such improvements typically centre around practical and very detailed knowledge (on what Lacroix calls 'savoir faire paysan'). External parameters and outside experience are less relevant within this particular framework. Instead *personal* experience is crucial. Progress then can only be measured using the yardstick of one's own previous experience. And that is exactly what Table 1.1 indicates, the kind of use these '*cowmen*' make of the available information packages. This constitutes a striking contrast with the way comparison is organised in other styles of farming. The '*thrifty farmers*' for instance, who are typically interested in the minimisation of monetary costs (that is, they tend to reproduce a historically guaranteed, relatively autonomous scheme of production and reproduction within their farm enterprise), are especially interested in comparison with other farms, from which they might gain new insights on ways to further reduce costs. Especially interesting is the case of the '*fanatical farmers*'. These model their enterprise more along the lines of the new technological designs, and are engaged in an accelerated expansion

**Table 1.1** The relative importance attached to the different possibilities of comparing within DELAR

| Comparing with: | Double goalers | Thrifty farmers | Practical farmers | Cowmen | Machinemen | Fanatical farmers |
|---|---|---|---|---|---|---|
| Previous years | + | − | + | + | − − | 0 |
| Other farms | 0 | + | + | − − | + | − − |
| Norms | − / + | 0 | − | 0 | 0 | + + |

| | |
|---|---|
| − | = relatively less important |
| − − | = relatively least important |
| + | = relatively important |
| + + | = relatively more important |
| + / − | = large range compared to others |
| 0 | = average compared to others |

of their farm enterprises (hence, their denomination by others as well as themselves as 'fanatical'). Their style of farming represents, as Table 1.1 makes clear, an 'adieu' to past and present. Comparison with previous years is irrelevant. Farm development, within their strategy, is a continuous rupture. The application of new technologies and the immediate 'response' to new market opportunities, do indeed make for sudden transformations: 'ruptures' are crucial. The same goes for the present. Comparison with other farms is irrelevant. According to their own 'project', these fanatical farmers are to be 'better than', to be 'ahead' of other farmers. That is what, in the still dominant discourse of Dutch agrarian policy, is labelled as a 'vanguard farm'. Only one criterion remains: the prospects (the 'norms') defined by applied agrarian sciences. In this style of farming, past and present are eliminated as points of reference, and the route defined by science becomes decisive. In a comparative analysis, this represents (as Table 1.1 indicates) a remarkable pattern of communication. It also illustrates, in its actuality, the impact of technological development. It is not only 'artefacts', but organisational patterns, 'norms', goals and new, quite exclusive patterns of comparison, and hence of communication[28] and cooperation, that are introduced into the practice of farming.

In synthesis, particular groups of farmers (those labelled 'fanatical' by their colleagues) indeed go along with the lines and perspectives entailed in the 'project' for scientification. Other groups, however, choose different routes (e.g. those labelled 'cowmen', 'thrifty farmers', 'double goalers', etc.). Thus, both homogeneity and differentiation occur. What is important is that in social practice itself, the one is argument for the other and vice versa. 'Cowmen' are convinced of their own rationale, when compared with 'fanatical farmers'; simultaneously the latter are convinced of the 'irrelevance' of the experiences lived and produced by the former, since they consider scientific 'norms' to be the main yardstick for evaluation and planning. In turn, this is embarking on development processes considered by the 'thrifty' ones, the 'double goalers' and others as being extremely risky if not crazy.

Nowadays, social practice in modern agriculture represents turmoil, confusion, debate and no conclusion whatsoever. Seen from some distance, modern agriculture is an arena that represents both very strong tendencies towards homogenisation (i.e. the liquidation of locality) and new, specific and local responses to these tendencies. It is impossible at this moment (admittedly, a very specific moment) to assess where validity might lie. It is impossible for the involved entrepreneurs themselves, and equally impossible for scientists. Available studies demonstrate that – whatever the size of farm operations might be – good income levels as well as good perspectives for continuity might be produced in all styles.[29] That is one point. The other is the extreme insecurity in the definitive lay-out of coming agricultural policies (including the re-ordering of markets). And wherever policy contains a specific distribution of benefits and costs (or opportunities and limitations), the articulation between new policies and a wide array of farming styles still remains one of the major questions. It is, in other words, no surprise that debates about this specific point are now leading to extensive discussions in the Netherlands, for instance, but also in Italy. Whereas the 'future' has been represented quite often as the 'unfolding logic' of scientific laws (or, as the leftist interpretation goes, the unfolding logic of 'capital'), today it is, probably more than ever, the object of social debate and struggle.

## On culture, patterns of farming logic and diversity

As argued above, farming always requires coordination. The virtually endless range of subtasks that together make up the labour process need fine-tuned coordination. In addition, the labour process must be coordinated with the most relevant parameters in those other domains that, together with the domain of production, constitute the 'fields of activity' (Vincent, 1977) in and through which farming as social activity is realised. The different forms of coordination are secured through continuous cycles of observation, interpretation, evaluation and (re)organisation. The crucial point is that this coordination should in no way be seen as a mere technical operation. The 'creation of the required balance' (as farmers often say) is no blue-print operation, nor is it simply a 'trial-and error' procedure leading to an a-priori assessed equilibrium. Although dealing largely with the technicalities of the process of production, the necessary coordination or 'balancing' is, in itself, not a technical operation. It is a conscious and goal-oriented process. What we are discussing here is the *social* coordination of subtasks,[30] of production and reproduction, of the different domains, of internal and external relations. All these aspects and relations should be 'balanced'. And *because* they are mutually coordinated, farming emerges as a *social construction*: as a coherent, multidimensional constellation, in which the unity and synergy of practices, internal and external relations, knowledge, norms, opinions, experiences, interests and perspectives are more striking than the tensions and contradictions.

It is precisely at this point, i.e. the mutual coordination of interests, perspectives, internal and external relations and practices (with all the implied technicalities), that *culture* as a relevant factor has its centre of gravity. In 'simple commodity production' (with its unity of 'mental' and 'manual labour', its characteristic room for manoeuvre vis-à-vis commodity relations, etc.), culture is not just another 'additional' factor. Culture is encountered in the *specific coordination* between internal and external relations, between experience and perspective, between past, present and future. Culture is not a phenomenon 'outside' the so-called 'hard' realities of market and technology. It is cultural models (or specific patterns of farming logic, as exemplified by the folk concepts already presented) that structure the interpretation of markets and technology, and which consequently structure the 'transfer of meaning', the 'translation' of, for example, market trends into action. A typical intensive (I) farmer in Emilia Romagna 'reads' the markets in a way that differs markedly from the interpretation of a typical extensive (E) farmer (Van der Ploeg, 1990). The same goes for the 'fanatical farmers', the 'cowmen' and the 'thrifty ones' from the

Netherlands. One and the same set of external parameters is interpreted in quite different ways and hence transformed into different practices.

Styles of farming are the nodal points of farm culture. The diversity in styles consequently emerges as the cultural repertoire of farming communities. Heterogeneity reflects – and contemporaneously reinforces – this cultural repertoire, that is, the range of available responses to all those limitations, opportunities and claims in which farming is embedded.

This cultural repertoire evidently interlinks with history, with locality, with new social movements, and with culture in a more general sense. That is, such cultural repertoires are not only the counter-images of prevailing market relations, technological designs and (agro)political settings, but are moulded by history, locality and culture in a general sense. This is why 'calvinist farmers' still differ from 'catholic ones from the south';[31] why Friesian farmers do not include pig-rearing in their farm-enterprises; why sons of 'mazzadri' are more often than not I- instead of E-farmers; and why a considerable proportion of the young farmers from the 1960s and 1970s, who formulated a radical critique of the then dominant agrarian policies, are now in the forefront of the movement for ecological agriculture. Thus, in agriculture (i.e. in SCP), culture is indeed a very relevant factor. Culture matters. New cultural conceptions materialise into new practices.[32]

It is evident that a far-reaching agenda for research is entailed by such considerations. Instead of conceptualising existing farming styles in terms of 'survival strategies' (i.e. like mere intentions to escape 'fate' as contained in 'structural trends'), the different models should be envisaged primarily as future-oriented projects in which *intentionality* is a crucial element. This raises the question of why some 'projects' fail while others succeed in the making of a specific future. The significance, scope and limitations of the 'cultural offensive' organised by the state, science and agribusiness on the 'rational' way of farming and on the 'inevitability' of the development-scenarios as forecast (and objectified) by these agencies, is yet another and highly strategic field to be considered by such an agenda.

Whilst this is the case, culture is not to be eliminated from the analysis, nor from the (theoretical) representation of agriculture. Culture is at the heart of it. Through the ways in which it is interwoven with particular patterns of farming logic it produces and reproduces heterogeneity and therefore locality. Markets and technology are increasingly translated, through the application of agrarian science, into specific cultural models ('the good entrepreneur' and the 'early innovator' are outstanding examples) – models that are accompanied by what I have called 'cultural offensives'[33] – whilst some segments of the agricultural sector align themselves with these kinds of 'role prescriptions', other and sometimes substantial parts take different positions. That is, they reject the proclaimed 'inevitability' of the prescribed behaviour. It is in this way that divergent 'projects' or styles of farming are created and realised. That is the power of culture.

**The end of globalisation: towards a 'relocalisation' of agriculture**

European agriculture is at the brink of a deep and far-reaching transformation towards more sustainable methods of production. In this respect, the pattern of scientification, externalisation and increasing incorporation into markets that has been dominant until now is like the pink panther: 'it strikes back'. The ecological crisis is to a considerable degree identical to the dependence of farming on markets for inputs. It is through this particular dependency pattern that huge quantities of nutrients, feed, fodder, chemicals and energy are concentrated in one place. It is through this inter-related standardisation of the labour process that technical efficiency is lowered. That is to say, a massive 'importation' of potentially contaminating elements is combined with low efficiency levels insofar as their 'conversion' is concerned.[34] The consequence is a high loss of such elements – whether this is into the soil, the ground-water, the air and/or into the end-products, as a high concentration of 'additives' or residuals. This situation increasingly provokes the concept of and struggle for 'de-linking'. The re-linking of agriculture to natural (instead of artificial) growth factors requires a 're-localisation'. The increasing importance of specific consumer preferences, specific attitudes of the farmers concerned and new interrelations between producers and consumers is re-emphasising the locality. In synthesis, locality again becomes relevant, if not immediately strategic. Hence sustainability in agriculture will require again 'art de la localité'; the 'art of farming' will, as it were, be re-invented and re-assessed.

There are, however, other tendencies and movements. As many writers[35] have illustrated, there is and remains in many so-called 'marginal' areas a remarkable 'resistenza sociale'. For many reasons – not the least important being regional culture – 'marginality' or 'superfluity' are no longer accepted but provoke new responses. There is now a large phenomenology of endogenous development patterns with which overall marginalisation is counterbalanced.[36]

In the 'growth-poles' there also appear to be new trends leading to a reinforcement of locality. Somewhat ironically, the deregulation and 'liberalisation' policies, now advocated and implied in many states, have actually become one of the main drives for a reconsideration of the globality constructed so far. The often neglected, but still existing and/or reproduced, heterogeneity is becoming, interestingly enough, one of the key arguments in this reconsideration. It is as if some forgotten facts start to talk in a new language. Take for instance the 'simple' fact that the production of 1.8 billion litres of cheese-milk (for the production of Parmesan cheese) in the Po Valley requires and generates productive employment in the primary sector for at least 26,000 labour units. In Friesland with its highly developed processing sector and intensive farming methods, the production of the same 'quotum' requires only 5,000 labour units. Income levels and perspectives on farm continuity are exactly the same (De Roest, 1990). Thus, where continuous expansion of total production is blocked (as is now the case for nearly all agricultural products and sectors), the variable distribution of value-added between agriculture and industry becomes necessarily a new and probably decisive factor in future patterns of development. Moreover, it is exactly this distribution of value-added that will probably emerge as the Achilles' heel of the scientification, externalisation and globalisation models that are currently dominant.

## Notes

1. Locality is not used here as a geographical notion, but as specific social space, i.e. the context in which social action acquires and reinforces its specificity. An excellent discussion is to be encountered in Marsden and Murdoch, 1990, pp. 24–40.
2. See for a detailed discussion of this concept Van der Ploeg, 1987 and 1990b.
3. Iron evidently being the 'famous' exception, that obliged the introduction of a 'culture d'or' into cropping schemes. Hence, 'economie nature' always was and still is a relational concept, and not an absolute category, as Bloch argued a long time ago (Bloch, 1939).
4. Evidently the relationship between ecosystem and farming was not a unilinear one. Ecosystems related to farming as a set of potentialities and restrictions. Initially the latter predominated, later the former became increasingly dominant as a guiding principle in the further development of farming (see Lacroix, 1982).
5. In the forms of theoretical agronomy that now predominate, the process of agricultural production is broken down into a far-reaching number of so-called growth factors. What was conceptualised in earlier approaches within agronomy as nature, ecology and/or as subtasks within the farm labour process, are now represented as independent elements, to be optimalised through chemical, physical, infrastructural and/or biological interventions (Van Heemst, 1983). It is assumed that both nature and the labour process can be subordinated to this particular perspective (see De Wit, 1983).
6. As a matter of fact, in 1990, several countries closed their borders to Dutch dairy products due to the high concentration of dioxines.
7. See for a further discussion and illustration, Van der Ploeg, 1985 and 1990a, pp. 26–8. A beautiful indication of the complexities of the different subtasks is to be encountered in Adams, 1966.
8. See Van der Ploeg, 1990a, pp. 18–23. See also Saccomandi, 1991, pp. 492–503.
9. Such as the construction of new buildings, irrigation infrastructure, mills, improving soil fertility (cf. Hofstee, 1985), etc. from labour available within the farm family. It should be noted that these forms are still omnipresent, also in so-called 'modern' agriculture (see De Bruin, 1991).
10. A well-known pattern, centred around the sexual division of labour, was associated with the concepts of 'voor' (in front of) and 'achter' (behind),

in the Netherlands, and 'resdoor' and 'resdora' in Emilia, Italy. The 'resdora' or matriarch typically managed the household-economy, which included production for self consumption (vegetables, chickens, bread, etc.) and also the production of minor goods for sale in order to obtain the money needed for family consumption. The resdoor or patriarch only controlled the part 'behind', that was the cow-shed. If earnings were realised these could be accumulated so as to enlarge the herd. The independent character of the household economy and the associated control over it by women, thus guaranteed the formation of capital.

11. Although it is to be stressed that this dependency in no way represents a uniform phenomenon. See for empirical data Van der Ploeg 1990a, Table 1.4 and Van der Ploeg 1990b, Table 12.

12. Capital formation evidently depended on the demographic cycle, on interrelations between generations and sexes and the other social activities in which the farming family was engaged.

13. See among others Brolsma, 1979; and Ledda, 1975.

14. See Van der Ploeg 1990a, pp. 92–5. Ample historical evidence is to be encountered in Bieleman, 1987; Hofstee, 1985; and Van der Zanden, 1985.

15. See Van der Ploeg, 1987 and 1990b. An illustration of the way 'time' is redefined is to be found in Van Heemst, 1983.

16. An empirical illustration of this change, based on a wide spread survey, is to be found in Van der Ploeg, 1987 and 1990b. See also Benvenuti, 1989, in which the same empirical data are linked to a solid theoretical discussion of structural changes in modern agriculture.

17. The reader is referred to Van der Ploeg, 1987 or 1990b, Chapter 5.

18. See especially De Benedictis and Cosentino, 1979, who developed a very powerful set of analytical concepts to explore and analyse the inter-relation between supply and demand of technologies.

19. Cf. Latesteijn for a publication of preliminary results. See also Lee, 1987. Lee, however, introduces several politico-economic dimensions into his analysis, which are typically missing in the current studies of Latesteijn *et al*.

20. See for a detailed analysis that includes Nestle's position, Van der Ploeg, 1987.

21. Specific in so far as it is predominantly based on the assumption of externalisation, whilst theoretically and practically it is quite possible to develop innovations that tend to re-establish the 'integrated' character of farming.

22. A good discussion of this problem is to be found in Busch and Lacy, 1983.

23. An empirical illustration of these problems is to be found in Frouws and Van der Ploeg, 1988.

24. In Saccomandi, 1991, one finds a discussion of this phenomenon within the framework of neo-institutional economic analysis; in my opinion, this framework is extremely interesting and powerful as far as the

representation of the different interlinkages between farming, and markets and technology development are concerned.

25. Cf. Maso, 1986; De Rooy, 1991. The point is that the labour process in farming is both a multidimensional *and* an integrated process: different 'aspects' are coordinated in specific ways, that is, brought in line with each other. The reasoning Mendras applied to 'work, time and the land', also applies to 'work, women and cows'.
26. Such as working with several small, second-hand tractors, each attached to a specific farm implement, instead of having one powerful tractor. This avoids the job of 'hooking on' machinery to the tractor each time it is needed, one of those 'invisible jobs' normally done by women.
27. This is, for instance, the case on farms where cheese-making remains (or is again) one of the central elements of the labour process (cheese-making is a woman's job). Cf. De Rooy, 1991.
28. This typically includes increased reliance on extensionists.
29. See especially Van der Ploeg *et al.*, 1992.
30. A theoretical discussion of the implications of this, at first sight, quite simple and evident fact, is to be encountered in Koningsveld, 1987.
31. This is not only manifest in the different degrees of land stewardship (*rentmeesterschap*), i.e. the different care that is paid to nature and landscape, but also in specific tensions, as expressed in famous slogans such as 'we don't want catholic shit on protestant soils'.
32. This has, of course, always been the case; the remarkable fact is that it is still the case.
33. Automation again is an excellent example, cf. Frouws and Van der Ploeg, 1988.
34. See Roep *et al.*, 1991 for an empirical illustration.
35. See, among others, Antonello, 1987; Barragan *et al.*, 1991; Lacroix, 1982; Osti, 1991; Pernet, 1982.
36. See De Haan (forthcoming), containing the proceedings of the seminar on 'Endogenous development patterns', held in November 1991 in Vila Real, Portugal.

### References

Adams, G. B. (1966) 'The work and words of haymaking', in *Ulster Folklife*, Vol. 72, pp. 66–91.
Akker, K. J. Van den (1967) *Van de mond der oude middelzee, schetsen uit het oude leven op het land en uit het boerenbedrijf*. Friese maatschappij Van Landbouw, Leeuwarden (fifth edition).
Antonella, S. and Bonati, F. (1987) *La Zootecnia Nell' Apennino Emiliano-Romagnolo: configurazione attuale e tendenze evolutive*, IRECOOP Emilia Romagna, Bologna.
Barragan, A., Gonzalez, M. and Sevilla Guzman, E. (1991) 'Revueltas campesinas en Andalucia', in *Cuadernos*, historia 16, No. 294.
Benedictis, M. de and Cosentino, V. (1979) *Economia dell'Azienda Agraria*, teoria e metodi, Il Mulino, Bologna.

Bennett, J. (1981) *Of Time and the Enterprise, North American Family Farm Management in a Context of Resource Marginality*. University of Minnesota Press, Minneapolis.

Benvenuti, B. *et al.* (1989) *Produttore Agricolo e Potere; modernizzazione delle relazioni sociali ed economiche e fattori determinanti dell' imprenditorialita agricola (ricerca CNR/IPRA)*, Coldiretti, Roma.

Benvenuti, B. (1991) 'Geschriften over landbouw, structuur en technologie', *Wageningen Studies in Sociology* 29, Wageningen Agricultural University, Wageningen.

Bernstein, H. (1990) 'Agricultural "modernisation" and the era of structural adjustment: observations on Sub-Saharan Africa', in *The Journal of Peasant Studies*, Vol. 18, No. 1, pp. 3–35.

Bieleman, J. (1987) *Boeren op het Drentse zand 1600–1910, een nieuwe visie op de oude landbouw*, HES Uitgevers, Utrecht.

Bloch, M. (1939) 'Economie-nature ou economie-argent: un pseudo dilemme', in *Annales d'Histoire Sociale*, No. I/1, pp. 7–16.

Bourdieu, P. (1982) *Outline of a Theory of Practice*. Cambridge University Press, Cambridge.

Brolsma, R. (1979) *Groun en Minsken*, De Tille, Ljouwert (fifth edition).

Bruin, R. de, *et al.* (1991) *Niet klein te krijgen, bedrijfsstijlen in de Gelderse Vallei*, Wageningen Agricultural University and Gelderland Province, Wageningen, Arnhem.

Burawoy, M. (1985) *The Politics of Production*. Verso for New Left Books, London.

Busch, L. and Lacy, W. B. (1983) *Science, Agriculture and the Politics of Research*, Westview Press, Boulder.

Columella (1977) *L'arte dell'agricoltura*, Einaudi Editore, Torino.

Frouws, J. and Van der Ploeg, J. D. (1988) *De automatisering in de Nederlandse landbouw, Mededelingen Van de vakgroepen sociologie*, Wageningen Agricultural University, Wageningen.

Gonzalez Chavez, H. (1991) 'Los empresarios en la agricultura de exportacion en Mexico: Un estudio de caso', in *Revista Europea de Estudios Latino-americanos y del Caribe*, No. 50, pp. 87–114.

Graham Brade-Birks, S. (1950) *Modern Farming: a practical illustrated guide*. London.

Haan, H. de (forthcoming) *Endogenous Development Patterns in Marginalizing Rural Areas*: concepts, methods and practices. CERES, Wageningen.

Heemst, H. D. J. Van (1983) 'Crop calendar, workability and labour requirements', in International Post Graduate Training Course, 'Modelling of agricultural production: weather, soils and crops', Wageningen, Geneva.

Hofstee, E. W. (1948) *Over de oorzaken Van de verscheidenheid in de Nederlandse landbouwgebieden*, Groningen.

Hofstee, E. W. (1985) *Groningen Van grasland naar bouwland, 1750–1930*, PUDOC, Wageningen.

Klaassens, K. (1985) *Verschillen in bedrijfsresultaten op moderne melkvee-houderijbedrijven*, LEI (publ. no. 3.131), The Hague.

42

Koningsveld, H. (1987) 'Klassieke landnouwwetenschap, een wetenschapsfilosofische beschouwing', in H. Koningsveld *et al.*, *Landbouw, landbouwwetenschap en samenleving, filosofische opstellen, Mededelingen Van de vakgroepen voor sociologie*, 20, Wageningen Agricultural University, Wageningen.

Lacroix, A. (1982) *Transformations du proces de travail agricole; incidences de l'industrialisation sur les conditions de travail paysannes*, INRA/IREP, Grenoble.

Latesteijn, H.C. Van, Rabbinge, R. and Hengsdijk, H. (1990) HteGemeenschappelijk landbouwbeleid ter discussie, in *Spil* 91-2, pp. 23-8.

Ledda, G. (1975) *Padre padrone: l'educazione di un pastore*, Feltrinelli Editore, Milano.

Lee, J. (1987) 'European land use and resources, an analysis of future EEC demands', in *Land Use Policy*, July, pp. 179-99.

Long, N. and Van der Ploeg, J.D. (1988) 'New challenges in the sociology of rural development; a rejoinder to Peter Vandergeest', in *Sociologia Ruralis*, Vol. XXVIII, No. 1, pp. 7-29.

Long, N., *et al.* (1986) 'The commoditization debate: labour process, strategy and social network'. Papers of the departments of Sociology, 17, Wageningen Agricultural University, Wageningen.

Marsden, T. and Murdoch, J. (1990) 'Restructuring rurality: key areas for development in assessing rural change', ESRC Working Paper, 4, London, Newcastle.

Maso, B. (1986) *Rood en zwart: bedrijfsstrategieen en kennismodellen in de Nederlandse melkveehouderij, Mededelingen Van de vakgroepen voor sociologie*, 18, Wageningen Agricultural University, Wageningen.

Mendras, H. (1970) The vanishing peasant; innovation and change in French agriculture, Cambridge University Press, Cambridge.

Mok, A.L. and Tillaert, H. Van den (no date) 'Beroepsorientaties in de varkenshouderij', unpublished manuscript, Wageningen Agricultural University.

Newby, H. (1980) 'Rural sociology', in *Current Sociology*, Vol. 28, No. 1.

Oasa, E.K. (1981) *The International Rice Research Institute and the Green Revolution: a case study on the politics of agricultural research*, University of Hawaii, Hawaii.

Osti, G. (1991) *Gli innovatori della periferia, la figura sociale dell'innovatore nell'agricoltura di montagna*, Reverdito Edizioni, Trento.

Pernet, F. (1982) *Resistances Paysannes*, INRA, Grenoble.

Ploeg, J.D. Van der (1985) 'Patterns of farming logic: structuration of labour and the impact of externalization; changing dairy farming in Northern Italy', in *Sociologia Ruralis*, Vol. XXV, No. 1, pp. 5-25.

Ploeg, J.D. Van der (1987) *De verwetenschappelijking Van de landbouwbeofening, Mededelingen Van de vakgroep voor sociologie*, 21, Wageningen Agricultural University, Wageningen.

Ploeg, J.D. Van der (1990a) *Labour, Markets and Agricultural Production*, Westview Special Studies in Agricultural Science and Policy, Westview Press, Boulder, San Francisco and Oxford.

Ploeg, J. D. Van der (1990b) *Lo sviluppo tecnologico in agricoltura: il caso della zootecnia*, Società Editrice Il Mulino, Bologna.

Ploeg, J. D. Van der, *et al.* (1992) *Boer bliuwe blinder, bedrijfsstijlen op de Friese klei*, Wageningen Agricultural University and CCLB, Wageningen and Leeuwarden.

Polanyi, K. (1957) *The Great Transformation*. New York.

Rambaud, P. (1983) 'Organisation du travail agraire et identités alternatives', in *Cahiers Internationaux de Sociologie*, Vol. LXXV, pp. 305–20.

Reynders, L. (1990) 'Additieven in he voedsel', pp. 22–6 in J. D. Van der Ploeg and M. Ettema (eds) *Tussen bulk en kwaliteit, landbouw, voedselproductieketens en gezondheid*, Van Gorcum, Assen/Maastricht.

Robertson Scott, J. W. (1912) *A Free Farmer in a Free State, a study of rural life and industry and agricultural politics in an agricultural country*. Heinemann, London.

Roep, D., *et al.* (1990) *Zicht op duurzaamheid en kontinuiteit, bedrijfsstijlen in de Achterhoek, Vakgroep Agrarische Ontwikkelingssociologie*, Wageningen Agricultural University, Wageningen.

Roest, C. de (1990) 'Een voorbeeld Van kwaliteit: de productie Van Parmezaanse kaas', pp. 77–87, in J. D. Van der Ploeg and M. Ettema (eds) *Tussen bulk en kwaliteit, landbouw, voedselproductieketens en gezondheid*, Van Gorcum, Assen/Maastricht.

Rooy, S. J. G. de (1991) 'Werk Van de tweede soort, boerinnenarbeid in de melkveehouderij in Midden-Nederland', in *Spil*, 93–4, pp. 20–7 and 'Werk Van de tweede soort (2), Sekse als structurerend principe in de arbeidsdeling op melkveehouderijbedrijven', in *Spil*, 99–100, pp. 55–60.

RPD (Rijks Planologische Dienst) (1986) *Ruimtelijke effecten Van technologische ontwikkelingen in de agrarische sector*, Wageningen.

Saccomandi, S. (1991) *Istituzioni di Economia del Mercato dei Prodotti Agricoli*, REDA, Roma.

Slicher Van Bath, B. H. (1978) 'Boerenvrijheid' (pp. 71–92), in B. H. Slicher Van Bath and A. C. Van Oss, *Geschiedenis Van maatschappij en cultuur*, Basisboeken Ambo, Baarn.

Staudenmaier, J. M. (1985) *Technology's Storytellers*, MIT, Massachusetts.

Thunen, J. H. von (1842) *Der isolierte Staat in beziehung auf Landwirtschaft und Nationalokonomie*, Rostock.

Vincent, J. (1977) 'Agrarian society as organized flow: processes of development, past and present', in *Peasant Studies*, Vol. VI, No. 2, pp. 56–65.

Wit, C. T. de (1983) 'Introduction', in International Post Graduate Training Course, 'Modelling of agricultural production: weather, soils and crops', Wageningen, Geneva.

Zanden, J. L. Van (1985) *De economische ontwikkeling Van de Nederlandse landbouw in de negentiende eeuw, 1800–1914*, A.A.G. Bijdragen, Wageningen Agricultural University, Wageningen.

CHAPTER 2

# Transformation of the Labour System and Work Processes in a Rapidly Modernising Agriculture: The Evolving Case of Spain[1]

*Miren Etxezarreta*

## Introduction

The modernisation of agriculture since the Second World War has involved extensive transformation of its productive system and of the relations between agriculture and the rest of the economy.[2] The position of labour in agriculture has also undergone far-reaching changes. The aim of this chapter is to identify the changes affecting labour in agriculture, and to assess their consequences in the context of a late developing European country like Spain. The recent and very rapid transformation of the rural world serves to analyse this process. Rather than giving a detailed account of Spanish agriculture per se, the chapter deals with the dynamics of labour in general, using the Spanish case to illustrate the arguments.

One of the important consequences of modernisation is that agriculture becomes closely integrated into the economy, both at national and world level. Whilst agriculture has always been related to the rest of the economy – remembering the Corn Laws and Ricardo – the productive system of modern agriculture has become much more closely intertwined with other economic variables. Therefore its evolution is increasingly related to the general dynamics of the macro-economy. Labour is no exception. It can be observed that the social relations of production in agriculture and the organisation of the work process increasingly follow the patterns of evolution of labour organisation in other sectors.

Since the beginning of the economic crisis of the 1970s, and with the neoliberal economic programmes of the 1980s, the labour market in the developed countries has experienced vast changes. Full and permanent employment is no longer even considered a feasible aim, and the flexibility for labour and wages has become the key objective for labour market policies. Many different methods are being tried to achieve those objectives, leading to important new – more often only renewed – forms of labour engagement and modifications in the organisation of work. It is the contention of this chapter that these trends can also be detected in the agricultural productive system despite its peculiarities and the importance of family labour, in such a way that the agricultural production system becomes fully integrated in the present capitalist re-organisation of production. It proposes to show, first, the different forms by which the organisation of economic life leads to the subsumption and commoditisation of labour in agriculture and, second, the different, often very ingenious, formula by which flexibility is enhanced, such as new forms of labour contracts, externalisation of tasks, pluriactivity and even self-employment. The chapter also tries to explore and assess the main consequences of these developments for workers, agriculture and the rural sector, and society more broadly.

Another important consequence of the modernisation of agriculture concerns the relationship between agriculture and rural development. The changes in the productive situation have brought about significant variations both in the capacity of agriculture to absorb manpower and the role of agriculture in modern economy and society. This new situation, together with important modifications in social values of developed societies about the use of space, signal important changes into the outlook for the rural world. Throughout Europe the discourse on the rural world has been altered.[3] Agricultural development is no longer considered the main base for rural development, but new ways and means to attain it must be found, as well as new venues for displaced agricultural labour. In the second part of the chapter the new forms of labour use in the rural world will be explored, their role in the transformation of the labour conditions investigated, and their scope to fulfill the newly sought aims evaluated.

The modernisation of Spanish agriculture has generally followed the same lines of other developed countries, albeit with a significant time lag.[4] The sector has made a major effort to modernise and become competitive on European and global terms, even if there is still a considerable gap in productivity and competitiveness for many agricultural products. Spain's 1986 accession to the EC is intensifying the modernisation process. This will need to continue and be accomplished rapidly since the country has to 'catch-up' with more developed economies. The speed and scope of change is leading to a variety of adjustment patterns depending on existing agrarian structures and levels of economic development.

Spanish agriculture has two very distinct production systems: family farming and commercial wage-labour farms. The latter historically consisted of 'latifundio' farms; but most of them are now modern agricultural enterprises. A new variety of 'absentee owners' are also becoming important, where commercial farms are owned by urban professionals and run with the help of farm foremen. Modernisation has brought about increasing differentiation of family farms. A minority of family farms, the more modern and economically more powerful, have become very entrepreneurial, while a wide range of different conditions can be found in the remainder. Most farms are owned and run as individual – nuclear family – undertakings rather than in extended family terms. The more modern the farm, the more this is true. Although no statistical information exists about it, it is clear that commercial enterprises account for a major and increasing part of agricultural output. With respect to labour, although family farms employ the bulk of the labour force, wage work is also important, accounting for more than a third of the population employed in agriculture.[5]

## Labour in agriculture

### Modernisation and differential subsumption in the 1980s

(i) Reduced labour requirements
The modernisation of agriculture leads to changes in the composition of the factors of production. New means of production and knowledge are incorporated, requiring heavy capital investment, whereas the socially necessary labour for the production of goods greatly diminishes.

In Spain, this process was retarded by the Civil War (1936–9) and then by economic autarky (1940–53). Agricultural workers still represented 54 per cent of the total working population in 1950. Significant modernisation began only in the 1960s as the by-product of the huge process of industrialisation and urbanisation leading to very rapid emigration from the countryside facilitating the introduction of new productive systems. The agricultural working population was rapidly halved: estimates indicate that 1,000,000 workers left agriculture during the 1950s and about 2,000,000 more from 1961 to 1970;[6] while other figures show a decline from 4,395,000 workers in 1950 to 2,619,000 in 1970 (27.6 per cent of the total working population).

This trend continued through the following decades. Even during the economic crisis, when there were very high unemployment rates for the economy as a whole – above 15 per cent throughout the 1980s up to the summer of 1991, with a peak of 22 per cent in 1985 – the labour force in agriculture was reduced very substantially. In 1990 there were 1,485,500 workers employed in agriculture, only 11.23 per cent of the total working population. Agriculture lost about one million working people in the midst of an industrial economic crisis, manpower diminishing at an annual rate of 4.3–4.7 per cent while the average rate of decline for EC countries is between 2.1 and 2.8 per cent.[7] These figures show that economic problems in the primary sector are still more acute than elsewhere, forcing people to look for outside jobs even in very difficult external circumstances. Agricultural unemployment figures are nevertheless lower than in other sectors, although they vary considerably depending on the source of data.

**Table 2.1** Unemployment rate per sector. Percentage of working population

| Year | All sectors | Agriculture EPA data[8] | Agriculture registered |
|------|-------------|-------------------------|------------------------|
| 1983 | 17.7 | 5.7 | 4.3 |
| 1985 | 21.9 | 11.7 | 5.1 |
| 1987 | 20.6 | 13.4 | 6.1 |
| 1989 | 17.3 | 12.8 | 5.4 |
| 1990 | 16.2 | 12.1 | 5.1 |

*Source*: La agricultura, la pesca y la alimentación españolas en 1990 MAPA, Table 23, p. 24.

The regional distribution of unemployment requires some explanation. In Spain agricultural unemployment figures refer mainly to wage labour, which is concentrated in the big farms of the south, where the major emigration movements of the industrialisation period took place. But the emigration outlet is now closed and the population remains, pushing unemployment rates up to the 30 per cent level.

**Figure 2.I** Rate of unemployment in 1987 (percentage of working population)

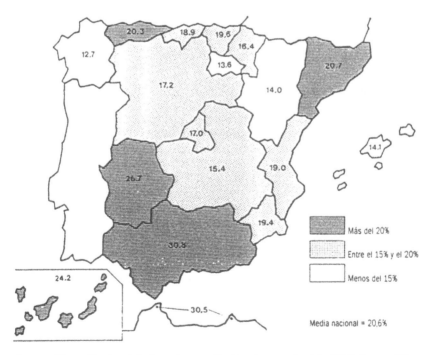

*Source*: Renta Nacional de España y su distribucion provincial, 1987, Banco Bilbao Vizcaya.

Table 2.2 provides information about the agricultural unemployment in the two large southern regions (Andalusia and Extremadura) showing how it rises to 78.7 per cent in 1989 of total agricultural unemployment of Spain. Estimates point to future increases in the area's unemployment.

**Table 2.2**  Agrarian unemployment in Andalucia and Extremadura

| Year | % of agricultural unemployed in Andalucia & Extremadura over Spanish total | % of unemployed agricultural wage workers (Average means) | | | |
| | | Andalucia | Extremadura | Total | Rest of Spain |
| --- | --- | --- | --- | --- | --- |
| 1983 | 60.8 | 26.6 | 18.6 | 25.7 | 10.5 |
| 1984 | 73.3 | 47.3 | 36.0 | 46.1 | 15.0 |
| 1985 | 70.7 | 43.7 | 44.2 | 43.6 | 16.7 |
| 1986 | 70.5 | 48.5 | 46.5 | 48.3 | 17.0 |
| 1987 | 74.2 | – | – | – | – |
| 1988 | 76.3 | – | – | – | – |
| 1989 | 78.7 | – | – | – | – |

*Source*: Agricultura y sociedad, No.54, pp. 181 and 238[9].

This high level of unemployment has led to a very special system of unemployment benefits in Andalusia and Extremadura. People who can prove they have worked 60 days a year are entitled to 190 days of unemployment benefit. The system is even enhanced by the provision of public employment to allow people to reach the 60 required days of work.[10]

It is difficult to estimate the amount of surplus labour and unemployment in agriculture. The extent of family farming means that one should account for disguised unemployment where, because of lack of employment elsewhere, members of the family work on the farm and do not consider themselves unemployed, even though their labour is not fully absorbed. Also, people who become unemployed in agriculture often leave the sector altogether and are thus not counted as unemployed in agriculture.

Moreover, surplus labour can manifest itself in other ways: excess labour in family farming shows up not only by lack of job opportunities but also through decreasing family incomes, widening income differences with other sectors, poorer standards of living and decreasing economic opportunities. Some indices based on income differentials with other sectors can be considered. Table 2.3 presents some data about relative incomes.

Considering all these elements it is likely that a better explanation could be obtained of why people leave agriculture even when facing almost impossible employment conditions elsewhere.

The differences in income between sectors clearly indicate the very unfavourable position of agriculture. In the 1970s and 1980s the agricultural incomes were estimated to be around one third of the Spanish average; from 1974 to 1982 net farm returns fell by about 38 per cent and the downward trend has not changed. The absolute level of agricultural wages stands at

**Table 2.3** Relative incomes among sectors

| Evolution of income parity among sectors. % of Value Added of agriculture over non agrarian sectors | | | % of Net Margin in total gross production Spain | |
|---|---|---|---|---|
| Country | 1973 | 1979 | 1973 | 1985 |
| Germany | 34.6 | 25.8 | | |
| France | 58.3 | 41.1 | | |
| Italy | 38.8 | 41.5 | | |
| Netherlands | 76.7 | 70.3 | | |
| United Kingdom | 81.5 | 64.7 | | |
| Ireland | 56.0 | 49.3 | | |
| Denmark | 70.3 | 61.5 | | |
| Spain | 35.4 | 36.3 | 43.8 | 36.5 |

*Source*: Garcia de Blas, A. Papeles de Economía No. 16, table 12, p. 91.

about one third of the average national wage. Between 1977 and 1986 productivity increased by 83.4 per cent while real incomes only increased by 9.7 per cent. At present, in 1991, high levels of uncertainty about new trends in agricultural policy and decreasing incomes mean that most farming families are increasingly confused and pessimistic about the future.[11]

(ii) From traditional to intensive labour

The impact of modernisation on labour concerns much more than the volume of work. It involves a transformation of the use of labour, the work process and the types of labour that are required. Among the most relevant aspects:

- *Diminished physical effort*: the greater ease of physical tasks is an important gain of modern agriculture. It affects not only the well-being of farm workers but also the division of labour within the family and decisions concerning investment.
- *Scale of production and labour use*: technology allows for a great increase in productive capacity, which is used by farmers not to reduce their labour input but to increase production to full capacity.

The search for higher profits is not the only reason to increase production. The need to pay off and valorise invested capital also means that equipment must be used to its highest capacity. The economic conditions of present-day agriculture also require an increased scale of production. Higher production and world competition have led to decreasing prices, tight markets and narrowing farming returns. Valorisation of invested capital and of labour, even the sheer economic survival of the production unit, requires production of a greater *quantity* of commodities. This in turn is feasible precisely because of machines. The high increase in productivity has thus been necessary to obtain almost the same income as ten years ago. Modern farmers do not work less hours than traditional farmers, but they do produce much more with the aid of machines.

When increased production is not possible, the farming family has to find new ways to increase their income. They find themselves taking up every opportunity to use available labour, within or outside of agriculture. New levels of farm family consumption according to urban models, with self-consumption becoming of almost no significance, also have a bearing on production. This means that the income requirements of the farming community are much higher than in the past. This leads to increased production and intensification.

It should be pointed out that farmers generally do not seem to resent the work they now have to do. This is because of its greater physical ease and the fact that they have always worked all day long. But younger generations and women are much more critical about labour requirements, mainly because of the lack of free time. This is especially the case in livestock rearing, where it is difficult to have free week-ends and annual holidays. Obstacles to a modern and more urban way of life are heavily and increasingly resented.

- *Increased intensity of work*: as in industry, much of the labour in agriculture nowadays consists in the operation of sophisticated equipment. Machines have to work at full capacity and their operators become dominated by their rhythm, leading to very attentive and regular work where all slack time, i.e. the *'porosity'* of work is eliminated. The means of production thus establish the conditions of work. If tools served the worker in the past, now, the worker has become a tool of the machine.[12] Moreover, not only does the work to be performed with machines increase, but competitiveness strengthens the trend in the intensity of all types of work. Table 2.4 provides an interesting example of increased intensity in the harvesting of three varieties of oranges which is performed without machines. Moreover, this increased intensity of production and work is postulated as the only valid method for a dynamic agriculture, becoming the normative work process conditioning the socially necessary labour for the production of agricultural goods and, ultimately, defining market prices.

**Table 2.4** Number of 'Arrobas' (12.5 kgs) to harvest required per day wage

| Oranges | 1960s | 1970 | 1979/80 | 1985/86 | 1989/90 |
|---------|-------|------|---------|---------|---------|
| Type 1 | 33.3 | 40 | 50 | 55 | 56 |
| Type 2 | 33.3 | 40 | 45 | 48 | 60 |
| Type 3 | 11.0 | 17.5 | 22.5 | 27 | 27 |

*Source*: Arnalte *et al.* (1990) Agricultura y Sociedad, No. 54, MAPA.

(iii) From independent to subordinate work
The independent work of the traditional farmer has thus been diluted into the machine. The requirements of technology and product norms have subsumed human effort in a 'farming' version of the subsumption of labour by capital. The internal decision-making process has thus radically altered.

Knowledge, technology and means of production are mainly externally induced and change very rapidly; work requires the operation of sophisticated machines and dealing with new breeds of expensive animals. The farmer needs the assistance of advisers of various kinds, the help of repairers of machines, and experiences the guidance of public policy makers, while food manufacturers increasingly establish product norms. He has lost more of his autonomy and has almost no scope for independent decisions. The priority of capital over labour becomes clear.

The subordination of work may also be based on social relations. This is shown by the so-called 'integration' contracts, whereby the farmer commits his farm to produce a specific commodity according to the contractor's specifications, with the contracting farmer providing mainly the labour force and equipment and bearing the risk of production failures. This form of production has produced a debate about the real nature of the contract farmer, with opinions being divided in considering him a real farmer or a peculiar wage worker. In any case it is clear that the farmer's ability to take independent decisions affecting the production process is greatly weakened. As Van der Ploeg argues, 'Agricultural work is reduced, degraded to executive manual work. Mental work, or at least substantial portions of it, is externalised.'[17]

### (iv) Conditions of work

Significant changes occur in working conditions. First, the intensive use of chemicals in agriculture presents the risk of gradually poisoning the people working with them. Second, there are an increasing number of very serious accidents caused by new and powerful machinery.[18] Third, the strain caused by the greater intensity of work and the economic problems associated with farming seems to be causing major psychological problems both for farmers and farm workers.

Farmers also often mention the loneliness of their work. This has consequences for social interaction, identity and on the feelings of having to bear a heavy burden in isolation. Since family farms are now mainly one-man undertakings, pressure of work makes social intercourse difficult. Isolation is often mentioned by younger family members when explaining their desire to abandon agriculture.

There are also some specific situations where new production systems have major negative consequences. Work in hothouses (most often under plastic in Spain) presents a serious case of unhealthy work conditions. In Southern Spain, particularly, there are many small farms solely devoted to out of season horticultural production under plastic, with very sophisticated irrigation and extremly intensive cultivation systems. The atmosphere under the plastic is extremely unhealthy due to the very heavy use of fertilisers and chemical pesticides, high temperatures and humidity. Analogous problems may exist in intensive chicken or pig production units.

Despite these conditions the deferential and 'familiar' nature of labour makes institutional control of professional sickness or poor working conditions more difficult.

*Changing requirements from labour*

(i) Composition of the labour force
The importance of capitalist agriculture in Spain can be seen by the fact that wage workers represent a much higher percentage of the agricultural labour force than in other EC countries (8 per cent EC average). Wage labour increased from 28.6 per cent in 1982 to 31.3 per cent in 1987, or from 36.5 per cent in the same base year to 38.9 per cent in 1990. All these figures have to be interpreted carefully, however, since the temporary character of much agricultural employment makes it difficult to calculate the real work performed. Other estimates made on the basis of the 1982 census and in terms of working days, account for wage labour at 21.1 per cent of the total, from which 9 per cent corresponds to fixed workers and 12 per cent to temporary ones.

Wage labour is strongly associated with the size of the farm and it is mainly concentrated in the southern half of Spain, being much more important in crop growing than in livestock rearing activities. Temporary, even daily, engagements are dominant.[14] Agricultural workers in Andalucia are generically called 'jornaleros', from 'jornal', meaning daily wage. Women represent a small proportion of wage workers (about 10 per cent in 1986) and are increasingly employed as occasional workers. According to some estimates, unemployment at various times among 'jornaleros' may reach 60 per cent.[15]

Wage labour is growing mainly at the expense of family helpers. In the first wave of emigration the wage workers were the ones that disappeared, but this trend changed in the 1980s. In 1990 almost all the decline in the number of agricultural workers was ascribed to family helpers.[16] This trend reflects the changing nature of farming. The new types of commercial farms require wage workers, a core minority of which are permanent. On the other hand, family labour is scarce and peak periods have to be covered with external labour. Also, since work has become more intensive and professional, it cannot be performed so easily by family members on an informal basis.

(ii) The new flexibility of labour
Flexibility seems to be the key word in current labour markets. Policy-makers and entrepreneurs are trying to promote and increase flexibility so that labour can become a variable cost, avoiding the rigidity of a fixed wage bill. Spanish economic policy was very permissive in this respect in the 1980s, allowing for temporary labour contracts, with the result that 30 per cent of wage workers are now employed on a temporary basis. This figure rises to 70 per cent for new entrants in the labour market and younger workers.

Agriculture has always practised labour flexibility, since seasonal work has always been related to agricultural production. Mechanisation curtailed partly these practices by reducing work peaks, thus introducing a certain rigidity in employment, even if with a greatly reduced work force. Family farming also involves a certain rigidity since, at least in principle, the labour available in the family might be considered a fixed factor. Maximising employment or total returns of the family has sometimes been more important than the attainment of maximum profits. However, capitalisation of farming activities, competition and higher returns make it more difficult to attain these aims. This is shown by the high number of youngsters leaving agriculture.

In many regions of Spain, the more modern farm enterprises face severe problems because of the lack of labour willing to accept the wages and work conditions offered. The problem is partly solved by bringing in workers from poorer agricultural areas, especially for seasonal tasks. When more perm-anent work is required, recourse is made to migrant labour from Africa or Portugal. The immigrants are paid lower wages and have very poor work conditions. Their presence in rural areas, where outsiders are traditionally rare, is generating numerous social problems, particularly outbursts of racism. When the farms do not require all the available family labour, external activities are sought in order to adapt the labour supply to manpower requirements. Pluriactivity thus constitutes an adjustment system directed to make more flexible fixed family labour.

Overall, modernisation has promoted the redifferentiation of labour. Farm holders with viable farms and farm foremen work as qualified agricultural productive agents with permanent employment, they are complemented by wage workers, temporary or seasonal unqualified workers or low-pay immigrants. On the other hand, many small farm families diversify their labour force by means of pluriactivity. There is thus an interesting duality here. The farmer traditionally sells his produce, not directly his labour; he is a commodity seller. But when the selling of produce is not enough to obtain the necessary income, he shifts and sells his labour, significantly altering his social status.

Traditional ways of organising flexibility are being re-formed by new systems of externalising agriculture and contracting labour. Some productive tasks are performed by external enterprises, as in the joint hiring of machinery and the services of its operator. There are different strategies developed either to cope with the indivisibilities related to mechanisation, to cover the labour requirements of a special nature, or simply to reduce regular or permanent employment and its costs on the farm. This represents the agricultural version of the modern trend towards subcontracting. In Catalonian agriculture, for instance, in 1989, wage labourers from contracting enterprises accounted for 1 per cent of all 'agricultural working units' and 5 per cent of wage work. Contract labour grows because of the increasing sophistication and price of new machines, the decreasing agricultural work force and the rise of pluriactivity. Its use is most frequent for bigger commercial farmers and especially by those 'absentee' farmers from the towns. Arnalte (1989) suggests that the agricultural structure of Mediterranean countries enhances the use of contract machinery, especially the tractor, in comparison with the northern countries of the European Community, although it seems the practice is also spreading in the latter.[20]

The supply of these services started with cooperatives but greatly expanded when farmers with medium or large farms bought expensive machines for their farming and found themselves with extra time. Some of them have become almost 'machinery hiring entrepreneurs' working full time as contractors; others supply these services, in very varied forms, as a very substantial complement to their farming incomes.

Modernisation has implied *externalisation* throughout the system. This increasing reliance on external inputs broke the self-contained character of agricultural production. The aspects we comment upon now represent a further step of externalisation; based on almost the only remaining input that the farmer still produces, his labour. This process will have important consequences for analysis of the concept of the productive unit, investment requirements, the elements that determine the scale of farming, and relations between farm structure and returns. The modern production system externalises the productive process itself. As a result its coherence no longer lies in the local production process but at national and international level.

### (iii) Labour qualifications

The growing externalisation places severe pressures on labour flexibility. However, there is a clear contradiction between the need for more flexibility and the need for better qualifications for that labour which assumes more regular employment. The situation is not the same for all types of work. Family farmers are the ones who have been compelled to change the most. The incorporation of capital, mass production and the speed of change compel the farmer to be extremely aware of variations in the general framework of agricultural production and marketing systems, as well as the market for inputs, technology and financial conditions.

Of more significance concerns the change in internal decision-making. There is now a much wider gap between knowledge and the carrying out of tasks. The farmer has to be much more of an entrepreneur even if in family farming he has to continue being the direct worker as well. As Van der Ploeg argues, productivity on an independent farm depends on the technical capacity of the farmer, but on commercial farm, productivity depends on entrepreneurial ability. The 'technological' know-how of farmers diminishes at the same time as their entrepreneurial capacity needs to develop.

In Spain there is still a general bias in favour of technical aspects in agricultural training, whilst management techniques tend to be ignored. Many observers of Spanish family farming in fact state that the lack of managerial capacity is the main factor limiting the future development of agriculture. However, when there is economic capacity, managerial capacity is developed. In the last twenty years Spanish farmers have convincingly proved their capacity for change, adaptation and entrepreneurship. It is always extremely difficult to be the manager of a farm when there is very little to manage. Lack of management capacity should not be confused with scarcity of resources for the new conditions of production. Such a confusion may lead to very wrong policy decisions.

The 'successful' farmer has to combine a high degree of entrepreneurial capacity with the ability to carry out the material tasks of the production process. This combination is, in itself, a difficult undertaking. It assumes heroic proportions when we consider the different types of knowledge, outlooks, and even personal tastes that both lines of development require. A very enterprising young farmer may find it difficult to devote a large part of his time to lonely work in the fields, while a person who likes working peacefully on his own in the countryside might find it difficult to be interested in the type of managerial work that his survival depends on. This contradiction is not alien to the problems experienced by some young farmers who decide to stay in agriculture because they like rural life. Conflicts appear when they become responsible for their holding and find themselves acting as tough businessmen.

The minority of permanent wage workers include farm foremen, qualified farm workers and machine operators. The first two categories are not easy to find since most people with agricultural training work on their own farms. Machine operators, mainly drivers of big machines, are trained in non-agricultural practices and gradually tend to become industrial-like labourers.

The picture is very different for temporary wage workers. The required qualifications have in fact been reduced to the level of simply following machinery. Tasks like fruit or cotton harvesting require totally unqualified work. Modern agriculture accentuates the divisions between the people working in farming. A minority of farmers with viable farms become much more entrepreneurially minded with highly diversified and flexible capacities.

The population of wage workers, mainly temporary, remains utterly unqualified. This dichotomy is affecting labour markets in all industrial countries. Such 'deskilling' tendencies also affect other family members on family farms. They have no specific agricultural qualifications (except in the case of aid from the 'retired' father of the farmer). They are usually wives or relatives working in other sectors. They may have acquired some knowledge on the job, but, with the significant exception of wives doing administrative and clerical work, they generally undertake manual tasks.

*Changing patterns of social organisation*

The uneven modernisation of agriculture has brought significant changes in key areas of social organisation. These are highlighted by considering the role of women; the lack of unionisation of hired farm workers, and the limited employment opportunities of the rural young. An appreciation of these features raises severe questions concerning the nature of rural development in the context of capitalist penetration and commodity led growth.

(i) The role of women

There has been more discussion recently about the changing role of women in Spanish agriculture. Statistics for Spanish agriculture show an increase in female labour from 20 per cent of the working population in 1967-9 to a maximum of 26.1 per cent in 1980, then a fall to 23.3 per cent in 1986 and a new increase in 1987 and 1988.[21] There must be some doubt as to whether these figures reflect real changes or merely improvements in computational methods. In any case, we once again have to distinguish between different regions and types of agriculture.

First, in *the minifundia livestock rearing farms of the north*, women have always played a crucial role in farming, filling in for absent males and being compelled to work very hard in agriculture all year round. Mechanisation, recent return migration and industrial unemployment have made their tasks easier, but they continue to play an important role.

The same can be said of cattle rearing areas like the Pyrenees, even if the holdings are larger and men stay on the farm. The work of women is also crucial in many vegetable growing areas with high labour requirements. On small farms, modernisation has sometimes deteriorated the women's position, since the decrease in family labour and the greater intensity of work means less free time. Physical work has become less strenuous, but the introduction of machines allows women to undertake tasks they did not undertake before. In addition, pluriactivity, of men as well as women, increases the overall requirements on labour. Leisure time disappears and the quality of life drops, even though income levels may be higher.

Women mostly carry out subordinate work in the sense that they are very seldom the real farm holders. They work as family helpers and rarely receive any sort of wage or remuneration. As far as wives are concerned, domestic and farm work are hardly differentiated and both are considered to be the obligation of a 'normal' wife. Very few single girls work in agriculture. Some of them may live with the family and help from time to time but their work is considered a normal, non-remunerated consequence of living with the family. In the few cases where the farm successor is a girl, it is assumed she will marry a man who will take over the running of the farm. It is very likely that the unpaid work of women is one of the main factors permitting the survival of many small family farms.

Work on the farm nevertheless can give women an enhanced status in the household. There is no regular evidence on this but, when interviewing farming women, it is very easily perceived that where they have an important role in the running of the farm they also count more in decision-making. However, there can be little doubt that farm women have a highly exploited life. In Galicia, rural villages are extremely small and offer poor living conditions. In the rest of the region most family farms are scattered in the mountains and social life is extremely poor. Although the ownership of cars and better roads have greatly improved this situation – and women rapidly took advantage of this improvement, using cars much more than the male farmers – it is still a difficult and isolated existence. As a consequence, far more women than men are abandoning the rural sector. In the mountainous and cattle rearing areas, this has led to a major 'marriage problem'.

The position is different for larger family farms. Mechanisation, the increase in the business size and improvements in the standard of living have led to a clear trend towards differentiation of the productive and home spheres. Work becomes an individual undertaking with little relation to the family, similar to work in other spheres of the economy. There a masculinisation of agricultural work and a corresponding decrease of female participation.

The position regarding marriage also changes. This problem affects farmers with traditional ways of life, generally but not always with smaller farms. When the farm is larger and its economy sound, the farmer tends to be a more educated person with a wider outlook. Difficulties may still exist but they can be surmounted, while marriage is extremely difficult for poorly educated, traditional farmers. As in many other countries, girls have attained higher schooling levels and more urban manners and aspirations, making a modern way of life crucial in personal relationships and marriage.

On economically viable farms run by young, well educated farmers, wives tend to come from a non-farming background and/or have attained good professional qualifications and jobs before marriage. They continue to work outside the sector. Both situations can be found in the mountains of north Catalonia. On the most traditional farms, there are no marriage prospects, while on the plain and near small towns some farmers' wives are teachers, nurses, social workers, clerical or industrial workers. These indicate the trend for the future.

The modernisation of farming – and its ways of life – is thus increasingly leading to a separation between the domestic and the farm spheres of the family farm. Meanwhile, the farm family does not retain its decision-making powers. The very hard-working farmer's wife with a very traditional outlook on life is rapidly disappearing, since small farms are themselves either rapidly disappearing or, where local conditions permit, becoming pluriactive.

Although many women may take care of the farm's 'internal' accountancy, once the paperwork becomes external it corresponds back to men. Applications for policy aids, tax declarations and especially dealings with banks are all handled by men.

Second, *central and southern Spain* presents a different picture. In the crop growing areas of the centre (cereal, sugar beet, etc.), women on family farms once worked hard but have had their lives vastly improved by machinery. Moreover, densely populated villages mean there is no social isolation. At present women continue to work in the fields, especially at harvesting time, but not too exhaustively or for long periods. Most girls nevertheless emigrate because they do not like the rural way of life.

In southern Spain, large agricultural businesses combine with very small minifundia family farms and labour is abundant. People live in rural towns and the fields are at a distance. Values and attitudes about female work are different and, with a lack of jobs, there is low female activity on farms. In Andalusia women may work as temporary wage field workers or may be employed for olive harvesting during the winter, when entire families are contracted, but it is not frequent to find them working on their own small farms. Female work is reduced to that of temporary wage workers. Machinery has worsened their work opportunities even more than it has done for men, since women's tasks were ancillary and have disappeared. Unemployment of women wage workers is thus still higher than for men.

Women are becoming increasingly important in the manufacturing or processing of agricultural products and in new forms of intensive agricultural production. In the rural areas of Spain – mainly in the south but also in the easterly and more northerly vegetable growing areas – seasonal work in agro-industries is an important income-earning outlet for young women. In general, these jobs are temporary and non-skilled, organised on 'industrial' lines but paying lower wages, requiring new and intensive rhythms of work and offering poor work conditions.

Overall, the labour of women will continue to be extensive and necessary in many regions if family farming is to survive. Although some physical tasks have been reduced and paperwork has increased, the subordinate nature of women's work has not changed and is not likely to alter in the near future. A dissociation of the family sphere and the farm sphere already existed in the poorer, temporary wage areas of the south and is now appearing in the more developed agricultural areas, although it may be interesting to consider how far pluriactivity tends to slow down or alter this trend.

(ii) Farming unions and labour

Farming unions in Franco's Spain were a complex illegal mixture of political struggle and economic demands. They were mainly based on family farming, although in the south, unions were mainly formed by 'jornaleros'. The position of unions was basically that of considering farmers as workers in agriculture and seeking an adequate return for their work, mainly through 'fair prices' for agricultural products.

Democracy and the modernisation of agriculture have very significantly altered this situation. The political aspect has given way to political parties. At the same time, the development of commercial agriculture and the differentiation of family farming have led to the development of a strata of modern farms. In some cases commercial farmers have created new unions to reflect the interests of bigger farm holders and, in others, viable family farmers have 'taken over' the old unions, giving them a much more entrepreneurial outlook. Their claims and demands now concern aspects like support for farm restructuring, rationalisation and improved competitiveness, not directly related to their labour but to entrepreneurial returns. The change is not simple and parts of the old philosophy remain, but the final outcome is clear. Lip service is paid to the problems of marginal farms and, except for a union of 'jornaleros', wage worker unionisation has virtually been eliminated.

(iii) Youth and the rural world

It is almost a general premise that the agricultural labour force is relatively old and there are no young successors. In Spain, rural young population diminished by 30 per cent in the smaller villages between 1960 and 1981, and by 10 per cent in medium size villages for 1960–70, then increased by 4.4 per cent between 1970 and 1981.[22] The economic recession reversed the outflow, but data from 1987 onwards shows that the decline began again very rapidly. Young people started leaving the rural sector as soon as they found economic opportunities elsewhere.

About half the young people occupied in rural areas work in agriculture, the other half in other sectors. The latter start work earlier than in towns, but about half of them work as family aids (50.8 per cent), of which a quarter are unpaid. For those working in agriculture the percentage of family helpers increases to 78.8 per cent. These figures indicate strong dependence on the family, but very little responsibility in the farm business. We thus find a group of people who are occupied but do not enjoy an independent income.

Formal education is substantially lower than in towns, and agricultural training is very seldom taken up. In general, rural youth is trained for jobs outside agriculture. These are difficult to find. Encouraged by a past expectation of industrial growth, a good percentage of rural youth have trained for trades that now lead nowhere, returning them to the same rural areas they very earnestly tried to leave. This situation can constitute the structural basis for depression and confusion of rural youth. As a result, unemployment amongst young people is 3.5 times the rate for rural people of 30–44 years. The overall picture for rural youth shows 'an image of economic depression and cultural marginality, where there is no room for the majority of them and where they feel parked waiting for the chance to escape' (ibid., p. 9).

### Non-agricultural labour: a way forward?

#### New approaches to the emerging rural world

Throughout Europe, it is now quite clear that agriculture is no longer able to absorb enough people to sustain active and dynamic rural communities. Rural development is no longer the 'natural' result of productive activities but a conscious social option. Many other outlets for rural labour need to be sought so that people can remain in rural communities.

As this chapter demonstrates these trends have reached Spain. Academics and politicians have fully and enthusiastically adopted the new outlook for rural development and have been successful in transmitting it to local leaders, opinion makers and rural families, even if farmers and their organisations seem harder to convince.

The general lines of such development in a semi-industrial country like Spain raise the following considerations:

(i) The current status of this approach is still secondary and only partially developed. That is, the rural world is still mainly associated with agriculture and with complementary sources of income. Although income from other sources might have increased and even become dominant for many families, agriculture is still paramount at the macro level.

(ii) This position is likely to be closely connected with the fact that opportunities for non-agricultural activities in the rural world are closely related to the general level of economic development. In poorer countries (and Spain is a poor country in the European context) there are fewer alternatives for the rural world than in richer countries. Moreover, as it can be seen in Figure 2.2, income

**Figure 2.2**  Economic growth and income differentials in autonomous communities (1985–8)

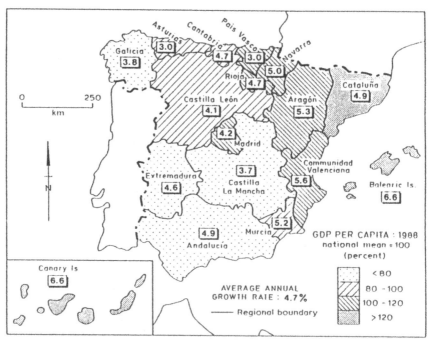

*Source*: El Pais. Anuario Economico, 1990, p. 429

differences are very important between regions. Those with lower incomes have the highest agricultural population making it difficult to find non-agricultural opportunities.

Except in rural areas where industry is traditionally established, few new opportunities appear. The new openings for the rural world are related to expectations for a higher standard of living. Although in Spain these desires are starting to be felt, they appear to be substantially lower than in wealthier European countries. For instance, the trend towards 'green tourism' is much weaker in Spain, where most urban dwellers are still connected with the rural world and do not feel such a strong urge to return to it. Even the sheer economic capacity to consume non-necessary and non-industrial goods is lower. This also has an influence on what is possible from the political point of view. When many basic public services are very weak, both in urban and rural areas, it is very difficult to devote resources to enhancing special projects for a distant rural space. Although there is extensive development in national theoretical and political lines of thought on stimulating new modes of rural development, there is a relatively weak demand for these kinds of activities and a low, if increasing, assignment of public resources.

The activities that have been created in the rural areas can be classified into different types. One group is related to tourist services. It still represents a rather weak demand, except for very specific locations like ski resorts. A second group is based on returning emigrants who establish small businesses to cater for local demand, very often pubs or small general stores. Thirdly there are new types of 'putting-out' home-based labour that have developed. Also, the rural people who work in nearby towns no longer abandon their villages as they used to do in the 1960s and 1970s. Having discovered the advantages of village living and, thanks to the spread of private cars, they tend to commute to work.

There is no data on the extent of these emergent activities, but they are clearly of limited importance, even if they seem to be increasing rapidly. Some unpublished and very partial data from inland Spanish regions shows that about 50 per cent of the rural working population is still in agriculture, whilst the other 50 per cent is working in industry or traditional services for the local population.

### Labour in non-agricultural activities

Generally, non-agricultural wage labour in the rural world is scarce and diminishing, since some traditional manufacturing firms located in rural areas have closed down with the economic crisis. In some regions, where industry and the services are widespread, farmers and rural people commute to work every day. But there is no sign that new industry may become important in the rural areas, nor is there any sort of public policy where spatial considerations for the development of industry or modern services can be perceived. In Spain the economic crisis and industrial restructuring have been very severe and all efforts have been devoted to enabling industry to just keep going. The geographical concentration of industry and modern services is thus increasing in favour of the great industrial and urban areas where the main markets and good communication networks are situated.[23]

It is also difficult to identify clear trends for non-agricultural wage-labour work conditions in rural areas. Many authors indicate that enterprises situated in rural areas tend to pay lower wages and offer their workers less social security benefit. These aspects, rather than being regarded as problematic, constitute what are seen as the comparative advantage of rural areas for industry. However, this 'advantage' is by no means clear when analysis is extended to the labour working in the enterprises. In Spain there are significant *regional* differences in wages; and regions are poorer or more affluent according to the extent of non-agricultural activities and on the type and combination of industrial sectors established in the region. There is some evidence that labour contracts are more irregular and for shorter periods in rural areas, but the differences do not seem that significant, particularly since temporary contracts have now become common in industry and the services.

It nevertheless seems true that workers make fewer demands in the less industrialised regions. Employers claim that even in industrial areas, people belonging to the rural world are less conflictual than urban industrial workers ('there is no harder and more disciplined worker than a farmer used to work for his independent income'). Industrial employers thus often give priority to applicants from farming backgrounds. On the other hand, in some very protracted industrial disputes in firms situated in rural areas, employers have complained bitterly that, since many workers could rely on their income from other sources, especially farming, they could muster stronger resistance. But these particular cases do not outweigh the more general trend.

There is little clear data on diffused industrialisation. Even in regions where such systems have traditionally existed, mainly in the País Valenciano – centre-east of Spain – it is difficult to tell if the labour they employ has increased. Informal or undeclared work is widespread in Spain and most instances of what could be considered diffused industrialisation are in fact small submerged industries of a rather traditional type, where most workers have no regular employment or social security benefit. The type that seems to have undergone most development concerns that of home workers being paid on piece rates. During the recession some big firms closed down shops in the industrial areas and replaced them with systems whereby women work at home at extremely low rates of pay and with no social benefit. These displacements of activity have taken place as much in urban as in rural areas, peri-urban areas or small industrial towns. Most economic initiatives for the new systems of rural development require either the creation of activities by the rural people themselves or public employment generated by the provision of government services.

Public employment could be important here. When new forms of managing natural resources and the environment are being sought, when the need to provide good physical and social infrastructure and cultural services is being stressed, and when new uses for rural space are explored, it is obvious that a generous provision of goods and services, fully or partly publicly financed, is basic to achieving those aims. This could be one of the most direct ways of increasing employment and economic activities in the rural areas (see Persson, Chapter 3). Public employment could provide major opportunities, even well above their quantitative impact. There are some good cases confirming the usefulness of this type of job creation. In the last fifteen years, in some Spanish regions a number of public jobs have been created in rural municipalities through the provision of social services. In spite of their small number these measures have provided jobs especially for women with medium professional qualifications – social workers, teachers, nurses. This is a crucial segment of the population if the number of families with higher education levels is to be increased in the rural areas and dynamic local communities are to be formed.

However, the present high pressure for the control and restraint of public expenditure makes it unrealistic to contemplate any significant expansion of public employment in rural areas. Despite the official discourse, national priorities do not seem to be going in that direction.

Other avenues do present more scope. Greater attention is paid to the economic opportunities which can be created by small private investments and personal or family labour. Internal financial and labour resources may complement each other so as to provide activity and income for rural families. Schemes based on such arrangements are variously called integrated rural development, harmonious development, eco-development and so on. Diffused industrialisation should also be included here. In many cases the combination of external activities and farming is contemplated as a pluriactive system for either the farm-holder or the family. Versions of rural tourism would seem to lend themselves to this arrangement, along with craftsmanship, direct manufacturing and selling farm products.

These schemes may at least provide a way of utilising surplus family labour and savings. This type of arrangement could also give rural families greater social intercourse with external networks, leading to a wider outlook and cultural expansion, as well as favouring the diversification and full use of the abilities of family members. They might also constitute very flexible and more autonomous working arrangements, since they are self-arranged and may be fitted to suit demand. They may be an emergent mechanism for rural development. However, in spite of the favourable light in which many of these opportunities are usually presented and evaluated it is necessary to raise a series of qualifications.

First, it is not clear that surplus family labour will be used to the full. This depends entirely on uneven levels of demand. One important feature of this type of arrangement is that the demands do not correspond to the main lines of the local economy, but cater mainly for scattered segments (for instance, they do not concern great flows of tourists but precisely people who try to avoid tourists, wanting selective forms of recreation). This type of demand is certainly on the increase, but it is vulnerable, often associated with a lower spending power. Moreover, the institutional arrangements to deal with it are imperfect. The uncertainty of these initiatives is high; the economic capacity to bear uncertainty is weak; and the low income levels earned are making such schemes more an emergency survival operation than a satisfactory diversified living arrangement.

Second, if the scheme is successful, the employment level reached may be too high. Although it is frequently asserted that pluriactive arrangements have the advantage of combining periods of slack labour with different activities, this is rarely so in the real world. Pluriactivity is often highly seasonal. The rural families involved often have every member working to the full, including old people and children. Overwork may exist both in the form of many hours for the active members of the family and in the full use of every member of the family, even if they are not of working age or do not have access to proper work conditions. Since there is no institutional control whatsoever, such practices are difficult to regulate.

Third, many people involved in those pluriactive activities are 'jacks of all trades' without professional qualifications. This does not mean that they are not intelligent, resourceful and imaginative. On the contrary, they usually have to be all of these things if they are to be successful. But very seldom can they utilise professional qualifications of any sort. It is possible that this is the case in Spain because of the present limited scope of this type of activity.

This further underscores the efforts made by families to educate their children. Once youngsters have acquired professional qualifications, it is rare that they envisage entering an activity associated more with *survival* than with modern professional *development*. Take, for instance a young man trained to become a car mechanic or a computer operator, or a girl trained as a nurse or a secretary. It is difficult to imagine they will be happy as seasonal tourist guides. More often than not the decision is to look for work outside the town or village and if necessary to emigrate rather than contemplate becoming a pluriactive self-employed worker. In a country where the official discourse is entirely devoted to working for modern qualifications, what sort of outlet can this type of system imply? It suggests that a significant part of the working population in the rural world have to rely on all sorts of unqualified activities that have little to do with the national trends towards professionalisation.

Fourth, many of these diversified systems involve the work of several family members in more or less regular arrangements. This implies a specific type of family arrangement and decision-making process that, in the Spanish context at least, cannot always be taken for granted. This type of setting can only be accepted for families with young children, where the parents are still dominant. It is not realistic when the children come of age. In the Spanish context, rural families are also nuclear families; with the extended family rare. The children want to become economically independent – even if they keep living at home – and it is to this end that all efforts are directed. Moreover, if they have any independent source of revenue, it is far from certain that the income will be pooled at the family level. This sort of 'family activity' is thus not favoured. Unmarried children can help a little, or parents may help a son who is starting a new business. However, there is no unity of economic organisation or decision making. Even in the farm families where the successor son lives and works on the farm, the unity of income is in fact one of the aspects that causes most problems. The current social trend towards increased separation of economic activity and the family is simply overlooked by integrated schemes. The kind of family implied in many ideas for rural development thus has little to do with the Spanish rural world in reality.

Do we have then to conclude that there are no or few possibilities for rural development outside agriculture? A negative answer, implies a very grim future for the rural world. What we want to emphasise here is that non-agricultural solutions are not as simple, cheap, general or sustainable as their often enthusiastic advocates seem to assume. The real scope for such activities has to be evaluated and assessed with realism in each particular regional and local contexts.

As for their labour implications, the main conclusions to be drawn are that these schemes may present some opportunities in quite a number of cases and care should be taken to develop them. It is not certain that these types of activity have the scope to absorb labour in enough quantities to make for flourishing and dynamic rural communities. They may involve long hours, uncertain and rather low incomes and risky investments. Above all, these activities are not in line with efforts to develop a highly qualified working population able to compete in the increasingly internationalised world economy.

### Summary and conclusion

The processes of homogenisation and convergence operate not only among sectors but also among countries. This analysis indicates how far the process in Spain is similar to those that have taken place in more industrialised countries (Van der Ploeg, Chapter 1). In spite of many differences in economic and social situation, and despite the considerable time lags, the main trends caused by the modernisation of agriculture within internationalised capitalism at the end of the twentieth century seem to be similar in Spain to those of other industrialised countries in Europe.

The current production system in agriculture incorporates the main features of wage work in industry and many services. Competition at world level and public policy make sure that product prices do not increase and labour is used more intensively, dispensing with redundant labourers. Modernisation, mechanisation and automation make for intense utilisation of fewer labourers, and almost Taylorist systems of work are brought in with machines and new techniques. The organisation of work is largely determined by the means of production, technical knowledge and outside advisers. Procedures to ensure the flexibility of labour are maintained and developed through new forms like contract labour, externalisation and expanded pluriactivity. Dualisation of the labour force and qualifications is intense, with the productive and family spheres tending to be differentiated as in industrial work. In short, the conditions of production and reproduction in agriculture are converging.

In the second part of the chapter the systems by which labour is made redundant in agriculture and adapts to new conditions have been explored. There seem to be two main developments for the residual farmers and labourers. Either they complement falling agricultural incomes by means of selling or reselling their labour power, gradually changing their nature of sellers of products to sellers of labour, very often as part-time workers and with very irregular periods of work; or they become self-employed on a more or less regular basis. The scope to absorb labour by these solutions appears limited and the resulting quality of life might be dubious. In both cases the rural population has to solve the problems by itself, with local solutions.

The problems should be squarely faced: significant elements of rural labour, as well as urban and industrial labour, are made redundant by the current conditions of production. It is interesting and useful to try to employ rural workers, as integrated rural development schemes propose, but care should be taken not to use such schemes to disguise the real extent of rural unemployment. Some of the longstanding problems should be considered again, such as the geographical distribution of economic activity, the function of rural unemployment benefits, the real cost of maintaining rural populations, who should pay for such maintenance, how many rural people does society wish to have, and what quality of life should rural people enjoy. These are certainly difficult questions, but they need to be advanced if rural areas are to achieve real development and rural labour is to find harmonious uses in this period of agricultural transformation and international integration.

## Notes

1. This article has greatly benefited from information and comments from Mario García Morillas, Lourdes Viladomiu, Josefina Cruz, Chema Fernández, Rocio Muñoz, Pencha Santasmarinas, Antonio Fernández, Ricardo de Andrés Mozo and Maria Pilar García Lozanos, to whom I extend my sincere thanks. Responsibility for what is said is obviously mine.
2. 'Agriculture' here refers to both crop and livestock activities.
3. Considerable documentation on this change can be found in the EC documents about rural policy starting from EC (1985) *The Future of the Rural World* to present day documents about the reform of the PAC. See also M. Etxezarreta (ed.) (1988) *Desarrollo Rural Integrado* (Madrid: Ministerio de Agricultura, MAPA).
4. See J.M. Naredo (1971) *La evolución de la agricultura en Espáñna* (Barcelona: Estela); J.L. Leal *et al.* (1975) *La agricultural en el disarrollo capitalista español 1940–1970* (Madrid: Siglo XXI). M. Etxezarreta and L. Viladomiu 'The restructuring of Spanish agriculture and Spain's Accession to the EEC', in D. Goodman and M. Redclift (1989) *The International Farm Crisis* (London: Macmillan), FIES (1983) 'La nueva agricultura española' *Papeles de Economía*, 16.
5. A. García de Blas (1980) 'Empleo y rentas en el sector agrario'. *Papeles de Economía* 16, 84; and *La agricultura, la pesca y la alimentación españolas en 1990* (1991) (Madrid: Ministerio de Agricultura).
6. J.L. Leal *et al.*, op.cit. p. 191. As can be observed the figures do not totally coincide, justifying caution with the use of statistics here.
7. C.S. Juan Mesonada (1990) 'Empleo y cambio técnico'. *Agricultura y Sociedad*, 54 (Marzo) 35, and *La Agricultura, la Pesca y la Alimentación españolas en 1990* (1991) (Madrid: MAPA).
8. According to estimated unemployment (EPA) it shifts from 5.7 per cent in 1983 to 12.1 per cent in 1990 with a peak in 1986 with 13.5 per cent, while registered unemployment goes from 4.3 per cent to 5.1 per cent for the same years with the peak in 1987 with 6.1 per cent.
9. J.L. Fernández-Cavada (1990) 'Remuneraciones y prestaciones sociales de los asalariados agrarios', *Agricultura y Sociedad* 54, 181–2.
10. For a detailed account of the system see J. Cruz Villalon (1990) *Context III: Andalusia. Implementation of agricultural policies*. Report for the Arkleton Project, Sevilla.
11. Data from A. García de Blas 'Empleo y rentas en el sector agrario'. *Papeles de Economía*, op.cit. 85–92; J.L. Fernández-Cavada op.cit.,

155–91; J. Colino (dir.) (1990) *Precios, productividad y renta en las agriculturas españolas* (Madrid: Mundi-Prensa/UPA) Cap. 4.

12. A. Lacroix (1981) *Transformations du procès de travail agricole* (Grenoble: INRA. IREP) 144. 'Porosity' is also Lacroix's expression.

13. K. Marx *El capital* (Madrid: Siglo XXI. 1975–81) T.1, Vols 1 and 2. Secciones 3 y 4.

14. See L. Ruiz-Maya (1989) 'El trabajo en las explotaciones agrarias: la influencia de la dimensión económica en la evolución de la estructura del trabajo'. *Revista de Estudios Agro-Sociales*, 147 (En-Maz).

15. L. J. Garrido and J. J. González (1990) 'La estimación de la ocupación y el paro agrarios', *Agricultura y Sociedad*, 54.

16. *Anuario de Estadistica Agraria* (1987); *La Agricultura, la Pesca y la Alimentación en España, 1990* (1991) (Madrid: Secretaria General Técnica, MAPA).

17. J. D. Van der Ploeg (1987) *La ristrutturazione del lavoro agricolo* (Milan, REDA) 35.

18. According to statistics from the Instituto Nacional de Seguridad e Higiene en el Trabajo.

19. A. Lacroix also indicates the value farmers place on that type of work in France. See op.cit. p. 116.

20. There is much research on the subject for Italian agriculture. In Spain E. Arnalte is the pioneer. See his article 'Estructura de las explotaciones agrarias y externalización del proceso productivo. Implicaciones para el debate sobre el proteccionismo'. *Información Comercial Española* 666, Febrero 1989, Ministerio de Economia y Hacienda. We have also used his draft 'El desarrollo de empresas de servicios agrícolas y su función en las agriculturas mediterraneas', for which I am grateful.

21. J. M. García Alvarez-Coque and E. Arnalte (1990) 'Factores demográficos y económicos en la evolución de la población activa agraria durante el período de la crisis económica'. *Agricultura y Sociedad* 54.

22. Data to 1984 are from J. J. González *et al.* (1984) *Sociedad rural y juventud campesina* (Madrid: MAPA). For later dates, from *La agricultura, la Pesca y la Alimentación españolas, 1987a, 1990*, MAPA.

23. The Gini index for spatial concentration according to production by square kilometre has been increasing since 1965, with exceptions in 1979 and 1985; in 1989 it reached the level of 0.62456. See *Renta Nacional de España y su distribución provincial* (1989) (Bilbao: Banco Bilbao Vizcaya). For a more qualitative assessment of regional policy: J. Rosell and L. Viladomiu 'La política regional en los ochenta, ¿continuidad o ruptura?', in M. Etxezarreta *et al.* (1991) *La reestructuración del capitalismo en España 1970–1990* (Barcelona: Icaria).

24. See M. Etxezarreta (ed.) *Desarrollo Rural Integrado*, op.cit. and M. Etxezarreta (1988) 'El Desarrollo Rural: Una proximación a planteamientos actuales', *Documentación Social*, 72 (Jl-Sp).

CHAPTER 3

# Rural Labour Markets Meeting Urbanisation and the Arena Society: New Challenges for Policy and Planning in Rural Scandinavia

*Lars Olof Persson*

## Introduction

Each with less than 20 inhabitants per square kilometre, the three Scandinavian countries of Finland, Norway and Sweden together constitute the most sparsely populated region in Europe.[1] Also, the function of the rural areas is continuously a question of major economic importance in Scandinavia. The forest industry, depending on domestic raw material from sparsely populated regions, is the dominant net export industry in both Sweden and Finland. Also, a substantial percentage of the electric energy is produced by hydroelectric plants largely located in the same rural regions; 99 per cent in Norway, 50 per cent in Sweden and 25 per cent in Finland. On the other hand, in the types of welfare economies that have been developed in the last three decades, total financial transfers via the central government are now substantially higher per capita to peripheral and rural regions than to other regions. This presents a dilemma when budget constraints and cutbacks are now introduced in many public sectors, partly as a response to the negative effects of high taxation levels in an international comparative perspective. Public consumption amounts to 27 per cent of the GNP in Sweden, 23 per cent in Finland and 20 per cent in Norway. Furthermore, agriculture which is supported well all the way up to the Arctic circle in all three countries, creates a persistent problem due to surplus production and heavy subsidies. Norway's support to agriculture corresponds to 70 per cent of the value of the production while the corresponding figures for Sweden and Finland are close to 50 per cent.

At the same time production based on rural natural resources continues to demand less labour.[2] Service production is becoming more and more important in all rural labour markets in Scandinavia.[3]

Although 'active development' of rural resources, human as well as material, is one of the goals that is stressed both in regional and agricultural policy, most of the governmental resources directed to rural regions are still spent on maintaining income and services and on consolidation of the settlement structure. This largely reflects the original location of the primary sectors; agriculture, forestry and fishery. This conservation strategy is most explicit in Norway, where the maintenance of the basic settlement structure is a primary goal in regional policy (*The Long Term Future of Regional Policy - A Nordic View*, 1989). In Sweden, the regional policy providing jobs and services in all regions, but the exact geographical level at which these goals should be fulfilled is not explicit. In the 1960s, it was made clear that the government could not take full responsibility for the provision of jobs and services in the rural periphery, but later the limitations of the policy became less sharp.

The increasing demand for international competitiveness, the challenges introduced also to the presently non-EC Nordic countries by the Single European Market, and technological renewal of industry has intensified the Scandinavian debate on regional development. In this debate, the somewhat artificial dichotomy of metropolitan and rural areas is often used to symbolise both the extremes of the settlement system and the necessity of more future-orientation in regional policy. Large cities and city regions are to an increasing extent associated with economic growth, creativity, early adoption of new technology as well as of import of cultural signals (Andersson and Strömqvist, 1988; Jacobs, 1984). Sparsely populated and rural regions are correspondingly considered to represent the old Scandinavian society in economic, cultural and social respects. The rural firms are mainly operating at late stages of the production cycle. The capacity for adjustment in such areas is assumed to be limited as a consequence, amongst other things, of the distances involved.

In the three Scandinavian countries, there is at the same time an established idea about the uniqueness of rural areas which motivates special policies for these areas: resources are geographically spread and bounded; the economy and the labour market is considered to be strongly tied to the exploitation of natural resources, even if to a large extent the profits of processing accrue to densely populated areas. Furthermore, it is commonly held that development strategies have to be built upon the basic resources and the local firms; that the ownership structure of the land should remain fairly fixed; and that the unique social and cultural systems are important to maintain and protect. This kind of perspective[4] guides most of the instruments used in rural policy by governments in Norway, Finland and Sweden; such as incentives to small enterprises and income support to small farms. Some of these instruments were introduced already in the 1940s, but most of them were initiated in the 1970s and later.

The aim of this chapter is to describe and analyse processes of change in rural Scandinavia from the rather isolated *short-distance*[5] *localities* – largely depending on resource-based production and self-employment – of the period before 1960; through the *local labour market areas* – largely with semi-urban character – of the 1970s and 1980s and currently into elements of the emerging modern *arena society*. The concept 'arena society' is used to describe the many-sided mobility that increasingly characterises the entire economy, the labour market and the population. Applied to rural Scandinavia, this may change the way both the rural and the urban resources are exploited in what can be labelled as the 'urbanised rural areas', i.e. the intermediate zones of the urban–rural continuum. In the future, the traditional function of the *local* labour market may be perceived as a less important issue in many rural areas.

The chapter also places emphasis on the role of public sector planning and policy in welfare states under the pressure of change, which is partly induced by internationalisation processes. Most of the empirical data used in this chapter refers to Sweden, but the discussion is partly relevant also to Norway and Finland. First, the general urbanisation processes influencing rural labour markets are discussed. Second, the changing structure and the labour adjustment of primary agriculture to the urbanisation process is analysed and compared in different locations. Third, the qualitative changes of labour supply and demand, in terms of the formal education of labour, is highlighted. Fourth and finally, the concept of the 'arena society' and its impact on the future of rural Scandinavia is discussed, i.e. the increasing importance of individuality and mobility.

### The rural-urban continuum: conventional characterisation of rural labour markets

In practically all regions – whether developed or not, industrialised or not, under a free market or a centrally planned regime – the settlement pattern is characterised by a rural–urban continuum, representing not only variable density, but also geographic differences in socioeconomic development (cf. Gade *et al.*, 1991b). It is likely that the slope of this continuum, from a high in urban centres and decreasing to a low in peripheral rural regions, will vary by stage of development. We expect that the steeper the slope the less developed the national condition, with the least slope likely to be found in advanced social welfare states, like Sweden. However, it is also true that in most cases of regional policy and planning, this continuity in socioeconomic development is not well recognised. 'Urban' and 'rural' are often treated as two quite opposite concepts. In most contexts urban is represented and visualised by built-up areas with intensive economic activity, high population density, and a relatively high quality of life when it comes to material resources. These areas have problems and options that are thought to be unique and planning has proceeded accordingly. On the other hand, rural is often visualised by a much more dispersed population with economic activities tied largely to the supply and quality of natural resources, plus a comparatively low quality of life in the limited sense mentioned above.

As an average condition, the economic as well as the social dynamics of the more urban region exceeds that of the more rural region. Consequently, in highly urbanised nations and regions, changes and development affecting metropolitan or city regions are often gaining more political interest than are those occurring in other regions. It is also true that public policies directed toward urban regions in general have more of a 'proactive' character, whilst policies toward rural areas are predominantly 'reactive'. That is, they are designed to *compensate* for perceived low quality of life in a wide sense. In traditional regional planning in Scandinavia the quality of life is generally reduced to three components; employment, supply of human services and good environment. With a view toward reconciling the dichotomies in regional policies that have resulted from these polarising perspectives, it is important to examine the changing character of urban–rural socioeconomic development from the perspective of its essential continuum condition. This perspective may prove to have greater credence in public policy formulation and planning for rural areas.

In Sweden, where compensatory and egalitarian elements are embedded in almost all sectors of the welfare system, the regional impacts are substantial and deep-seated. This suggests, that an analysis of the different aspects of the welfare system is crucial for understanding recent and potential development in rural regions. Toward the end of this century several changes are anticipated in the Swedish welfare system, including an increasing influence of market forces in service production, and additional elements of decentralised problem solving and planning. The form and scope as well as the regional implications of these changes are still very much under debate. For instance, after Sweden's formal application in July 1991 for full membership in the EC, questions are raised about the legitimacy of the municipal monopoly in producing childrens' day-care as well the admissibility of a basic element in rural policy, the investment grant to small firms.

Today, most peripheral and rural areas in Scandinavia in several respects are *more integrated in the urban economy* than is usually portrayed in debate, as well as in policy and planning. The national public programmes for social welfare and infrastructure development have contributed to increased rural–urban integration and to thorough restructuring of the local labour markets. This implies that future regional policy should take into account a vision of how to develop certain urban characteristics of the rural areas, without depleting the unique rural features.

The concept of 'urbanisation' of rural areas is used here to describe processes that lead to city characteristics - in terms of supply and demand of labour, consumption patterns, supply of services and life-styles (Persson and Wiberg, 1988; Persson, 1990). There are different processes that constitute the general urbanisation trend and these processes have advanced to a specific point in each rural area in Scandinavia. As shown later in this chapter, the urban characteristics of the economy and of the labour market are obvious in most peripheral regions in Scandinavia, whilst at the same time rural characteristics are still important when it comes to the lifestyle of the population and the housing conditions. The urban features of the regional economy and the local labour market is for instance registered in terms of employment in non-agricultural activities and in services. Public services are important parts of the rural labour market, more so in Sweden than in Finland and Norway. The importance of urban lifestyles in rural areas is reflected by increasing number of wage-earners. The increasing dependence of farm households on wage-labour is described as the 'sub-urbanisation' of the family farm in the next section of this chapter. An increasing number of commuters from rural areas generates a more urbanised – or suburbanised – housing standard and mobility pattern. The taxation system with the same local tax rate within the administrative units, the municipalities, covering both urban and rural regions adds further to the integration.

This integration is not yet well recognised in the present public rural policy. For instance, when the Swedish government initiated various types of subsidies for the rural areas during the 1970s, the following criteria were used as a basis for discussion: weak conditions for manufacturing industry, receding population basis, difficulties of maintaining services, the urgency in regional policy in fixing population and the lack of employment opportunities within reasonable distances. It is calculated that some 6 per cent of the total population live within this sparsely populated area.[6] It covers an areas which comprises more than half of Sweden, especially the large northern interior (Figure 3.1). This so called 'Aid area' is the main target for regional as well as rural policy in Sweden.

According to the interpretation of the urbanisation process in rural areas, a quite different concept is suggested: *urbanised rural areas* (Johannisson *et al.*, 1989). This is a type of area where there is an acceptable population base for most types of daily basic services and an ordered – even if limited – wage labour market, although at the same time conditions are poor for advanced services for both households and businesses. This proposal concerns – under Swedish conditions – smaller central places with a commuting area which is located relatively far from bigger settlements.[7] According to the definition, the urbanised rural areas are local labour markets that are found in most parts of Scandinavia and altogether contain almost 20 per cent of the total population. This consequently excludes remote areas with scattered settlements with households which are almost completely dependent on their own enterprise or guarding of natural resources. It involves important functions, covers a large land area, but only a few per cent of the total population and could be considered marginal when dicussing general regional problems. Consequently, we leave these areas outside the discussion in this chapter.

The geographical pattern of the *urbanised rural area* in Sweden is shown in Figure 3.2. It shows a more concentrated pattern than the region which is now subject to traditional rural policy, the 'Aid area' (Figure 3.1). This, in turn, reflects the point that the present rural policy is more inspired by the

**Figure 3.1**   Sparsely populated areas subject to special policy measures in Sweden.

rural characteristics of the large sparsely populated areas, while the point of this chapter is that the parts of rural Sweden which contain most of the economic activities and most of the population are in fact located within the urbanised rural zones with presently quite well functioning local labour markets areas, largely depending on service jobs. One important question is whether this type of region is also well prepared for the anticipated changing conditions, including the increasing demand for jobs requiring higher education, the need for cut-backs in public budgets and further increases in individual mobility.

**Figure 3.2** 'Urbanised rural areas' (Intermediate Socioeconomic Zones) in Sweden

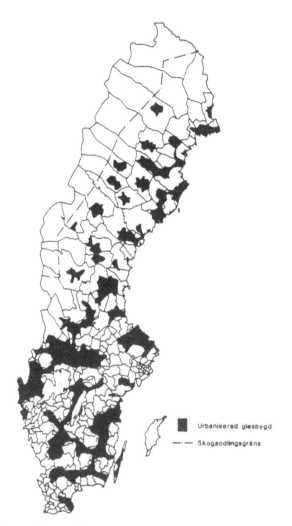

Urbaniserad glesbygd

—·— Skogsodlingsgräns

## Processes in rural urbanisation

In the urbanised rural areas public 'production of welfare' – i.e. education, health care, social services – now accounts for most of the jobs in the labour market for younger as well as older women. Agriculture and forestry accounts for 30 per cent of the labour market for middle-aged men, but less than 10 per cent for younger men (Johannisson *et al.*, 1989). The present long-term economic plan for Sweden assumes that employment within agriculture shall be substantially reduced up until the turn of this century (SOU, 1990, p. 14). The main reason is state budget restrictions, which implies that the world market prices in food products will reach the farmer more or less directly. In fact, agriculture will be the sector which experiences the biggest decline in employment – even in absolute numbers greater than manufacturing industry. At the same time, employment in both private and public services is forecasted to expand more than employment in agriculture, and forestry is expected to decrease. It is evident, according to a regional analysis of the impact of this national plan, that:

> at the same time as the transition to a post industrial information and knowledge society is in progress in Sweden, a strong structural transformation is occurring within the natural resource based industries. (op cit)

Statistics and surveys show that the urbanised rural areas are well equipped when it comes to basic services, both in terms of human and of business services. On average they have almost 80 per cent of what is generally found in fully urbanised regions. However, when it comes to more specialised services, primarily for business purposes, the situation is different. On average, the level of such services is represented by only one third of what is found in metropolitan regions (Johannisson *et al.*, 1989). In the long run, this creates a problem for economic growth and renewal in these regions. The importance of the supply of advanced producer services in rural development is increasingly recognised (cf. Sjöholt, 1991).

The labour markets in urbanised rural areas are generally small but are able to offer employment at almost the same level as in larger regions. The average employment ratios are only a few percentage units lower than in other regions (Johannisson *et al.*, 1989). The differences in unemployment rates are correspondingly small.

The transformation of the labour market in the urbanised rural areas is more powerfully influenced by sectoral policy within different sectors than by regional policy. The importance of this statement motivates some detailed statistics derived from recent research. It is calculated that resources for regional policy in a country like Sweden correspond to less than 0.7 per cent of the total governmental resources to the average region (SOU, 1989, p. 65). The rural policy is in turn only a fraction of regional policy. Subsidies to the agricultural sector only – which is located in practically all parts of the country, but the bulk of production is in or near central urban areas – account for at least five times that sum (Persson, 1989). At the same time, direct welfare transfer within the social security system accounts for almost 50 per cent of total transfers and another 11 per cent to compensate for general weak conditions in the regions, for example, expressed by high unemployment. Until recently relief work was used as one important instrument within the labour market policy, but is now replaced by labour market training schemes. Only 5 per cent of the resource transfer is explicitly or implicitly directed towards future development (higher education, research, etc.). Governmental services and infrastructure maintenance and construction accounts for 27 per cent and generates many jobs, directly and indirectly. The consequence of the extensive welfare programmes – largely managed by the municipalities and financed both by governmental resources and local income taxes – is that employment as well as buying power is effectively spread even to peripheral regions, primarily without any geographical intentions. These programmes are oriented primarily towards individuals, not regions. One of the direct results is less evidence of rural poverty in Sweden – as well as in Norway and Finland – than in many other countries in Europe. These programmes have meant an important shift not only in the level of service production in these areas, but also in the labour market situation, especially for women.

The geographical profile of all these governmental resources is, however, distorted to some extent. For instance, resources for higher education and research are directed much less to peripheral and rural regions. The per capita spendings for these purposes are generally less than half of the national average in these areas. This is clearly reflected in the quite low educational levels of the labour force in the urbanising rural areas, which is important in assessing the potential for future development of these areas. The relative frequency of labour with post-secondary education in rural areas is less than half of that in metropolitan regions, and in spite of an overall growth, the gap seems to widen over time.

When considering infrastructure the situation is different again. Due to the specific geographical conditions – mainly distances and climate – the northern peripheral regions in Sweden have for a ten-year period of 1978–87 received an amount in public investments in the transport and communications systems that clearly exceeds the population share of the region (Sundberg and Carlén, 1989). Major investments are provided for in the road systems, and also in the telecommunications network. This is another way of saying that the development of public infrastructure has facilitated the progress of urbanisation in peripheral areas. One question is whether the level of public investments in and maintenance of the infrastructure will be sufficient to meet the needs of the still more mobile population in the future.

In summary, in the countries in northern Scandinavia, especially in Sweden, the concept of 'urbanised rural areas' is relevant to describe the present situation in most rural regions. National programmes for social welfare and infrastructure development have more or less unintentionally promoted increased integration between rural and urban areas. Female participation on the formal labour market has increased to a high level. Although the explicit direction of rural and regional policy aims at the active development of rural resources, in practice the major state resources are directed towards the maintenance of local labour markets and basic services. This is provided for by both the labour market policy and as a side effect of the social policy. The strong consensus up until recently on equal opportunities for individuals is one driving force behind these policies. This has created integrated and continuous rural–urban peripheral regions in Scandinavia that prove to be viable in the short run. They are nevertheless at risk in terms of the future orientation of their economic structure.

**Decline of the agrarian basis of rural labour markets**

The structural changes involved in the urbanisation process of rural labour markets are realised at the household level. A graph tentatively showing the emerging social structure in many rural areas in Sweden is shown in Figure 3.3 (Grade *et al.*, eds 1991a). The traditional peasant family with more or less subsistence economy – in the short-distance society – was largely transformed into the politically desired 'rational' family farm structure. The subsequent deregulation in the 1980s of agricultural policy has made it possible and necessary to develop more of entrepreneurship in rural areas (Peterson, 1990). However, in most rural areas 'new' households with little or no dependence on agriculture and forestry are becoming the dominant social strata. A possible prolongation of this transition is made until the year 2000. In this section we examine the pattern of adjustment of rural labour markets at the household level.

**Figure 3.3**   Structure of rural population in Sweden 1940–2000

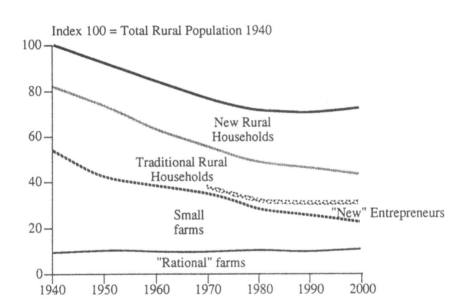

In a historical perspective, all Scandinavian countries were industrialised and urbanised quite recently and these processes have now proceeded most far in Sweden. Around the year 1940 the rural population in Sweden constituted 2.5 million or 40 per cent of the total population.[8] About 50 per cent of this population resided on what was, at that time, defined as farm units in the agricultural statistics.[9] Excluding all the farm families and a certain number of farm workers, it can be estimated that, in 1940, as many as 1 million people lived in rural areas without being directly involved in agriculture. However, many of these were indirectly involved, in the provision of farm services or in the food industry.

Fifty years later, in the early 1990s, the remaining population amounts to almost 1.5 million, but with no more than 20 per cent of them belonging to a household with a farm enterprise. Precisely like 50 years ago, more than 1 million rural inhabitants live in rural areas without having any direct contact with farming. However, few of these are now indirectly dependent upon agricultural production, since food industry and farm services are now largely centralised. A farm enterprise is now defined as cultivating more than 2 hectares of arable land and they amount to approximately 100,000. In practice, many of them are too small to be called a business, but rather constitute rural households. Counting only the large farms, i.e. those who give full employment the year around to at least two persons, these produce 80 per cent of the agricultural output, but generate only 10 per cent of the total population in rural areas.

The exodus of labour from agriculture was intensive already in the 1930s, but the rate of contraction increased in the 1940s and 1950s. The exodus from rural areas was, however, not only explained by labour surplus in agriculture and lack of employment in other sectors, but as much by the supposed cultural and social deficiencies of the rural communities. This opinion was also reflected by the comparatively wide development programme for rural regions that emerged in the 1930s and the 1940s. The smallest farms were also recognised and accepted in agricultural policy as what were called the 'personally owned rural homes'. Loans were provided with low interest rates to families who wanted to buy or build a house with or without some limited area of arable land in rural areas. Loans were also provided to rural workers who wanted to acquire some land for small-scale agricultural production.

In the 1940s it became clear that the different policy instruments to rural areas and to the rural population were not enough to stop depopulation or to solve the rural poverty problem. A public committee explained that the main cause for rural poverty was the large number of small farms. In a proposal to the Parliament (1947) the new agricultural policy was defined. It was decided that the farmers should have the right to an income that was equal to that of industrial workers and that the 'rationalisation' of farms should be stimulated, by means of structural policy and price supports. Although the major goal was social – increased incomes for the farm families – the policy instruments were directed towards the farm enterprise. For 40 years the income goal has been dominant in Swedish agricultural policy although the number of people dependent on agriculture has decreased to only a few per cent of the economically active population. In order to implement a proper price policy it was necessary to make income comparisons between farmers and industrial workers; a 'Normal Farm' should give the farm family a reasonable income and be of a specific size: between 20 and 30 hectares of arable land.

In order to implement the new policy central and regional agricultural boards were introduced – with a substantial bureaucracy. Also, public R&D efforts were intensified – in real terms the public expenditures on agricultural research increased 400 per cent between 1945 and 1965. For a long period of time – until the second part of the 1970s – the only active policy instrument directed towards employment in rural areas was support to agriculture.

The conception of 'rational' agriculture became heavily impressed upon both the farmers and the consumers. There was no doubt that social scientists contributed to the development of the concept of 'rationality'. Agricultural economists developed and used analytical tools such as linear programming in order to decide which optimal mix of production factors should be promoted at the farm level. In short, these and other factors and actors contributed to develop a perspective on optimal farming as depending on rather homogenous production units using scale economies.

The problems that developed in the 1980s in Sweden as well as in many other Western countries due to surplus production and increasing demand for price support certainly changed this view, among researchers, planners as well as among the farming population. The farmer as an entrepreneur is becoming the new 'ideal actor' in rural development. In Sweden this is obvious from new support programmes, stimulating investments in rural areas through monetary subsidies and extension services in more or less every rural community. Researchers try to show the potential advantages of new rural production. As will be shown later, however, it seems to be a rather slow process until a substantial number of the farmers have accepted a new role and found it economically worthwhile to fulfill. Furthermore, it seems that this process is quicker and easier to maintain in urbanised rural localities than in peripheral areas.

It is sometimes argued that the structural policy in Swedish agriculture has been successful, pointing to the fact that starting from a structure with not more than 10 per cent of the farms larger than 20 hectares of arable land (the minimum size for the Normal farm) in the early 1940s, we now find that more than 40 per cent of the farms meet this requirement. However, it certainly seems inappropriate to estimate the rationality of a farm only by its physical size. If one considers the basic element of the Swedish agricultural system to be a farm which is large enough to provide full employment for at least one person, we find that about 40 per cent of all farms meet their requirement. Only one out of five farms is entirely dependent on agriculture as the source of income.

About 80 per cent of all farms in Sweden are located in the more urbanised areas; i.e. less than 30 km from a medium-sized or big town. The basic production factor, the arable land, is even more concentrated. This means that – contrary to what is often argued in the public debate on rural development – farming is largely an activity which is geographically linked to urban areas. Agriculture is of limited interest when it comes to production, employment and population base in the sparsely populated – and peripheral – rural areas. Only 5 per cent of all full-time farms in Sweden are located in the rural periphery, i.e. outside commuting distance from a medium or large urban centre.

The traditional ways to meet the income problem at the farm level is expansion of the specialised production on farm or off-farm jobs. The diversification whilst increasingly advocated in rural and agriculture policy is still limited. Somewhat more than one fifth of the farms have introduced some sort of 'special production' but on a limited scale (Table 3.1). As an average for all farms the labour input is less than 3 weeks per annum in this kind of production, or about 10 weeks per annum at farms with such production. Full-time farms are more devoted to on-farm activities and consequently most interested in new products or services linked to the farm resources. Farmers in the Urbanised Plains[10] put in much more labour in these kind of activities than in the Rural North. This is partly a reflection of the bigger and more diversified local demand for such services that farmers can provide and partly a reflection of the more favourable climatic and other natural conditions in the southern Plains. Also the frequency of non-traditional agricultural production is higher there. As one would expect the younger farmers are more inclined to introduce non-traditional service production based on farm resources.

**Table 3.1**  Involvement in non-traditional production based on farm resources. Percentage of different farms and average labour input, hours per annum, 1988

| Percentage of farms with any kind of non-traditional production | | | | | | |
|---|---|---|---|---|---|---|
| REGION | Farmers >65 years | Hobby farms | Part-time farms | | Full-time farms | TOTAL all farms | Hours per annum (average) |
| | | | Small | Big | | | |
| Urbanised Plains | 8 | 22 | 21 | 32 | 25 | 23.3 | (140) |
| Intermediate | 5 | 18 | 26 | 24 | 24 | 19.9 | (73) |
| Rural North | 12 | 15 | 23 | 36 | 29 | 21.3 | (55) |
| SWEDEN | 8 | 18 | 23 | 30 | 25 | 21.4 | (89) |
| Hours per annum | (24) | (83) | (97) | (63) | (123) | (89) | |

*Source*: Deltidslantbrukets struktur och betydelse, 1989.

Agricultural production now contributes at the most one third of the average farmers' incomes, least in the Rural North and most in the Intermediate Region (Table 3.2). Some 20 years ago the corresponding figures were close to 50 per cent. Approximately two thirds the total income is now provided through off-farm jobs. In all regions off-farm service jobs contribute to almost 40 per cent of the farm families' incomes. The advancement of the welfare state into urbanised rural areas is clearly reflected by the fact that in many regions a larger proportion of the farm household incomes are derived from service jobs. Incomes from agriculture on full-time farms play their most important role in the Intermediate Region. Among the farm families, hobby and part-time farmers are relatively the most important generators of incomes in most types of rural areas; more than 50 per cent – and much more in the Urbanised Plains – of the incomes are generated from

**Table 3.2** Sources of income for farm families in three Swedish regions. Percentage of total income, 1985

|  | Urbanised Plains | Intermediate | Rural North |
|---|---|---|---|
| Agricultural incomes (on farm) | 28 | 32 | 20 |
| Capital income | 8 | 8 | 8 |
| Entrepreneurial incomes (farm-based) | 3 | 3 | 3 |
| Income from off-farm jobs: | 61 | 57 | 69 |
| in | | | |
| *Agriculture, forestry* | 5 | 5 | 6 |
| *Manufacturing industry* | 10 | 12 | 14 |
| *Construction* | 5 | 5 | 6 |
| *Commerce, transport* | 14 | 13 | 16 |
| *Public administration* | 3 | 3 | 4 |
| *Social and health care* | 14 | 13 | 16 |
| *Education* | 4 | 4 | 5 |
| *Other* | 3 | 3 | 3 |
| Total income for families | 100% | 100% | 100% |

*Source:* Estimated from 'Deltidslantbrukets struktur och betydelse'.

such farm families. In most regions in Sweden, incomes from agriculture constitute less than 10 per cent of total incomes in any rural area.

There is a substantial in-migration to most rural areas, even if the net migration may be negative. For a typical rural area in central Sweden the average cumulative in-migration during a 15-year period exceeds the present population in the area. In the northwestern interior, where the major regional problems are located, the number of the last 15 years' in-migrants generally exceeds half of present population (Persson, 1990). This 'renewal' of the population, which has little to do with traditional farming and/or job opportunities, but rather housing preferences, is important to realise in policy and planning. An analysis based on personal interviews in two rural regions in the north and in the south of Sweden shows that the new rural households are well aware of the unique combination of rural and urban resources and that this combination is an element of their perceived quality of life (Ennefors, 1991). Traditional rural problems – lack of employment, long distances to commercial and other services, etc. – are seldom mentioned in these interviews.

In summary, income and structural policy within the agricultural sector has not been able to slow down the continuous decrease of agricultural employment in rural areas. However, while the rural labour market changes suggest more dependence on service jobs many farm households obtain non-farm income. In the short run, this facilitates adjustment during the present agricultural 'crisis'. However, in many rural labour markets, the low formal quality of the local jobs may be a problem now and in the future. As shown in an earlier section, most subsidies or public resources reaching rural areas are not intended to, and do not develop or contribute to, a new viable economy.

This suggests that – in order to encourage further integration of the continuous rural–urban labour market – the policies should be redirected in order to increase the quality of the labour market, the supply of business services and support those households which find living in the urbanised rural area to be unique and attractive.

### Rural labour markets facing the knowledge economy

From one point of view most Scandinavian regional labour markets are vulnerable, being elements of small and increasingly open national economies. One reason is that the economically important and widespread forest-based as well as the manufacturing industry, both operating at rising levels of technology, are to a large extent export-oriented and dominated by a few big companies.[11] The ownership pattern is getting less local and more international. In the most northern region of Sweden, more than one third of employment is controlled by companies which have their head office located outside the region (Snickars *et al.*, 1989). Another feature is that the competitiveness of important growth branches depends almost entirely on advanced research linked to increasing international standards. Also, since many small and medium-size firms are subcontractors to the large export companies, their competitiveness depends on their ability to meet the quickly changing requirements on product quality and technology. Although high levels of technology and competence of labour in a region may imply vulnerability, it seems that most regional planners and policy makers favour this risk over and above the risk of the region of being 'left behind' with an obsolete industrial structure and an undifferentiated labour market.

In countries with a sparse urban system, with a comparatively small population and quite strong political consensus both on established objectives for regional balance and on the responsibility of the state to fulfill these objectives, these conditions mean strong demand on the provision of effective infrastructure, support for services and for the supply of qualified labour in practically all regions. Nevertheless, in spite of decades of regional policy in Scandinavia, many of these conditions still differ markedly between regions.

From another point of view there is already an element of built-in stability in most regions, since the local labour markets are largely oriented towards local and regional demand. The export industry is economically most important, but its demand for labour is limited. In Sweden, the total volume of service jobs is still increasing in most regions, but slower than before. The comparatively ambitious national labour market policy underlines this stability. Furthermore and at least until now, national sectoral standards have been the primary guides for the distribution of welfare and thus the number of public service jobs over the country. Such standards include criteria for formal competence; certificates of special education are now required in more of the public service professions and in each region. This leads to increasing demand for specialised education in most regions, in order to maintain objectives in terms of welfare distribution and to ensure the reproduction of local labour for public services.

In the national context there is an increasing demand from both private and public firms for qualified labour and new technology; in order to increase industrial competitiveness, to facilitate renewal and to produce and distribute household services of desired quality. This demand has been met by increased resources to education and the number of students at post-secondary level has almost tripled during a 20 year period. However, since Sweden covers a large land area but has only six university towns with significant research capacity, it seems unavoidable that many peripheral and rural regions lag behind – or at least differ markedly from central regions – in the supply of labour of certain levels of education and modern technology. This is, at the same time, a reflection of the location preferences of old and new industry. The main trends are usually illustrated and projected as simply as in Figure 3.4, showing the increasing but regionally differentiated

**Figure 3.4** 'Knowledge-orientation' of jobs on regional labour markets in Sweden 1960–2000.
*Source*: after Andersson, 1985.

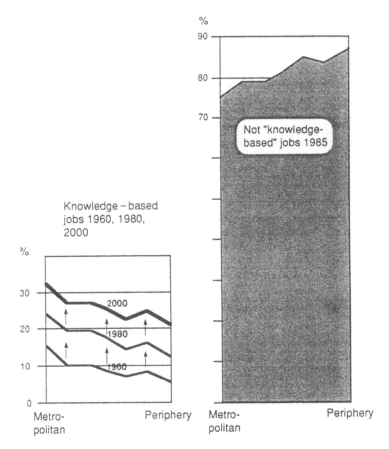

proportion of 'knowledge-oriented'[12] jobs (left) in the labour markets. The other side of the coin (right) is now usually shown in current debates. In the future it is likely that the vast majority of the population will be occupied in jobs with little or no 'knowledge-orientation' of the defined kind.

Central as well as local governments eagerly attempt to promote and launch programmes or projects in order to cope with these imbalances, which are generally assumed to increase spontaneously over time. Private firms try to overcome the problem by internal education and active recruitment policy, but also through relocation to sites close to university towns or 'import nodes'. However, empirical and theoretical knowledge is scarce when it comes to which instruments are effective in eliminating certain problems. It is fully conceivable that, given lasting financial transfers between regions within a welfare state, rural labour markets could perform quite well socially without the direct presence of knowledge-based industry.

In terms of employment the fastest growing industrial sectors of the Swedish economy for the last 20 years have been what is sometimes classified as the knowledge- and the R&D-based industrial sector.[13] However, out of total employment in the country still less than one tenth is found in these sectors. Within these sectors, the proportion of white-collar labour ranges from 30 per cent (in the knowledge-based sector) to 50 per cent (R&D sector). Consequently, in the average regional labour market, only a few per cent of total employment is expected to be directly related to the expansive knowledge-intensive sectors of industry. In peripheral and rural regions this percentage is much less (Table 3.3). One should not overestimate the importance of the knowledge-based industrial sector when it comes to demand for labour with long formal training. The present level of formal training in this sector is illustrated by the following figures; economists and technicians with university certificate represent less than 10 per cent of all white-collar workers in this industry in 1985, which is slightly more than 10 years earlier (Ohlsson and Vinell 1987). This means that economists and technicians with post-secondary training employed in the knowledge-based sector represent less than 2 out of 1,000 employees on the total labour market, as a national average. In this perspective the provision of competent labour in order to develop, maintain or expand 'knowledge-based' industries

**Table 3.3**  Employment in different sectors of manufacturing industry, 1985 (by percentage

|  | SWEDEN | Four peripheral counties |
| --- | --- | --- |
| 'Knowledge-oriented' | 5.5 | 3.8 |
| 'R&D-oriented' | 2.6 | 2.0 |
| Other manufacturing industry | 9.8 | 9.0 |
| TOTAL MANUFACTURING IND | 17.9 | 14.8 |
| Other economic sectors | 82.1 | 85.2 |
| TOTAL EMPLOYMENT | 100.0 | 100.0 |

*Source*: Ohlsson and Vinell, 1987.

in any region may appear as a quantitatively marginal problem. At least, one conclusion is that it is feasible to use selective, or even individually adjusted, instruments in order to ensure that this kind of labour is available for industries which may demand it in peripheral locations. On the other hand, the size of each urbanised rural labour market may present an obstacle for development of this kind of industry. Since most labour markets in Sweden encompass less than 10,000 employees, the local 'community' of competent labour within knowledge-based industry will probably always be very small, maybe too small to reach some kind of 'critical mass'. We will return to this problem later, when discussing the regional reception structure for competence.

If the presence and the size of the 'knowledge-based' industrial sector is generally considered a symbol and a guarantor of future-orientation of the economy and the labour market of a region, this is even more so for the R&D-based industrial sector. In Sweden as in many other countries, R&D-related jobs are concentrated in a few larger regions. For labour with post-secondary training belonging to this category, concentration is even more pronounced. Two thirds of the labour force with long training is found in the two largest city regions. Industries in five peripheral counties, accounting for one seventh of the population, together employ only a few per cent of this kind of labour. In practice and at present, hardly even one person with post-secondary certificate will be found in any kind of R&D-based enterprise in peripheral or rural municipalities.

In Sweden the great majority of the economically active population with higher education (post-secondary) are employed by the public service sector, i.e. in the municipal or governmental services. This may lead to the conclusion that public management could play an active and effective role in planning and matching supply and demand for that kind of competence at the regional level. If the public sector, as an employer, could be used more systematically in order to upgrade the quality of local labour markets, this would probably be more effective, than other public attempts to influence relocation and/or the technological level of private firms. In practice, this might imply relocation and decentralisation of specialised medical care, advanced education and certain governmental services and authorities. The question is, however, to what extent this reasoning is relevant at the present stage, i.e. when the pressure is rather to increase productivity and decrease inputs in public activities.

When it comes to the distribution of governmental resources for higher education, Sweden favours a quite centralised policy. Most resources are directed towards the old university cities, in or close to metropolitan regions (Table 3.4). Peripheral regions, which together have almost the same total population as the metropolitan regions, in practice do not receive any governmental resources of this kind.[14] In spite of the reform 20 years ago when 14 regional institutes for advanced studies were located to 'Regional Educational Cores' all over the country, their share of resources is still limited. Together, they receive less than 10 per cent of what is transferred to metropolitan regions, in spite of the fact that these regional centres are important nodes for the rural periphery.

**Figure 3.5** Labour of different levels of education in economic sectors in Sweden, 1986 (by percentage).

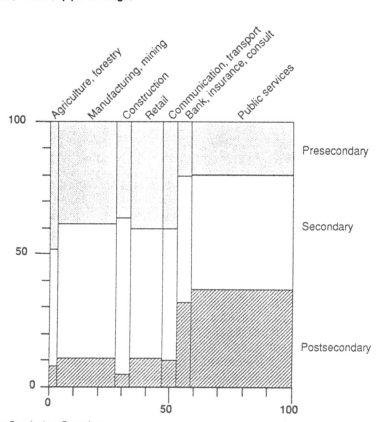

*Source*: Statistics Sweden.

**Table 3.4** Governmental resources for research and university-level education distributed to different regions, 1987/88

| REGION[15] | Percentage of Sweden's total of: | |
| | Population | Transfers for R&D |
| --- | --- | --- |
| Metrop cores | 39 | 76 |
| Reg univ cores | 6 | 17 |
| Reg educ cores north | 5 | 2 |
| Reg educ cores south | 10 | 5 |
| Rural periphery south | 30 | 0 |
| Rural periphery north | 10 | 0 |
| Total | 100 | 100 |

*Source*: Statistics Sweden.

Given this location pattern of facilities for higher education, it is not surprising that recruitment to post-secondary education shows a varied regional pattern which is quite stable over time. For the last 10 years it has been ranging annually around approximately 95 per 10,000 inhabitants in the capital county (Stockholm) and approximately 65 per 10,000 in one of the least urbanised counties (Kopparberg). The major differences, however, are shown between individual municipalities. For instance, the most 'educated' municipality within the capital region (Danderyd) shows an annual recruit-ment frequency as high as 160 per 10,000, whilst the least educated munici-pality (Älvdalen) shows a corresponding figure of only 23 per 10,000. As mentioned before, variation is great even within one single county. Typically, we find that the cores of each county – whether this core includes a full university or an institute for advanced studies – shows a recruitment frequency which is 65 per cent higher than in the rest of the county. This means that the reform mentioned above – including 14 regional institutes for advanced studies – is nowhere near effective enough to mobilise students from the rural periphery to attend post-secondary education. Low frequency of post-secondary studies here coincides with poor demand for that kind of labour. The general reception structure for competence is weak in the urbanised rural area as a whole.

Against this background, it is not surprising that when it comes to the development of regional differences in level of formal education, there seem to be small changes over time. Rather, the gaps between centre and periphery seem to widen. A simplified way to describe the situation is that compared to service regions and metropolitan regions, the peripheral regions have a 'lag' of about 10 years when it comes to the proportion of labour with short post-secondary education and more than double when it comes to longer education. Given the present rate of change there is little chance that this lag would decrease over time, since the main structure remains unchanged when it comes to the regional economy, the education system and social behaviour. The present differences in educational level between extreme regions – the capital region of Stockholm and the peripheral rural regions in the northwestern part of the country – is shown in Figure 3.6.

The migration pattern for the population with higher education strengthens the concentration trend. Data for one cohort – born in 1955 – show that whilst three metropolitan regions in Sweden 'gained' 11 per cent of post-secondary educated from other counties, the six most peripheral counties 'lost' as much as 24 per cent of this type of labour up till 1985 (Välfärdsbulletinen, 1988, p. 1). This happened in spite of the already mentioned fact that institutes for post-secondary education were located also to this peripheral region during exactly this period of time. This reinforces the argument for a strong reallocation of resources to create a distribution system and/or a reception structure for competence which more than marginally could influence the trend towards concentration.

In summary, we have touched upon three types of problems associated with the regional distribution and reception of formal competence. The demand for labour with long formal training in manufacturing industry and

88

**Figure 3.6** Population classified after different background of education, 1986. Stockholm region and sparsely populated regions. Three age groups in the range 16–74 years

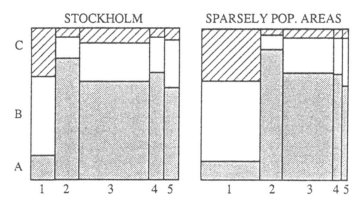

*Source*: Statistics Sweden.

*Notes*: 1: Pre-secondary < 9 years; 2: 9–10 years; 3: secondary; 4: post-secondary < =3 years; 5: >3 years.
A: 16–44 years; B: 45–65 years; C: 66–74 years.

private services in peripheral and rural regions is presently small in absolute numbers. This is partly a consequence of the existing branch structure, partly because of the low level of technology. In the short run, it should be possible to ensure regional supply of competent labour by use of selective instruments. Roughly, the task would be to attract such labour by offering good 'quality of life', in a wide sense, within the urbanised rural areas.

Recruitment to higher studies is substantially lower in the peripheral regions of the counties. This implies that further decentralisation of advanced education would be necessary in the long run to develop the formal competence in these regions. Since there is a problem of small and sparse population in the peripheral areas, it seems necessary to develop new systems of interaction between educational centres and periphery.

An underlying problem – largely hidden behind the present welfare policy with its geographical outcomes – concerns the standard and variation of business services, local labour market and infrastructure in most rural regions. The lack of resources for advanced studies corresponds to the already low standard of the secondary school system. The short supply of 'knowledge-oriented' industrial firms corresponds to a short supply of business and other important services. There is also an indication that any strategy to fundamentally 'raise' the general competence level of labour in peripheral regions needs to take into account how resources are to be spent on all these sectors. This forms a dilemma, since it is not obvious from empirical data how either the technological level of firms, their branch structure or the disposition of the population to attend post-secondary education, or return from such education to their home region, can be effectively and lastingly influenced by means of public policy.

An alternative planning strategy would be to accept that urbanised rural areas are different and that they will not necessarily be integrated in the 'knowledge-economy' based labour market of the 1990s as they have become in the labour market of the public service economy of the period 1970–90. In that case, the future comparative advantage of this intermediate zone of the rural–urban continuum would rather be its residential qualities.

## Rural labour markets facing the 'arena society' – conclusions and new challenges

Present policy and planning directed towards rural labour markets in Scandinavia is more or less implicitly based on a perception of the original rural character of these areas: the dependency on natural resources and low levels of income. When formulating political programmes, the differences between rural and urban areas are stressed more often than the continuity.

This analysis shows that it is more relevant now to speak about urbanised rural areas. In spite of the sparse population and the economic dependence of resource-based industry, the majority of rural regions in Scandinavia show many urban characteristics when it comes to the labour market. The dependence on rather uniform service jobs has increased as a result of the expansion of the public services. The generation of service jobs in rural labour markets is more an unintended effect of the welfare programmes than a result of intentional regional policy.

For the population involved in traditional agriculture, which is now in a period of pressured change due to state budget constraints and international market competition, the expansion of urban or semi-urban labour markets has facilitated adjustment, at least in the short run. As long as demand for public service labour remains high, the predicted decrease in agricultural employment will not necessarily mean severe disturbances on the labour markets in the urbanised rural areas.

Sectoral public policy is important in explaining the processes towards urbanisation of rural regions. In practice, the major resources have been directed towards the maintenance of labour markets at relatively low levels in terms of formal qualifications required. The future orientation of the governmental resource transfer is weak. Resources to higher education are geographically concentrated and the gap between rural and urban regions widens concerning the level of education. In this respect there is more of a rural–urban dichotomy than a continuum. However, with the present prospects for the public sector, which demands two thirds of the labour with university education, it is not probable that decentralisation of qualified services and jobs will be put on the agenda for regional and rural policy.

On the one hand, our analysis of the present structural problems of the labour market in urbanised rural areas suggests that policies would have to change in order to be more future oriented; i.e. to realise the problems of low quality of the labour market and that of poor supply of business services as well as to support those households which find living in the urbanised rural area to be unique and attractive. Given that the national motive for a development policy concerning rural areas is to intensify and to effectively use all the rural resources, it seems reasonable that the policy should include support to the enterprises and households that use these resources. But a new policy has to realise that the rural resources today are not mainly within traditional farming and that most of them contain variably integrated rural and urban elements. Rural areas and rural households have a 'suburban' character, i.e. they use and depend on resources and markets that belong to both the rural and the urban environment.

However, on the other hand, two ongoing changes are important in assessing the future of rural Scandinavia. First, the cutbacks in public budgets now likely, may call for a withdrawal of standardised service jobs from urbanised rural areas towards more central locations, as well as hamper any efforts to consciously use the public sector as a vehicle of raising the quality of rural labour markets. Second, stress on creating 'modern' and 'urban' labour markets in rural areas may diminish as the mobile 'arena society' advances. Mobility, individualism and post-materialistic values – embedded in what is labelled as the arena society – may increase the attraction of rural space as residential areas, in spite of their often poor performance in terms of regional policy goals concerning qualified employment and services.

Several factors contribute to the emergence of what can be labelled the 'arena society' in the Scandinavian countries. Internationalisation processes widen the scope for firms as well as some social groups. Increasing standard of living and increasing stress on individual and private alternatives – instead of public – means that the geographical links at the household level are slackened between the workplace, the residence and the place for education. This is reinforced by new models for labour organisation and improved infrastructure, i.e. for telecommunications. This has a general significance in all regions, but is especially noticeable and important in rural areas. More and more households are becoming less dependent on only local resources and local incomes. Some residents migrate to rural areas in certain phases of the lifecycle and the rationale for rural living has more to do with the perceived quality of life than with the quantity and quality of local labour demand and the local supply of services. Some of the new residents are more or less independent of local sources of income, partly as a consequence of their profession and the way work is organised around new communications technology.

The traditional function of the *local* labour market is consequently becoming less important for many people in rural areas, whilst the dependence on the economy and technology of other regions increases. The somewhat settled and static character of rural areas that has – at least implicitly – been one image guiding the public support system in all Scandinavian countries is thus challenged. At the same time, planning and policy based on collectivism and solidarity is losing its ideological support. Among the youngest generation there is a movement towards increased individualism. There is a diffusion of postmaterialistic ideas and values, for example in form of environmental concern, partly from the urban areas.

Collectivism versus individualism and public versus private organisational modes are important factors in analysing efforts to provide quality of life in different regions in Scandinavia. The traditional welfare model is still stressing the combination of collectivism and public institutions. The uniformity of services and employment has been considered an important welfare goal, and has meant some reduction of regional disparities. In the ongoing reorientation, privatisation, decentralisation and deregulation confront these assumptions. The welfare services developed in the urbanised rural areas are heavily dependent on transfer of governmental financial resources, awarding low interest loans for private risk-taking projects. A possible attractive alternative for these areas is a combination of decentralisation and deregulation which promotes higher adjustment to local needs and goals. In this case the geographical variation of the standard of services and the labour market can only be expected to increase. It is quite possible, that the intermediate zones in the rural–urban continuum provide unique and attractive combinations of rural and urban resources that are available for individuals and households choosing and experiencing different lifestyles at the turn of this century. They thus represent a key window through which the social scientist can assess both the development of 'arena society' and the reorientation of the welfarist model.

**Notes**

1. Except Iceland with two inhabitants per sq km.
2. In 1985 (1980) the share of total employment in agriculture, fishing, mining and oil production was 12 (13) per cent in Finland, 18 (9) in Norway and 5(6) in Sweden. Source: Statistical Abstract of Sweden 1990.
3. Throughout this text, labour market areas are defined as regions where demand and supply of labour is matched by means of daily commuting. Sweden's 284 municipalities aggregate to 111 labour market areas. According to a cluster analysis, 17 of these are classified as rural, 5 as sparsely populated (Expert Group on Regional and Urban Studies and Statistics Sweden).
4. This is obvious from a statement of the Swedish Parliamentary Delegation for Sparsely Populated Areas (1986) which suggests the following key concepts for rural policy
    > Development should be based on a better protection of the local resources, with equal attention to nature, people and capital. Those industries which are land intensive have an important place here ... An increase in additional local processing of the rural raw material is a prerequisite for positive development. A development of small-scale systems of production is needed ... Unconventional solutions which are adjusted to conditions in the rural areas are required.

5. The concept 'short-distance society' is used by Hägerstrand (1988) in order to describe localities where all rapid and most heavy transports are made within short distances.
6. The corresponding regions in Norway and Finland cover larger proportions of the land area as well as of the population. It is estimated that 24 per cent of the population in Norway live within sparsely populated areas, 29 per cent in Finland (Eriksson, 1989).
7. Definition: smaller central places or other population centres (2,000–10,000 inhabitants) with commuting area (30 km) which is located relatively far (>30 km) from bigger urban centres.
8. Rural areas are here defined as areas outside localities with more than 200 inhabitants.
9. In 1940 there were in total 415,000 units with more than 0.25 hectares of arable land and some agricultural activity. Most of these units were very small. In addition there were about 60,000 small holdings with on the average less than 0.1 hectares of arable land.
10. Urbanised Plains: plains with favourable conditions for agriculture in central and southern Sweden; Rural North: all agricultural districts in northern Sweden; Intermediate Regions: regions with less favourable conditions for agriculture in central and southern Sweden.
11. It became obvious that forestry as a traditional and indisputable rural resource-base is not protected from international challenge as imports of timber increased by 75 per cent between 1984 and 1986, mainly as a result of high production costs in Sweden.
12. The referred definition of 'knowledge-oriented' includes jobs requiring long training and handling of information rather than goods. Classification is based on census data 1960–85.
13. The knowledge-based industrial sector includes branches with little raw material orientation, such as production of household capital goods. The R&D sector includes branches such as electronics and medical industry.
14. Refers only to direct resource transfers to the regions, not the distribution generated by the geographical pattern of recruitment of students at each university. This means that we present a more 'centralised' pattern than is actually the case.
15. Metropolitan cores – counties of Stockholm, Malmöhus, Göteborg and Uppsala, with large universities. Regional university cores: Municipalities within appr. 50 km from other universities with research capacity (Umeå, Luleå, Linköping). Regional educational cores: Municipalities within 50 km from institutes for advanced studies (without research capacity). Periphery: other municipalities. North: six northernmost counties.

## References

Andersson, Å. E. (1985) *Kreativitet. Storstadens framtid.* Värnamo.
Andersson, Å. E. and Strömqvist, U. (1988) *K-Samhällets Framtid.* Stockholm.

93

*Deltidslantbrukets struktur och betydelse*. Lantbruksekonomiska samarbetsnämndens rationaliseringsgrupp (1988) Stockholm.

Ennefors, K. (1991) *Atto bo mellan land och stad - livskvalitet i den urbaniserade glesbygden 1991*. CERUM working paper 1991, p. 15. Umeå.

Eriksson, O. (1989) *Bortom storstadsidéerna. En regional framtid för Sverige och Norden 2å 2010-talet*. Stockholm.

ERU, Expert Group on Regional and Urban Studies, *Det omedvetna valet - nationell politik och regional obalans* (Bilaga 12 till Långtidsutredningen 1990).

Gade, O., Miller, V. P., Jr. and Sommers, L. M. (eds) (1991a) *Planning Issues in Marginal Areas*. Boone, NC: Appalachian State University, Department of Geography and Planning, Occasional Papers, Vol. 3, Spring.

Gade, O., Persson, L. O. and Wiberg, U. (forthcoming 1991b) *Processes Reshaping the Rural-Urban Continuum*, in The Proceedings of the PIMA Seminar, Galway July.

Hägerstrand, T. (1988) 'Krafter som fomat det svenska kulturlandskapet', *Mark och vatten 2010*. Ds 1988, p. 35. Stockholm.

Jacobs, J. (1984) *Cities and the Wealth of Nations*. Vintage Books, New York.

Johannisson, B., Persson, L. O and Wiberg, U. (1989) *Urbaniserad glesbygd - verklighet och vision*. Ds 1989, p. 1.

Jones, J. (1991) *The Intermediate Socioeconomic Zone: a comparative analysis of Sweden and North Carolina*. Boone, NC: Appalachian State University, Department of Geography and Planning, masters thesis, August.

Ohlsson, L. and Vinell, L. (1987) *Tillväxtens drivkrafter*. Industriförbundets Förlag.

Persson, L. O. (1991) 'Urbanizing processes in peripheral areas in a welfare state', in O. Gade, V. P. Miller, Jr. and L. M. Sommers (eds) *Planning in Marginal Areas*. Boone, NC: Appalachian State University, Department of Geography and Planning, Occasional Papers, Vol. 3, Spring, pp. 61-9.

Persson, L. O. and Wiberg, U. (1988) 'Policy and planning for the urbanized rural areas', in *Scandinavian Housing and Planning*, Vol. 5, No. 4. Stockholm.

Persson, L. O. (1989) 'Support for agriculture - an appropriate regional policy instrument? The case of northern Sweden', *Journal of Rural Studies* Vol. 5, No. 4.

Persson, L. O. (1990) 'Urbanization processes in peripheral regions in a welfare state', *Journal of Rural Studies*, Vol. 6, No. 4.

Peterson, M. (1990) 'Paradigmatic shift in agriculture: global effects and the Swedish response', Chapter 3 in T. Marsden *et al., Rural Restructuring: global processes and their responses*, Vol. 1, Critical Perspectives on Rural Change. Fulton, London.

Sjöholt, P. (1991) 'Producer services: a new panacea for marginal regions?' In Lundqvist, L. and Persson, L. O. (eds) *Nätverk i Norden* Ds 1990, p. 78.

Snickars, F., Hjern, B., Johansson, B., Lindmark, L. and Åberg, R. (1989) *Chans för Norrbotten*. Luleå.

SOU (1989) *Staten i geografin*, p. 65 Stockholm.

SOU (1990) *Långtidsutredningen 1990*, p. 14 Ministry of Finance, Sweden.

Sundberg, L. and Carlén, G. (1989) 'Allocation mechanisms in public provision of transport and communication infrastructure', *The Annals of Regional Science* Vol. 23, pp. 311–27.

*The Long-term Future of Regional Policy – a nordic view* (1989) OECD/NordREFO, Borgå.

*Utbildningsstatistisk Årsbok.* SCB. (Statistics Sweden).

*Välfärdsbulletinen* (1988) p. 1 (Statistics Sweden).

CHAPTER 4

# Class-based Social Mobility on the Rural/Urban Fringe: Cambodian Farmworkers in Philadelphia[1]

*Max J. Pfeffer*

## Introduction

This chapter focuses on the class-based social mobility of Cambodian refugees living in Philadelphia's inner city. This refugee group represents an interesting mix of persons who fled that country in the wake of Khmer Rouge purges and/or the subsequent Vietnamese invasion. Some have peasant backgrounds and were dislocated from their rural villages, others are relatively well educated, many of them former Cambodian civil servants. The chapter argues, that because of the diversity in social backgrounds some Cambodians, like many other new Asian immigrants, experience rapid social mobility, whilst others are likely to join the ranks of the urban multi-ethnic underclass.

The paper concentrates on Cambodian immigrants living in Philadelphia, and their involvement in day-haul agricultural labour in nearby New Jersey. Day-haul workers come to the farm on a daily basis with a care leader who contracts with the farmer(s) to supply workers. This labour recruitment strategy has been an especially important labour source since the years following World War II, when Afro-Americans began to be employed in this way. Over the past decade, Cambodians have replaced Blacks as the majority component of this work force. The focus on Cambodian involvement in this activity serves as a useful device for examining some of the major issues involved in the development of the contemporary urban underclass, representing strong interdependences between urban and rural labour processes.

95

The chapter begins with a review of competing explanations of the nature of the contemporary urban underclass. It then outlines major socioeconomic changes that took place in Philadelphia during the 1970s. It argues that these changes, rooted in global industrial restructuring, established the basis for the racial recomposition of the day-haul agricultural workforce in the city. The social mobility of Cambodians involved in day-haul agricultural labour is the focus of the remainder of the chapter. It concludes with a discussion of the findings on class-based social mobility and their implications for theories of the urban underclass.

## Theoretical issues

The Cambodian experience with day-haul labour is of special interest because of the contrast with the Black experience. The contrast between these two groups bears directly on competing explanations of the rise of the urban underclass. One thesis is that there is a *culture of poverty* with basic values that define patterns of behaviour not conducive to economic success. This theory was originally articulated by Lewis (1968), and was most recently given renewed attention by Lemann (1988, 1991). He argues (both explicitly in 1988 and implicitly in 1991) that the poverty of inner-city Blacks is due to various types of dysfunctional behaviour (e.g. drug use, out of wedlock child bearing, lack of family/marital stability) rooted in a *culture of poverty* that developed in response to social injustices emerging from slavery and Jim Crow. From this perspective, an autonomous culture exists and is reproduced by the individuals themselves as they conduct their normal daily affairs.

Wilson (1978, 1987) argues in opposition to the culture of poverty thesis. According to him, pronounced ghetto poverty and associated dysfunctional behaviour are consequences of recent economic restructuring that lead to the concentration of poverty and transformation of the class composition of inner-city neighbourhoods. Wilson (1987, p. 60) contends that the ghetto poor are effectively cut off from the 'sustained interaction with individuals that represent mainstream society'. In other words, they are 'socially isolated'. This notion implies that the growth of the urban underclass is not the result of ethnic or racial discrimination, but part of a process of socioeconomic development that leads to class subordination of those with the least skills and most limited educational credentials.

Because of the expansion of salaried positions in the government and corporate sectors, and the pressures of affirmative action programmes, more educationally qualified minority individuals were able to leave the confines of inner-city neighbourhoods (Wilson, 1978). These working and middle-class people were 'social buffers' that provided the structural basis of social stability in ghetto neighbourhoods. They invest in neighbourhood stability by patronising the churches, stores, banks and community organisations and sending their children to the local schools (Wilson, 1991). Thus, Wilson argues that the culture of the ghetto underclass cannot be attributed to an autonomous culture of poverty. Rather, negative behavioural patterns are social artifacts rooted in the current lack of economic opportunities and rewards available to ghetto residents, as well as the absence of neighbourhood stability provided by social buffers.

Recent Cambodian involvement in day-haul agricultural labour raises several specific questions with regard to the culture of poverty/social isolation debate. First of all, the issue of the racial recomposition of this workforce demands explanation. Why have Cambodians taken over this type of labour as Blacks abandoned it? Are there structural explanations, or are the cultural attributes of either group the basis for this change? Second, there is the issue of class composition and social mobility. Do Cambodians use employment in day-haul agricultural labour as a successful means of social advancement? The use of this type of employment as a vehicle of social mobility by Cambodians *as a group* would support the culture of poverty argument. That is, the finding that Cambodians use this type of employment effectively as a means of social advancement would suggest that cultural traits are a key element in overcoming ghetto poverty. On the other hand, the existence of social mobility differences within the Cambodian community would support Wilson's social isolation thesis if this development is part of a process of social, and perhaps geographical, mobility that results in the ghetto poor being cut off from the people who provide the structural basis for community stability.

## Urban restructuring and day-haul farm labour

Day-haul workers are employed mostly to harvest blueberries and peaches in New Jersey. They arrive daily with a care leader who contracts with the farmer(s) to supply workers. Technically the workers are employed by the crew leader. The vast majority of all day-haul workers in New Jersey come from Philadelphia. Although this form of labour recruitment goes back to the 1930s when Italian immigrants from the city worked as pickers, some farmers became more dependent on urban-based workers in recent decades, given both the declining pool of local farm workers and increased government enforcement in the late 1960s of farm housing regulations that discouraged the use of migrant farm workers (New Jersey Department of Labor and Industry, 1970). Currently, New Jersey farmers employ a peak of about 7,200 day-haul workers (Brooks *et al.*, 1991). For most of the post-World War II period until the early 1980s, Afro-Americans from Philadelphia constituted most of the New Jersey day-haul workforce. Blacks now account for only about 12 per cent of the state's day-haul workers (New Jersey Department of Labor, 1990). A slightly higher percentage is made up of Hispanics, but the bulk of these workers come from rural New Jersey, not central Philadelphia. More than half of New Jersey day-haul workers are Asian, and almost all of them come from Philadelphia (Brooks *et al.*, 1991). The dominance of Asians in the day-haul workforce came about rapidly over the past decade.

No estimates of changes during the 1980s in the actual number of workers are available, but recent changes in crew leaders offer some sense of the pattern of changes occurring. Crew leaders usually include people from their own racial or ethnic groups on their crews. Thus, changes in the racial/ethnic composition of crew leaders provide a sense of overall change in the composition of the day-haul workforce. Table 4.1 shows that the recomposition of the crew leader population has continued in recent years. There is a clear trend of decreased participation of Blacks which is almost directly compensated for by Asians. There is turnover in all segments of this population from year to year, but four or five Blacks retire for each new person involved in this activity while there is only a slight reduction in Asian crew leaders due to attrition.

**Table 4.1**  Crew leaders in New Jersey 1989 and 1990 (by percentage)

| Racial/ethnicity | 1989 | 1990 | Ratio of Retiring to New Crew Leaders |
|---|---|---|---|
| Black* | 16.5 | 12.8 | 4.5 |
| Hispanic | 19.7 | 20.2 | 2.3 |
| Asian | 63.8 | 70.0 | 1.3 |
| Total | 100.0 | 100.0 | 1.6 |
| Number | 127 | 109 | — |

*Note*: *Not Hispanic.
*Source*: New Jersey Department of Labor, Wage and Hour Division, unpublished documents.

Asian day-haul workers include Cambodians, Vietnamese and a few Loatians, Hmong and Thai. While no exact estimates of the ethnic composition of the Asian day-haul workforce exist, interviews with farmers, government officials and crew leaders leave no doubt that Cambodians make up the vast majority of this group. The question posed in the forgoing theoretical discussion thus stands: why have Cambodians taken over this type of labour as Blacks have abandoned it.

Cambodians began to enter the US in large numbers in the early 1980s. Those who settled in central Philadelphia encountered an economy rocked by changes in the local industrial structure. These were especially pronounced in inner-city neighbourhoods inhabited by large concentrations of Afro-Americans. The economies of older industrial centres like Philadelphia have been restructured over the past few decades. In the face of saturated and less profitable domestic markets for manufactured goods, many firms have attempted to maintain profit margins by reducing production costs. This has often meant the relocation of production facilities out of the inner cities of older industrial centres. Efficient communications and transportation systems have increased the mobility of capital, and have made it possible for corporations to shift a substantial portion of their manufacturing activities to other areas in the United States and overseas (Hymer, 1972; Evans, 1979; Cox, 1987). This movement of capital has led to industrial decline, especially in manufacturing activities, in many industrial cities in the midwestern and northeastern US (Jargowsky and Bane, 1991).

Philadelphia is one of these centres with a heavy concentration of manufacturing facilities. These are precisely the types of industrial plants that were leaving production centres in the northern cities for the suburbs, the south, and Third World countries in recent decades (Falk and Lyson, 1988; Wilson, 1978). Job losses resulting from such industrial relocation tend to be concentrated in labour-intensive, low-skill areas of production (Grunwald and Flamm, 1985).

These changes had particularly marked consequences for the inner-city residents of Philadelphia. The inner areas hold the highest concentration of abandoned factories. One clearly sees by their dilapidated state that these typically large structures are abandoned. The decline in employment opportunities in the inner city made the Philadelphia metropolitan area rank eighth in 1970 and third in 1980 in the number of ghetto poor (Jargowsky and Bane, 1991).

Employment statistics from the 1970 and 1980 Censuses of the Population paint a clear picture of changes that established the context for the transformation of the day-haul agricultural workforce. Table 4.2 shows that employment in central Philadelphia dropped rather sharply during this decade for both Blacks and other races. This trend is especially pronounced for manufacturing employment. Comparison of the central city with the suburbs indicates that these changes cannot be attributed to some conjunctural downturn in the economy; whilst employment declined in the central city, it grew in the suburbs, the only exception being a slight drop in manufacturing employment for non-Blacks. In 1970 there were only slight differences between central city and suburbs in labour force participation and employment rates. By 1980 sizeable differences had appeared.

The Black working-age population grew in both the central city and the suburbs, but only in the suburbs did employment and labour force participation rates keep pace with population growth. More central-city Blacks were entering the labour force in the context of dwindling employment opportunities. For non-Blacks in the central city, the working-age population fell along with employment and labour-force participation, as there was an actual net outmigration of working-age non-Blacks during this time. Thus, the number of central-city non-Blacks wishing to participate in the labour force dropped at a rate closer to the change in employment than was true of Blacks. This created less of a gap between those employed and those wishing to be, but unable to find a job.

Contraction of economic opportunities in the central city left more families living in poverty and receiving public assistance in 1980 than had been true in 1970.[2] By 1980 almost 30 per cent (43,005) of all central-city Black families had an annual income below the official poverty threshold, and more than one third (51,442) received public assistance income. There was an even more rapid increase in reliance in public assistance than in the poverty rate over the decade.

These changes established the basis for the reduction of Black participation in the day-haul agricultural workforce. Crew leaders and other informants knowledgeable about the day-haul labour system indicate that an

**Table 4.2** Selected family and employment characteristics, metropolitan Philadelphia, black and non-black, 1970 and 1980

| | Central city | | | Suburbs* | | |
|---|---|---|---|---|---|---|
| | % of total | | % change | % of total | | % change |
| | 1970 | 1980 | 1970–80 | 1970 | 1980 | 1970–80 |
| – Black – | | | | | | |
| **Persons 16 + years** | | | | | | |
| In labor force** | 59.1 | 52.8 | – 2.3 | 61.6 | 61.5 | 41.0 |
| Employed | 54.9 | 43.6 | –13.3 | 53.9 | 51.6 | 35.2 |
| Manufacturing | 26.0 | 19.6 | –34.6 | 30.3 | 24.6 | 9.9 |
| Total | 422,816 | 461,871 | 9.3 | 121,477 | 171,538 | 41.2 |
| **Families** | | | | | | |
| Income below poverty | 20.9 | 28.6 | 22.6 | 19.4 | 7.3 | 178.1 |
| Receive public assistance | 18.9 | 34.3 | 62.1 | 17.0 | 21.4 | 254.1 |
| Total | 167,903 | 150,117 | –10.6 | 20,127 | 56,677 | 181.6 |
| – Non-black – | | | | | | |
| **Persons 16 + years** | | | | | | |
| In labor force** | 56.7 | 54.9 | –16.3 | 57.3 | 63.9 | 22.7 |
| Employed | 54.1 | 49.9 | –20.3 | 54.1 | 59.8 | 21.6 |
| Manufacturing | 29.1 | 21.5 | –41.2 | 32.8 | 25.7 | –4.5 |
| Total | 981,279 | 848,769 | –13.5 | 1,940,186 | 2,134,980 | 10.0 |
| **Families** | | | | | | |
| Income below poverty | 6.0 | 9.8 | 40.7 | 4.3 | 4.5 | 10.4 |
| Receive public assistance | 3.0 | 8.1 | 126.7 | 2.5 | 5.7 | 99.8 |
| Total | 311,362 | 265,774 | –14.6 | 695,568 | 737,363 | 6.0 |

*Notes:* *Represents all of metropolitan Philadelphia outside of Philadelphia city;
** At work or actively looking for work.
*Source:* US Bureau of the Census, 1970 and 1980 Census of the Population.

important source of these workers has until recently been Afro-American migrants from the rural south. Persons already familiar with agricultural labour would often use the day-haul system as a means of establishing a foothold in the local urban economy. Indirect evidence suggests that such strategies were an effective means of integrating the migrants into the economic life of the city. A lower proportion of recent Black migrants from the south had incomes below the official poverty level or relied on public assistance income than other Blacks (Long, 1974; Long and Heltmann, 1975; Ritchey, 1974; Wilson, 1987).[3]

Sometimes these newcomers would join the crews on an annual basis as a means of supplementing their own or the family's income. Those who moved on to more regular employment were replaced from the pool of migrants regularly arriving from the south. However, the industrial restructuring described above eliminated many unskilled and semi-skilled manufacturing jobs that paid relatively well and were available to migrants with low levels of educational attainment. By 1980 Philadelphia's economy offered little sustainable economic incentive for persons to move from the rural south, compared with employment opportunities appearing in the expanding metropolises of the south (Campbell *et al.*, 1974; Farley and Allen, 1987; Long and Hansen, 1975; Pfeffer, 1991).

A number of additional developments made day-haul farm work unattractive to Philadelphia's inner-city residents. As indicated above, the decline in employment opportunities for persons with limited employment qualifications in Philadelphia's central city was accompanied by increased reliance on welfare payments. By 1980 more than one third of all Afro-American households in the centre city received some form of public assistance income. Finding steady employment that would raise one's income above that offered by welfare became a relatively remote possibility for persons from these households. A number of informants report that they cannot afford to take many of the jobs that are available, because the pay would not match the household's welfare income, especially when the costs of health insurance are considered. Day-haul farm work offers only temporary employment, and like low-level jobs generally, offers no health benefits.[4]

In 1981 the Reagan administration increased restrictions on the earnings of women receiving Aid to Families with Dependent Children (AFDC). Between 1967 and 1981 welfare recipients could keep the first $30 earned and one third of all additional earnings after deducting work-related expenses. After 1981, AFDC payments were reduced by the full amount of earned income (Jencks, 1991). As a result, there was a significant economic risk in taking short-term employment in agriculture as part of an effort to enhance personal or family income. The risks of losing welfare benefits could be minimised as long as earnings from agriculture could be concealed. However, because of regulatory changes in agriculture in the 1980s, many day-haul workers became wary of the possibilities of hiding this supplementary income.

The Migrant and Seasonal Agricultural Worker Protection Act (MSPA) of

1983 has several provisions with direct implications for day-haul farm workers. The law requires that all crew leaders register with the US Department of Labor contractors. Among other things, registered crew leaders must keep payroll records and provide each employee with a written statement of earnings and deductions. These requirements meant that crew leaders collected personal information like names, addresses and social security numbers of employees. The possibilities for continuing to conceal these earnings by providing the crew leader with false information was limited by frequent on-site inspections of crew records by agents of the Department of Labor, and after 1986 by inspections conducted by agents of the the Immigration and Naturalization Service to enforce the Immigration Reform and Control Act (IRCA) of 1986 (Runyan, 1989; Slesinger and Pfeffer, 1991).[5]

As a result of this formalisation process, crew leaders who served as the conduit between inner-city residents and agricultural employers also began to lose interest in performing this role. MSPA created a bookkeeping nightmare for crew leaders. Interviews with former crew leaders, farmers, government officials and others reveal that many Black crew leaders had little education or bookkeeping experience and felt that this task was beyond their capabilities. Many felt that the cost of hiring an accountant cut too far into already restricted earnings. Interviews with crew leaders reveal that earnings from labour contracting declined throughout the 1980s.

The income of most crew leaders depends on the quantity of work done by the crew. That is, the more product the farmworkers pick, the greater the profits of the crew leader. As the pool of persons interested in day-haul farm work dries up, crew leaders have fewer workers to choose from. In particular, strong young people are increasingly uninterested in farm work, moreover most young Blacks in Philadelphia's inner city were born and raised there, and have very little or no connection with farm work. Many crew leaders believe that other informal economic activities like drug dealing offer a more lucrative and interesting means of earning an income. Thus, Black day-haul crews are now mostly composed of less productive individuals like alcoholics, drug addicts and the elderly. With the earnings potential of operating a crew thus limited, and governmental regulations increasingly onerous with the strict enforcement of MSPA and IRCA, many Black crew leaders ended their involvement with day-haul labour.

Cambodian immigrants to Philadelphia came to dominate the day-haul agricultural workforce in this conjunctural context of urban, industrial and regulatory change. That they arrived to take this work as Afro-Americans abandoned it was partly coincidence. Nevertheless, limited job opportunities available to Cambodian refugees arriving in Philadelphia during the early 1980s made agricultural employment an important survival strategy of many households. In the following section the chapter considers the sociological significance of Cambodian involvement in this type of employment. The examination of the effectiveness of this activity as an economic stragegy, highlights key aspects of class-based social mobility.

**Cambodian social mobility and day-haul labour**

As noted in the earlier theoretical discussion Wilson maintains that certain working and middle-class people can act as social buffers within the community, providing a structural basis for social stability. Social isolation results when these social buffers leave the community. It is argued here that social mobility differences within the Cambodian community will support Wilson's thesis if this development results in the Cambodian inner-city community being severed from the structural support offered by working and middle-class individuals. On the other hand, the evidence would be consistent with the culture of poverty thesis if Cambodians *as a group* use day-haul labour as a means of social advancement. This finding would suggest that Cambodians are able to muster some sort of collective cultural capital toward social advancement.

A consideration of Cambodian immigrants' social mobility affords a methodologically appealing opportunity to evaluate the theoretical issues raised, because Cambodians occupy the same urban ecological niche as the Black underclass.[6] In other words, Cambodians have no obvious advantages in access to mainstream social institutions. Most Cambodians reside in the poorest inner-city neighbourhoods on Philadelphia's south, north and west sides. They often live in tight clusters interspersed with Afro-American neighbours. Furthermore, they have no clear advantage over their neighbours in terms of access to social or job networks. In fact, they may be at a relative disadvantage.

The bulk of all Cambodians in the US began to arrive after 1980, so statistics to compare Cambodians with other groups are limited. In 1980 there were only 531 Cambodians residing in the Philadelphia metropolitan area. This population skyrocketed over the past decade.[7] Although detailed data from the 1990 Census are not yet available, summary data at the national level from the 1980 Census show that the first Cambodians to come to the country were concentrated in metropolitan areas, and more than three-fifths lived in central city areas. Nationally, Cambodians were even more urban than Blacks and persons of Spanish origin. They also exhibited lower rates of labour-force participation and much higher rates of personal and family poverty than the other groups. Other data show that Cambodians, like other Southeast Asians, have lower income and employment rates, lower levels of educational attainment, poorer health and nutrition status, and higher rates of welfare programme participation than other Asians in the United States (General Accounting Office, 1990).

Primary data were collected by the author in interviews with Cambodians in Philadelphia during late 1990 and early 1991 (175 individuals from 71 households). Contact was made with all Cambodian crew leaders registered with the New Jersey Department of Labor who gave a Philadelphia address. Although concentrating efforts on crew leaders, interviews were conducted with other Cambodians whenever possible. Review of the data collected suggests that the sample is not systematically biased in any obvious way, other than the over-representation of crew leaders, and to a lesser

**Table 4.3** Residence, labour force and poverty status of Cambodians, Blacks, and persons of Spanish origin, 1980 (by percentage)

| | Cambodian | Black | Spanish origin | Total population |
|---|---|---|---|---|
| Residing in: | | | | |
| SMA* | 92.8 | 81.1 | 87.6 | 74.8 |
| Central city | 61.2 | 57.7 | 50.3 | 29.9 |
| In labor force** | 50.8 | 59.4 | 63.4 | 62.0 |
| Personal income | | | | |
| below poverty*** | 48.7 | 25.8 | 20.2 | 11.0 |
| Family income below | | | | |
| poverty | 46.9 | 26.5 | 21.3 | 9.6 |
| Number of persons (000) | 16 | 26,495 | 14,609 | 226,546 |

*Notes*: *Standard metropolitan area defined by US Bureau of Census;
**Persons 16 years or older;
***Persons 15 years or older for Cambodians, 16 years or older for all others.
*Source*: US Bureau of the Census, 1980 Census of Population.

extent farm workers. The over-sampling of these two sub-groups is the result of the way in which the survey was implemented, and is desirable given the questions under consideration. More complete information on the implementation of the survey may be found in the Appendix.

To address the issue of social mobility within the Cambodian community, households were classified on the basis of their main economic activity. This classification refers to the employment that generated the most income for the household. As in other groups, Cambodian individuals have a variety of jobs to generate income that is channelled into the household economy. However, in Cambodian households one main income source takes precedence over other activities. That is, individual economic activities are structured around the household's main activity. For this reason, the household's main economic activity serves as a valid indicator of the individual's class position. 'Class' is used here in the Weberian sense, to refer to the social relations of exchange (Weber, 1978). As I show below, the class position of Cambodian refugees is largely determined by the human capital assets at the disposal of the household.

Table 4.4 shows the distribution of individuals by five basic household types. Not surprisingly, given the survey design, more than one half of the households received most of their income from either labour contracting or farm work. Persons living in households that rely on wage work for most of their income were also a numerically important group, and a sizeable number of persons lived in households where no one was employed.

Examination of the social background characteristics of individuals confirms that the main economic activity of the households is a valid indicator of individuals' class positions. In questioning individuals about their background, it was ascertained what their family had done for a living in Cambodia, and whether their family lived in a city, a village or in the countryside. Individuals were grouped by occupation of the person who

**Table 4.4** Distribution of Cambodians grouped by main household economic activity

| Main economic activity | Number | Percentage |
| --- | --- | --- |
| Labour contracting | 44 | 25.1 |
| Farm work | 48 | 27.4 |
| Business | 10 | 5.7 |
| Wage work | 44 | 25.1 |
| Unemployed | 29 | 16.6 |
| Total | 175 | 100.0 |

headed the household in Cambodia. Individuals were also grouped by whether or not they had lived in a major city (almost always Phnom Penh).

When the social background characteristics are crosstabulated with the main household economic activity, an interesting pattern emerges. Table 4.5 shows that persons living in labour contracting and business households tend to come from a business or civil service background, and the majority are from the city. Wage-work households are an intermediary category coming from a mix of civil service and peasant backgrounds, and about as many come from the city as do not. Those in unemployed households overwhelmingly come from rural areas and a majority from peasant backgrounds. Farm-work households display a similar pattern, but come almost exclusively from a peasant background.

The education of individuals in Cambodia, measured in years of school attendance, is related to social background and shows a clear pattern when averages are disaggregated by the household's main economic activity. Persons living in farm-work and unemployed households have low levels of education, those in business and labour contracting households have the highest levels, and those in wage-work households fall somewhere in between. Differences in social background by main household economic activity are not artifacts of the age and gender composition of households. Average age and the percentage of persons that are female are almost identical across household types, with the exception of persons in unemployed households that are slightly higher on both of these measures.[8]

The diversity of migrant social backgrounds reflects the international political realities. As noted above, Cambodians entered the US in large numbers in the 1980s. After Vietnam's invasion in 1979, many Cambodians were granted refugee status and allowed to enter the US. Many of these refugees had been civil servants and business people that supported the Sihanouk regime prior to its fall. They were unable to apply to the US for refugee status after the Khmer Rouge takeover in 1975, because the US supported the new regime which was also allied with China in opposition to Vietnam. Thus they went into hiding and posed as peasants to avoid execution by the Khmer Rouge. Not until the Vietnamese invasion in 1979 could they flee Cambodia with a clear chance of being granted refugee status by the US, based on the claim that they were in danger because they were loyal to forces that opposed the Vietnamese (i.e. the National Sihanoukist

**Table 4.5** Selected characteristics of Cambodians by main household economic activity

| Selected characteristics | Labour contracting | Farm work | Business | Wage work | Unemployed | Total |
|---|---|---|---|---|---|---|
| Father's occupation | | | | | | |
| % Peasant/farmer | 13.2(5)* | 95.2(40) | 20.0(2) | 31.7(13) | 58.6(17) | 40.0(77) |
| % Business/merchant | 55.3(21) | 0.0 | 40.0(4) | 12.2(5) | 3.4(1) | 17.7(31) |
| % Civil servant | 31.6(12) | 0.0 | 40.0(4) | 46.3(19) | 20.7(6) | 23.4(41) |
| % Urban residence in Cambodia | 63.2(24) | 11.9(5) | 80.0(8) | 53.7(22) | 13.8(4) | 34.9(61) |
| Mean years schooling in Cambodia** | 9.1(44) | 3.0(48) | 9.0(10) | 5.8(44) | 4.1(29) | 4.5(175) |
| Mean age | 33.7(44) | 34.6(48) | 35.1(10) | 31.5(44) | 37.1(29) | 34.1(175) |
| % Female | 36.8(14) | 40.5(17) | 40.0(4) | 41.5(17) | 48.3(14) | 37.7(66) |

*Notes*: *Number of cases in parentheses;
**Age 30+

Army of Prince Sihanouk and the Khmer People's National Liberation Front headed by former Prime Minister Son Sann) (Alagappa, 1990; Jones, 1990).

A large number of Khmer Rouge supporters were also granted refugee status, but this group came from a much different social background. The Khmer Rouge had been committed to eradicating all bourgeois influence from Cambodia and embarked on rebuilding the country on an agrarian foundation. They built their entire military and political apparatus from a peasant base. Given the low level of economic development in Cambodia, these peasants were almost always poor, with little education. Very often they were illiterate. Because the Khmer Rouge were allied with Sihanouk and Son Sann against the Vietnamese, their peasant supporters who fled the country were granted refeeee status by the US alongside those from quite different social backgrounds who supported the other factions.

The flight from war and political turmoil had a downgrading and equalising effect on Cambodian refugees. They all came to the US poor, but the differences in social background gave households quite different human resources to draw on to survive once they arrived in the US. Those from a peasant background typically had little education, few language skills, and were almost completely unfamiliar with the complexities of the urban world. Better-educated persons often had well-developed language skills. If they did not already speak English, they had often already mastered French and had the confidence and experience to learn another language. Persons with a business background had an idea of how to manage people and money. Former bureaucrats often had accounting skills that could be used in business. Persons from the city generally had an idea of how to move in an urban environment to capture some of the diverse opportunities available.

By coincidence day-haul farm work was one significant opportunity that appeared just as the Cambodian refugees began to arrive in Philadelphia. This work provided initial employment to a relatively large proportion of Cambodians. Table 4.7 shows that, overall, almost 40 per cent of all the Cambodians interviewed reported that their first job in the US was a farmworker. However, reliance on farm work varied a great deal by household type. Persons in households where the main economic activity is currently farm work relied most heavily on such work as their initial source of employment. Almost 60 per cent of these persons were initially employed in this activity. About two fifths of persons in wage work and about one third of those in labour-contracting households started in farm work. Persons in unemployed and farm-work households were less likely than those in any other type of household to be employed as wage workers. Wage work was the initial form of employment for the majority of all persons in labour-contracting, business and wage-work households.

Farm work differs from other forms of wage work in some significant ways that bear directly on the issue of social mobility. Day-haul farm labour requires almost no skills and can be obtained simply by arriving at the appropriate pick up point each morning. Considerably more skill is required to obtain regular wage employment. Communications skills are important in enquiring about employment and then completing application forms. Often workers must be literate so they can follow written instructions necessary to operate complicated machinery. Possession of such skills also opens a wider range of opportunities to individuals and households. Labour contracting households best illustrate this point. Table 4.6 shows that persons from such households secured a wider range of jobs than those in other households when they first entered the workforce in the US. Household circumstances improve considerably when at least some household members are able to secure better paying and more stable employment. Perhaps most impressive is that all persons from labour contracting households had held a job at some time. This finding is in stark contrast with that of farm-work and unemployed households. The vast majority of persons in both these household types had never been employed or had been limited to farm work.

Table 4.6 also shows the present employment of persons living in different household types. Comparison of the initial employment with present employment allows us to assess the social mobility of persons living in different household types. The most important finding emerging from a comparison of the upper and lower panels of the table is how little mobility persons in farm-work and unemployed households experienced. In fact, the relatively large and statistically significant Chi-squares for these household types suggest that initial employment predicted present employment with a higher degree of accuracy than in the other categories.

An important change in terms of social isolation was the substantial increase in joblessness in unemployed households. People in unemployed households moved from farm and wage work into joblessness. Persons in wage-work households also exprienced an increase in unemployment as they left farm work, but others moved into wage work. Some of the most substantial changes in employment took place in business and labour-contracting households. These households had the lowest rates of unemployment. Most persons in business households started as wage workers and ended up self-employed. This pattern is about the same for labour contracting households. These people left farm work, and to a lesser degree wage work, to become crew leaders. Crew leaders are another type of self-employed business person and they must have most of the same skills. This point was not as true prior to the early 1980s. However, with the passage of Migrant and Seasonal Workers Protection Act, the Immigration Reform and Control Act, and recent revisions of the Internal Revenue Code to include agriculture in income tax withholding requirements, crew leaders require the use of the same accounting skills as any other business person.

Although the refugee experience had an initial levelling effect on the wealth of Cambodian immigrants, advantages based on differences in social background helped immigrants from more privileged backgrounds to recapture a superior position in terms of income. Table 4.7 shows that crew leader households enjoyed an advantage in total household income and this edge remained even after controlling for differences in the number of workers per household.[9] These large differences cannot be attributed to variation in the number of years in the US. This variation was slight and

**Table 4.6** Initial and present Cambodian employment by main household economic activity* (by percentage)

| Type of employment | Main economic activity | | | | | |
| --- | --- | --- | --- | --- | --- | --- |
| | Labour contracting | Farm work | Business | Wage work | Unemployed | Total |
| | | | – Initial Job – | | | |
| Unemployed | 0.0 | 26.5(9)** | 0.0 | 3.2(1) | 56.0(14) | 18.2(24) |
| Farmworker | 34.4(11) | 58.8(20) | 10.0(1) | 41.9(13) | 16.0(4) | 37.1(49) |
| Wage worker | 50.0(16) | 14.7(5) | 80.0(8) | 54.8(17) | 24.0(6) | 39.4(52) |
| Crew leader | 9.4(3) | 0.0 | 0.0 | 0.0 | 0.0 | 2.3(3) |
| Self-employed | 3.1(1) | 0.0 | 0.0 | 0.0 | 0.0 | 0.7(1) |
| Professional | 3.1(1) | 0.0 | 10.0(1) | 0.0 | 4.0(1) | 2.3(3) |
| Total | 100.0(32) | 100.0(34) | 100.0(10) | 100.0(31) | 100.0(25) | 100.0(132) |
| | | | – Present Job – | | | |
| Unemployed | 5.9 | 35.3(12) | 0.0 | 19.4(6) | 92.0(23) | 32.1(43) |
| Farmworker | 14.7(5) | 41.2(14) | 0.0 | 12.9(4) | 4.0(1) | 17.9(24) |
| Wage worker | 35.3(12) | 17.6(6) | 20.0(2) | 67.7(21) | 0.0 | 30.6(41) |
| Crew leader | 44.1(15) | 0.0 | 0.0 | 0.0 | 0.0 | 11.2(15) |
| Self-employed | 0.0 | 0.0 | 70.0(7) | 0.0 | 0.0 | 5.2(7) |
| Professional | 0.0 | 5.9(2) | 10.0(1) | 0.0 | 4.0(1) | 3.0(4) |
| Total | 100.0(34) | 100.0(34) | 100.0(10) | 100.0(31) | 100.0(25) | 100.0(134) |
| Chi-squared (initial χ present) | 11.1 | 27.4*** | 4.7 | 2.8 | 28.3** | 98.3*** |

Notes: * Age GT 22;
**Number of persons in parentheses;
***P < 0.001.

there was no clear linear relationship between years in the US and income either within the groups or for the sample as a whole.

Labour-contracting households depend little on public assistance, but show about an equal reliance on wage and salary and self-employment income. Other households display a greater reliance on a single income source. This finding re-emphasises the point that households from more privileged backgrounds are better prepared to take advantage of a wider range of new opportunities.

Labour contracting households display a distinctive economic strategy that is based on a relatively lucrative main activity supplemented by a variety of other types of employment. This strategy allows households to take full advantage of their human resources and to capture a wide range of employment opportunities. Low-paying farm and wage jobs are used to *round out* the household's more lucrative self-employment income. However, this strategy is effective only for those households that have members with qualifications that enable them to capture more lucrative economic opportunities.

### Discussion: the sociological significance of day-haul farm labour

Labour contracting presented a relatively lucrative and immediate opportunity in the early 1980s when the Cambodian refugees began to arrive in large numbers. Newly arriving refugees lacked access to job networks, local labour markets, and the welfare system. They were available for day-haul farm work at a time when the demand for this labour was no longer being satisfied by Afro-Americans because of changes in the local economy and labour regulations. Nevertheless, the refugees needed a means to gain access to this employment. Educated Cambodians with organisational and communications skills provided a bridge between the refugee community and the farm labour market. These educated Cambodians sometimes began as farmworkers themselves, and learned the labour contracting business from existing crew leaders who employed them. They were able to *capture* this business opportunity by drawing on their social skills. Some Cambodian crew leaders have since become prominent community leaders, or 'social buffers', based on their economic success and service to their community. Their service, in part, consists of *providing labour market access* to other Cambodians with fewer social skills.

As a group, the crew leaders have done well economically. They were able to capitalise on the demand for day-haul labour and to start to invest in a number of other businesses. These businesses include real estate, restaurants and a variety of other sales and service establishments. Some of these businesses continue to serve the Cambodian community, but others have begun to diversify and serve other consumers as well.

At least part of their interest in diversifying into other business activities is a reflection of difficulties in attracting quality day-haul workers in recent years.[10] Cambodian crew leaders express a marked degree of scepticism about the continued profitability of labour contracting. Newly arrived

**Table 4.7** Cambodian income and proportion of income from different sources by main household economic activity

| Income and source | Main economic activity | | | | |
| --- | --- | --- | --- | --- | --- |
| | Labour contracting | Farm worker | Wage worker | Unemployed | Total |
| Mean total household ($) | 67,464 (46,428)* | 25,243 (23,540) | 42,188 (20,825) | 12,289 (3,696) | 38,800 (36,076) |
| Mean per worker ($) | 27,911 (31,988) | 14,715 (4,488) | 17,507 (6,282) | 11,936 (3,363) | 18,514 (18,780) |
| Mean years in US | 5.3 | 4.1 | 3.4 | 4.4 | 4.4 |
| Percentage of total household income from: | | | | | |
| Public assistance | 3.9 | 70.7 | 9.8 | 93.4 | 40.8 |
| Wages and salary | 46.6 | 29.3 | 90.2 | 6.6 | 42.5 |
| Self-employment | 49.5 | 0.0 | 0.0 | 0.0 | 16.7 |
| Total | 100.0 | 100.0 | 100.0 | 100.0 | 100.0 |

*Note:* *Standard deviations in parentheses.

refugees had been the core of the Cambodian day-haul workforce. However, fewer refugees are arriving since 1990. The US government changed its official position and began supporting a negotiated settlement to fighting in Cambodia that includes the Vietnamese backed government as well as all three opposition groups (Jones, 1990). The earlier refugees now express decreasing interest in farm work. Some of them have found more steady and better paying employment, but others are mired in what will likely become persistent social isolation. This group is chronically unemployed or employed in marginal jobs (such as farm work). They increasingly rely on public assistance income (see Table 4.7 above). Most persons in unemployed households have given up on the prospect of regular employment altogether. They shun farm work because it represents a threat to continued receipt of welfare payments. Those who continue to participate in day-haul work depend on it, because they lack either the qualifications for other work or the social skills needed to find alternative employment. This group includes mostly teenagers and the elderly for whom there are relatively few employment opportunities in the inner city. The upward mobility of crew leaders and other business people stands to leave less qualified Cambodian refugees socially isolated in an inner city with dwindling job opportunities for the Black or Asian unskilled.

**Conclusion**

On the surface, racial recomposition of the day-haul agricultural workforce in New Jersey appears to support an explanation grounded in cultural differences between Afro-Americans and Cambodians. However, closer empirical inspection reveals that Blacks were withdrawing from this workforce for several reasons related to the rather profound structural changes in Philadelphia's inner-city economy. At the same time and for different reasons Cambodians arrived to take the day-haul work just as Blacks left it.

Examination of the employment histories of Cambodians also reveals little basis for any simple cultural characterisation to describe their experience in the US. Marked differences in economic success are apparent *within* the Cambodian community. These differencs reflect variations in the social resources immigrants brought with them. Cambodians from more privileged backgrounds have been able to utilise these resources to gain a clear economic advantage over others. Some have translated this advantage into economic capital enabling them to enter mainstream social and economic activity, whilst the less fortunate remain socially isolated.

The analysis presented here points to the importance of considering *class-based social mobility* as a key basis for ghetto poverty and the *isolation* of some persons from mainstream social and economic institutions. As already noted by Wilson (1987), this understanding sets a basis for the development of policies that attack the roots of ghetto poverty rather than its symptoms.

**Appendix**

*Data on recent Cambodian immigrants*

To gain entrance to the Cambodian community, I contacted social service agencies that assisted refugees in settling in the area. This contact introduced me to Cambodian social workers who in turn provided an introduction to a Cambodian civic group active in Philadelphia. One member of this group agreed to work with me in the capacity of a guide and a translator, and later helped me recruit another person in this capacity.

We began interviewing by attempting to contact all Cambodian crew leaders registered with the New Jersey Department of Labor who gave a Philadelphia address. Although we concentrated our efforts on crew leaders, we interviewed other Cambodians whenever possible. Sometimes crew leaders had moved from the address listed. If other Cambodians lived at the location, we asked to interview them. Sometimes crew leaders and others suggested additional people to interview, and we contacted them and requested an interview. This survey method was preferred over a formal random survey. First, no adequate sampling frame was available for a formal random survey. Any list that might have been available for the purposes of drawing a sample would quickly be outdated and incomplete, because of the continuous arrival of Cambodians from abroad and other parts of the US. Second, and perhaps most importantly, random contacts raised considerable suspicion. Cambodians are fearful of government officials and other strangers. Cambodians attribute some of this fear of government to memories of atrocities committed under the Khmer Rouge regime, but others are afraid that providing sensitive information could jeopardise their welfare status. In this context, anonymous visits based on random selection tend to undermine the completeness and quality of the interview data. By attempting to contact registered crew leaders throughout the city, we established an air of legitimacy in the eyes of the interviewees. Furthermore, we established contacts with Cambodians throughout the city and avoided bias that might have resulted from the peculiarities of one location.

By working with two translators, I was able to get a sense of the reliability of the translations. Minor difficulties in the translations were corrected by means of additional probing during the interviews. One of the translators was female, and the other male, but I detected no important differences in the quality of the interviews based on gender.

The interviews consisted of a series of questions covering the social background of individuals in Cambodia, their employment history in the US, their record or receipt of public assistance, and the composition of their households. Whenever possible all working-age members (age 16 +) of the household were interviewed. When all these individuals were not available, the household head was asked about those not present. I conducted more extensive interviews with crew leaders. Crew leaders have rather extensive knowledge about the Cambodian community, because they come into contact with a wide range of individuals. Crew leaders were asked about their experiences with farmworkers, and changes in the farm workforce and Cambodian community at large in recent years.

## Notes

1. The research reported here was funded by the Social Science Research Council's Program on the Urban Underclass, with additional funding provided by the New Jersey Agricultural Experiment Station. Valuable research assistance was provided by Thierry Hua, Charlie Lor and Katherine Panagokos. The helpful comments of Baruch Boxer, Bill Friedland and Gary Green on an earlier draft of this chapter are gratefully acknowledged. All errors or omissions are my sole responsibility.
2. The comparison of percentage change figures for the incidence of poverty and receipt of public assistance between central city and suburbs is misleading. The large percentage change figures in Table 4.4 for the Blacks living in suburbs and all non-Blacks reflects the small base from which the rates were computed. The fact is that in sheer numbers both poverty and reliance on public assistance is concentrated in the central-city Black population, and became more so between 1970 and 1980.
3. This evidence is important because it directly refutes arguments that Blacks from the south had been reared in a 'culture of poverty', and that migration resulted in the diffusion of this culture to northern cities. Lemann's (1988, 1991) popular account of the great migration is flawed in this respect (Duneier, 1991).
4. Most agricultural employment in New Jersey is seasonal and, as elsewhere, the labour process in specialised agriculture is organised such that labour requirements during the season are uneven (Pfeffer, 1983a). Only the harvest offers employment to a relatively large number of day-haul workers for an eight to twelve week period each year. Day-haul farm work is not steady employment, and cannot be considered an occupation. Most individuals are only involved in this activity casually. People who lack access to more stable employment opportunities are most attracted to this work (Pfeffer, 1983b). However, earnings whilst the work lasts can be substantially above those of other jobs in the city available to persons with limited qualifications.
5. I observed the enforcement of MSPA whilst working with a day-haul crew picking blueberries during the summer of 1991. As in past years, inspections were widespread and many citations were issued. The crew I worked with was inspected on three occasions; twice in the field and once at a roadblock operated by state troopers. Our crew leader was cited at the roadblock for minimum wage violations, and subsequently fined. Whilst these violations were relatively minor, other crew leaders were issued citations at the same roadblock and subsequently received substantial fines. The important point here is that roadblocks and other inspections are very intimidating especially when workers are trying to conceal facts such as their earnings in the fields from authorities. Such close contact and

questioning by authorities acts as a real barrier to continued participation in day-haul work for many individuals.

6. ·Studies of problems like poverty that focus on different racial and ethnic groups are not always relevant to the problem of social isolation, because they do not control for differences in the possibilities for access to mainstream social institutions offered by different social settings (Wilson, 1987).

7. Detailed census figures for 1980 are not yet available, but preliminary figures for the Asian and Pacific Islander Population which include Cambodians indicate that this group grew by more than 139 per cent compared with growth rates of 62, 6 and 53 per cent respectively for Native Americans, Blacks and Hispanics. The growth of Asian and Pacific Islanders in Philadelphia exceeded the national rate which was 108 per cent. By 1990 there were more than 123,000 Asian and Pacific Islanders living in metropolitan Philadelphia (*USA Today*, 8 July 1991). Asian day-haul workers who are overwhelmingly Cambodian are estimated to number about 3,700 (Brook *et al.*, 1991). This figure underestimates the total number of persons involved in this activity, because of the extremely high turnover in this workforce. Furthermore, only a relatively small proportion of the total Cambodian population is engaged in this activity. Still, if we compare the number of Cambodians living in Philadelphia in 1980 with the number of day-haul workers in 1990, we observe more than a 600 per cent increase in the Cambodian population. This example simply illustrates that the Cambodian population in Philadelphia skyrocketed in the 1980s, even though no exact figures are yet available.

8. The higher average age of persons in unemployed households is the result of older persons being unable or unwilling to take work and actually increases the variation in social background in this category. Because unemployment is in part age related, regardless of social background, estimates of differences in social background between household types are more conservative than they would be if I had controlled for age. The higher proportion of females in this category reflects the presence of female-headed households. Almost all female-headed households I encountered were the result of recent separations in the US and the women were typically in their twenties. I cannot say whether this represents a widespread trend based on so few cases, but this is an interesting finding given the attention placed on the growth of female-headed households in the urban underclass debates.

9. Business households were excluded from Table 4.7 because of missing data.

10. This difficulty is confirmed through interviews with farmers. Those who relied heavily on Cambodian day-haul workers have experienced increasing difficulty in attracting crews of sufficient size and quality in recent years. Farmers have responded to this problem by recruiting Mexican migrant workers to replace the Cambodian day-haul crews. This observation is confirmed in a recent study of the supply of and demand for farmworker housing which found that more than 52 per cent of all

116

farmers hiring Asian day-haul workers expressed an interest in investing in migrant worker housing (Brooks *et al.*, 1991).

## References

Alagappa, M. (1990) 'The Cambodian conflict: prospects for a negotiated settlement', *Disarmament*, Vol. 13, No. 1, pp. 59–90.

Brooks, F. A., Pfeffer, M. J. and Panagakos, K. (1991) *The Supply and Demand for Farm Labor Housing in New Jersey*. Unpublished manuscript.

Bureau of the Census (1987) *1987 Census of Agriculture*. Washington, DC: US Government Printing Office.

Campbell, R. R., Johnson, D. M. and Stangler, G. (1974) 'Return migration of Black people to the south', *Rural Sociology*, Vol. 39, No. 2, pp. 514–29.

Cox, R. W. (1987) *Production, Power, and World Order*. New York. Columbia University Press.

Duneier, M. (1991) 'Black migrants have done better', *New York Times*, 11 June.

Evans, P. (1979) *Dependent Development: the alliance of multinational state, and local capital in Brazil*. Princeton: Princeton University Press.

Falk, W. W. and Lyson, T. A. (1988) *High Tech, Low Tech, No Tech: recent industrial and occupational change in the south*. Albany: State University of New York Press.

Farley, R. and Allen, W. R. (1987) *The Color Line and Quality of Life in America*. New York: Russell Sage Foundation.

General Accounting Office (1990) *Asian Americans: a status report*. Washington, DC: General Accounting Office.

Grunwald, J. and Flamm, K. (1985) *The Global Factory: foreign assembly in international trade*. Washington, DC: The Brookings Institution.

Hymer, S. (1972) 'The Multinational Corporation and the Law of Uneven Development', pp. 113–29 in J. W. Bhagwati (ed.), *Economic and the World Order*. New York: Macmillan.

Jargowsky, P. A. and Bane, M. J. (1991) 'Ghetto poverty in the United States, 1970–1980', pp. 235–73 in C. Jencks and P. E. Peterson (eds) *The Urban Underclass*. Washington, DC: The Brookings Institution.

Jencks, C. (1991) 'Is the American underclass growing?' pp. 28–102 in C. Jencks and P. E. Peterson (eds) *The Urban Underclass*. Washington, DC: The Brookings Institution.

Jones, S. (1990) 'War and human rights in Cambodia', *New York Review of Books*, July, pp. 15–22.

Lemann, N. (1988) 'The origins of the urban underclass', *Atlantic Monthly* (Part 1) June, pp. 31–55, (Part 2) July, pp. 54–68.

Lemann, N. (1991) *The Promised Land: the great black migration and how it changed America*. New York: Alfred A. Knopf.

Lewis, O. (1968) 'The culture of poverty', in D. P. Moynihan (ed.) *On Understanding Poverty: perspectives from the social sciences*. New York: Basic Books.

Long, L. H. (1974) 'Poverty status and receipt of welfare among migrants and nonmigrants in large cities', *American Sociological Review* Vol. 39, No. 1, pp.46–56.

Long, L. H. and Hansen, K. A. (1975) 'Trends in return migration to the south', *Demography*, Vol. 12, No. 4, pp. 601–14.

Long, L. H. and Heltmann, L. R. (1975) 'Migration and income differences between black and white men in the north', *American Journal of Sociology*, Vol. 80, pp. 1391–409.

New Jersey Department of Labor and Industry (1970) *Seasonal Farm Labor*. Trenton: State of New Jersey, Department of Labor and Industry.

New Jersey Department of Labor, Wage and Hour Division (1990) Unpublished internal memorandum.

Pfeffer, M. J. (1983a) 'Social origins of three systems of farm production in the United States', *Rural Sociology*, Vol. 48, No. 4, pp. 540–62.

Pfeffer, M. J. (1983b) 'Industrial farming', *Democracy*, Vol. 3, No. 2, pp. 37–49.

Pfeffer, M. J. (1991) 'Black migration and the legacy of plantation agriculture', Chapter 11 in J. Singlemann and F. A. Deseran (eds), *Inequality and Labor Market Areas*. Boulder: Westview (forthcoming).

Ritchey, N. P. (1974) 'Urban poverty and rural to urban migration', *Rural Sociology*, Vol. 39, No. 1, pp. 12–27.

Runyan, J. L. (1989) *A Summary of Federal Laws and Regulations Affecting Agricultural Employers*. Agriculture Information Bulletin Number 550, Economic Research Service, United States Department of Agriculture.

Slesinger, D. P. and Pfeffer, M. J. (1991) 'Migrant Farm Workers', Chapter 8 in C. M. Duncan (ed.) *Rural Poverty in America*. New York: Auburn House (forthcoming).

Weber, M. (1978) *Economy and Society*. Edited by G. Roth and C. Wittich. Berkeley: University of California.

Wilson, W. J. (1978) *The Declining Significance of Race: blacks and changing American institutions*. Chicago: University of Chicago Press.

Wilson, W. J. (1987) *The Truly Disadvantaged: the inner city, the underclass, and public policy*. Chicago: University of Chicago Press.

Wilson, W. J. (1991) 'Public policy research and *the truly disadvantaged*', pp. 460–82 in C. Jencks and P. E. Peterson (eds) *The Urban Underclass*. Washington, DC: The Brookings Institution.

CHAPTER 5

# Local Culture, Life Mode and Development in a Norwegian Rural Community

*Mariann Villa and Reidar Almås*

## Introduction

This chapter is based on data and approaches developed in the project 'Public Policy and Regional Development in Selected Rural Communities of Mid-Norway' at the Centre for Rural Research, Trondheim. The research project is financed by the Agricultural Research Council of Norway, as part of the research programme 'Rural Development'. The project is presently ongoing, and this chapter attempts to systematise some of what is at present available for analysis. The paper focuses on one of four communities studied.

We intend to apply the analysis of life-mode and community studies to *Stordal*, an industrial and agricultural municipality in Møre and Romsdal county. Stordal has, as have many rural district communities, a small and declining population. But, the municipality differs from the usual pattern in its low unemployment level. This is connected to the development of the small-scale furniture industry. In addition to this, agriculture is an important way of living.

In this research we are asking three central questions. These are:

(i) How valuable is the use of life-mode analysis, in order to explain industrial growth and labour processes in a small rural community?

(ii) Can concepts of rural community and local culture help explain deviations from what is traditionally meant by 'wage labourer' and 'self-employed'?

(iii) What is the competitive advantage of a community like Stordal, considering the changing international division of labour?

118

**Methodological premises**

Several research strategies have been employed, using different types of data. This approach is called triangulation, or the combination of different methodologies to study one phenomenon. Denzin (1978), who introduced this methodological concept, holds that 'no single method ever adequately solves the problem of rival causal factors; because each method reveals different aspects of reality, multiple methods of observation must be employed' (Denzin, 1978, p. 28). He identified four different types of triangulation:

(i) Data triangulation – the use of a variety of data sources.
(ii) Theory triangulation – the use of different analytical perspectives to interpret data.
(iii) Methodological triangulation – the use of multiple methods to study a single problem.
(iv) Researcher triangulation – several researchers taking part in one study with different attitudes and approaches.

The research design employed in the Stordal study attempts to include all four types of triangulation in addressing the local development in the community. First, we have used statistical data from the Central Bureau of Statistics. The population census and the census of agriculture are the two most important sources. Second, we have gathered data by personal interviews of key informants of the local administration and politics. Third, we have used in-depth interviews with key figures of local public life. Those might be retired entrepreneurs or teachers, or local historians. Fourth, we use archives of the municipality, anniversary and jubilee reports of firms and organisations, and other relevant records. We are also intending to use essays on their own future, written by local schoolchildren (aged 15). We may also ask local personalities, entrepreneurs and leading social figures to write their own autobiographies.

Our theoretical perspectives are influenced by holistic approaches in historical sociology, life-mode analysis from ethnology and sociology of culture, and neo-Chayanovian rural sociology. In our view, the historical perspective is essential in examining the rural community. We start our structural analysis of the communities in the early 1950s, and follow the key variables up to 1990. By using a modified life-mode analysis we hope to show how different people in a rural community will act, compared to people in an urban context. We also include Chayanov's perspective on the family firm, showing how a 'peasant economy' might survive as a modern adaptation to a capitalist market.

We use both quantitative and qualitative methods in our study, arguing that the protracted either/or attitude emerging from the debates on positivism was quite inadequate. Villa has worked mostly with qualitative methods, while Almås has mostly experience from quantitative survey analysis. We use statistical methods to analyse census data from the Central Bureau of Statistics, while employing content analysis to address the in-depth interviews, veteran autobiographies and schoolchildren's essays.

Research triangulation in this study is thus made possible by the different backgrounds and approaches of the two researchers. Villa is interested in cultural sociology and has worked with the concept of life mode in a previous community study. Almås is more macro-oriented and has worked with sociology of agriculture from a neo-marxist standpoint. Both take part in all stages of the research process and discuss each methodological step to ensure that we both share a common understanding of the research enterprise. Whilst our analytical contributions are quite distinct, taken together we hope to illuminate our research problem more fully. Also, even if we do not aspire to be objective, we intend to attain a common understanding through a focus on the *intersubjectivity* of the crucial developmental factors observed in our studied communities.

## The Stordal municipality

Stordal municipality belongs to the interior rural districts of Sunnmøre, in Western Norway. Ålesund, the nearest city, is about one hour away by car (see Figure 5.1). Most of the district is mountainous, and the valley Stordalen cuts right through the mountains. The tall mountains shut out the sun from the valley for long periods of the year; in central Stordal it is absent from October to March.

From 1965 until 1977, Stordal and two neighbouring municipalities (Skodje and Ørskog) constituted one large municipality. During the years up to 1977 the inhabitants of Stordal, led by the local entrepreneurs, successfully fought to be an independent municipality. Until 1980 the number of inhabitants was increasing, but then the development reversed. By the beginning of 1991, the municipality had a population of 1025 persons. At the same time there were 115 self-employed persons.

Furniture production is an important industry. The municipality has five furniture factories. They are all led by entrepreneurs who come from local families. There is also a factory making fishing tackle and some smaller enterprises in woodworking and engineering. There has been a gradual concentration in employment. Whilst in 1980, seven enterprises employed 235 people, in 1989 six employed 346. In addition, three grocer's shops do business in the municipality. Industry and trade in Stordal also give employment to people from the neighbouring communities, and, according to the Mayor, there are between 80 and 100 daily commuters to the municipality.

Stordal's cultural landscape differs from that of other fjord villages in the prominence of the numerous furniture factories located side by side along the innermost shore. These factories started their activities as cottage industries in cellars and basements in private houses in the community. Initially, production might not have been associated with furniture at all, but with commodities like chandeliers and canned goods. However, the reconstruction period immediately following the Second World War, saw a large demand for furniture, and the extra effort and initiative of the time, gave rise to this new industry. Now, the well-established Stordal furniture

**Figure 5.1**  Møre og Romsdal

**Table 5.1**  Stordal population change

| 1950 | 1960 | 1970 | 1980 | 1990 |
|------|------|------|------|------|
| 989  | 1060 | 1042 | 1079 | 1028 |

*Source*: Population Census.

industry exports its products both within and beyond Europe. Several of the furniture factories have found significant niches in the market; for instance in capturing main deliveries to public offices and institutions. The furniture industry produces for export to Denmark, Iceland, Holland, US, Germany, Belgium and Luxembourg. An important part of the business is to develop the sales inside and outside Norway. One factory exports 48 per cent as a result of this strategy. There has also been a growth in the national market; and the industry emphasises quality production and work in order to strengthen markets. The factories also have sales agents in other parts of Norway as well as abroad.

Despite variations in the market, the need to import raw materials, and severe transportation problems – even today the roads are narrow and of an inferior standard for the transport of heavy machinery and furniture – the enterprises prosper. This contributes to Stordal's comparatively low unemployment (1.7 per cent as of February 1991). Unemployment elsewhere in Norway currently averages more than 5 per cent.

Norwegian regional policy has had an overall aim to ensure equal living conditions for people in all parts of the country, and to maintain the existing population pattern. A part of the regional policy is rural development funds. As Stordal has deviated from the high degree of unemployment that occurs elsewhere in Norway, the community has minimal support (15 per cent) on investments from the rural development funds. In fact there is no local apparatus for taking care of such interests. The lack of a local public job-creating apparatus in Stordal may be seen as a result of a strong and growing private economic sector, which up to now has secured employment and settlement in the community. Stordal also shows deviations in development in the service sector. This sector has for the country as a whole had a very rapid growth, especially in the 1970s and the 1980s, and today public and private services employ most of the rural population. In Stordal this is, in comparison, a small sector.

Agriculture represents the other important industry. Most people in agriculture combine farming with other sources of income. The typical production is dairy produce and meat. Farmers who keep young cattle and sheep often have factory work as well.

**Table 5.2**  Number of farm units (above 0.5 hectares)

| 1949 | 1959 | 1979 | 1989 |
|------|------|------|------|
| 131  | 118  | 80   | 63   |

Source: Census of Agriculture, RS 4/90.

From 1950 there has been a steady decline in the number of farms, whilst those still in production acquire more acreage. This trend is consistent with the country as a whole. In the 1950s and 1960s there were many small farm units, with approximately a third of the working population being employed in the primary industries in 1960.

**Table 5.3** Employees by industry (Norway, by percentage)

|  | 1960 | 1980 |
|---|---|---|
| Agriculture, forestry, fishing | 34 | 17 |
| Manufacturing | 35 | 49 |
| Power production and water supplies, building and construction | 9 | 6 |
| Trade, transport, services | 21 | 28 |
| Total | 99 | 100 |

*Source*: Population and Housing Census.

The 1980 census shows a reduction in the number of employed persons in the primary industries since 1960. Although agriculture experienced difficult times through low incomes, the situation tended to stabilise during the 1970s. The 1975 Government resolution, to ensure equal income for people in agriculture and in manufacturing, created more optimism. Many of the present farmers started their careers in the late 1970s when the policy was very favourable to communities in the marginal agricultural regions of Norway. In Stordal this contributed to a modernisation and concentration in agriculture, especially of the largest farms.

*The labour symbiosis between furniture factory and farming*

A common occupational combination in the community is factory work and farming. According to evidence from the enterprises, as of 1991, 25 per cent of the farms in the municipality had supplementary income from furniture manufacturing.

The interactions between farming and other activities is longstanding. The farmers work in the factories during the winter season, and take the time off to work on their farms in the summer season. In summer the factories receive less orders, and they have an additional supply of student labour. The pressure of work in agriculture alternates with the rush of business in manufacturing, and the employers avoid the need to dismiss workers. Another solution for farmers who have this occupational combination, is to start work in the factory later in the morning.

The combination of manufacturing and farming can also represent conflicting interests, particularly when the farms are drained of a labour force by the manufacturing industry. On the other hand, the factories are a necessary source of income to the smaller farms. One of our informants argued that farmers in Stordal ought to be grateful to the furniture factories, as a handy source of supplementary income. Small-scale farmers have found their necessary income supplements by developing these different labour–time combinations with the local manufacturing industry. This mutual dependence of farming and manufacturing in Stordal may have suppressed or moderated conflicts, that otherwise might have arisen. Moreover, it has contributed to the sustainability of the agrarian-based population even if it has engendered more flexibility on their part.

**Life-mode analysis**

Life-mode analysis is a conceptual tool employed to analyse people's adaptation and behaviour on the basis of the cultural and economic structure of a locality. It starts with people's basic way of life; how they organise everyday life, and the values and ideology which is created within the life mode. Its originator was the French historian Paul Vidal de la Blache, who worked to develop an analytical concept ('genres de vie') which could capture the interaction between society and nature (Bærenholdt, 1991). The concept was later developed by Lucien Febvre, who together with March Bloch founded the journal which gave name to their 'Annales-school'.

In recent Scandinavian social science life-mode analysis has re-established itself on the basis of supplementing the more conventional structural and Marxist analysis of community life. The Danish ethnologist Thomas Højrup introduced this new structural school of life-mode analysis through his book *Det Glemte Folk* (*The Forgotten People*) (Højrup, 1983). In this adaptation, the *mode of production* and *the ideology* create the total concept which is called *life mode*. Lone Rahbek Christensen and Thomas Højrup (1989) summarise the structural analysis of life mode in this way:

> Culture is defined here as contrasts in a community and as being the center-pin of our social world. With this starting point, it becomes the mission of cultural analysis to localize cultural contrasts in the community which can often seem to be invisible. However, this must be done with the help of a well-defined theoretical apparatus where different concepts are held in precise relations to one another. As a starting point, the authors seek these contrasts in different production forms: simple as opposed to capitalistic production of wares – where concepts such as work, reproduction and family become central. (1989, p. 152)

Three main life modes are outlined by Christensen and Højrup: *The self-employed life mode, the wage-labourer life mode* and *the career life mode*. These life modes are based on the simple and on the capitalistic modes of commodity production. We shall give a brief outline of the three main life modes as they are presented as typologies.[1]

*The self-employed life mode*

The self-employed life mode is rooted in the simple mode of commodity production. The life mode is not primarily built on economic relations. Instead, the producers are tied together in family relations, relations to colleagues and so on. This life mode can be found in smaller enterprises or in the core of larger enterprises.

If we look at the family farm, we see that the important principle is to sustain the farm production and to secure a self-employed and independent future for the next generation. To be self-employed and independent is a goal in itself. To do wage labour for others is looked upon as a misfortune.

Independence is achieved by owning both the means of production and the qualifications and skills necessary in order to do the work. The distinction between work and leisure is obscure. Due to different concepts of work and leisure in the various life modes, some might claim that the farmer works in his 'leisure' as well; that is, if 'leisure' is defined as the time after six o'clock in the afternoon or on Saturdays and Sundays.

### The wage-labourer life mode

The wage-labourer life mode is more centrally a characteristic of the capitalistic mode of production. In this life mode the family may be a place where the labourer can relax and reproduce his capacity for work. The family may also be looked upon as a service institution for a worker who in his turn contributes financially with his income.

In this life mode, work is opposed to leisure, and the worker declares his solidarity with his workmates - not with his job or the factory. The worker is told to do a job, and it is not worth doing more than strictly necessary. The intensity of work is secured through force and control.

### The career life mode

The *career life mode* is another type of wage labour in the capitalistic mode of production. This wage labourer usually starts on a lower level, but works up an organised career hierarchy. In this life mode work may be a painful duty but it is also a way to a career. The employee thinks it is important to be independent, avoiding routine work on a lower level because it diminishes the value of his job.

As in the self-employed life mode there is no clear distinction between work and leisure. Spare time can be used to strengthen one's own career. It is important to be able to show off a presentable home and façade which *traditionally* has been run by a woman who has given up her own career for the benefit of her husband.

### Criticism of life-mode analysis

Dating back to its origin, life-mode analysis has been met with some criticism. There has been a debate whether Vidal's concept of 'genres de vie' implied a natural evolutionary determinism. Vidal himself makes a point against determinism, but the concept is rather descriptive and clearly influenced by a Darwinist attitude on human adaptation to nature (Bærenholdt, 1991, p. 33).

The lack of regional and local variations in life-mode analysis is also problematic, given the salience of local cultures. These debates have raised some important questions concerning the nature of cultural change. Through socialisation the members of a community learn the whole conglomeration of values, ideas and customs. But why does deviance emerge? If communities, villages and tribes live side-by-side for centuries with very little cultural contact, why do we see acculturation? The diffusion of values, techniques and cultural institutions may take different forms, and life modes may be changed. But what are the mechanisms through which life modes are changed?

The most severe criticism against the Højrup school emerged from those claiming that there is too little room for social action and cultural creativity in his model. The very close connection between mode of production and life mode leaves very little space for actors to create their own way of living. Because Højrup is very much against hermeneutically developed typologies from real life, his life-mode analysis somewhat loses the dynamics of social action.

In the Stordal research, we employ and adapt life modes as *synthetical cultural categories*; developed from and linking both modes of production and real social life. In a modern, or post-modern setting, people's life modes are partly creations of their own. The components of these life modes are chosen, not at random, but to show other people where you belong (Gullestad, 1990). They are thus inherently social phenomena. They are based on modes of production, but strongly influenced by regional affiliation (for instance, the rural counter cultures versus the urban elite culture) and gender (for instance, house decoration is mainly supposed to be a female obligation (Gullestad, 1990)).

Whilst being influenced by aspects of local and regional affiliation, life modes are independent of regional context, in the sense that they are not exclusive to the city or the countryside. Even if we see the career life mode and the wage-labourer life mode as stereotypically urban (i.e. associated with the capitalistic mode of production), and a self-employed life mode (simple mode of production) as primarily rural, empirical research increasingly shows that these life modes in reality exist side by side and in different combinations in rural and urban localities.

In this analysis we must also focus on workers whose employment situations *combine* self-employment (for instance on their own farm) with wage labour (in the furniture factory). This further complicates the application of life-mode analysis. A wage-labourer with his own enterprise will have his life pattern and ideology influenced by both the wage-labourer and the self-employed life mode. Nevertheless, these labourers have without regard to their home situation, contributed to the industrial development in Stordal. We will also consider the rural wage-labourer as different from the urban wage-labourer, by the ways that the former is strongly contextually influenced by the self-employed life mode and by the local community.

## *A neo-Chayanovian perspective: an adaptation of life-mode analysis*

As an alternative conceptual understanding of the adaptation and social actions of the people in Stordal we wish to employ the perspective of the Russian agricultural economist, Chayanov. The rediscovery of the Chayanovian concept 'peasant economy' has created a fruitful theoretical discussion in order to understand the logic of persistent simple commodity production and the cultural ways of life attached to it (Reinhardt and Barlett, 1989; Bodenstedt, 1990).

Chayanov argues that the family farm, as opposed to a capitalist farm, is based on a distinctive behavioural logic. The goal of the production is not the desire for profit, but the consumption needs of the household (Chayanov, 1966). The amount of work the family is willing (and able) to contribute is dependent on the age and number of working members of the family. The aim of the family farm lies in finding an equilibrium in the labour–consumer balance. Increasing prices may lead to reduced input of labour, because the needs of the family will be met with less output to the market. On the other hand, production in a family unit may increase when prices fall because the consumption needs of the family are the same. However, in times of crisis, the farm family will accept a return on labour lower than the market wage (Reinhardt and Barlett, 1989, p. 204).

Both Marxist and neo-classical schools of political economy have argued against the Chayanovian premises. Eventually, they have claimed, family farming has to give in to capitalist penetration. However, as time passes, family farms seem to persist, both in Europe and elsewhere (see Marsden, 1991). They even re-emerge, as in Eastern Europe today. Also, the logic of the family farm, especially the aspect of accepting a lower return for family labour than market wage, is widely seen in other trades. Both because of the high unemployment rates, and the renewed efforts in all post-industrialised states to create new jobs, we now see a re-emergence of family firms both in manufacturing and in the services.

Such an extended neo-Chayanovian perspective may thus be especially fruitful when examining a rural community where furniture factories were established by part-time farmers still living in the community. Several family members may work on the factory floor as well as in the farm yard. If not thoroughgoing peasants any more, they may still follow the *logics* of a peasant family, working to make family ends meet, and not for profit. In such cases we need to ask whether their life mode is dominated by their role as wage-labourer or as self-employed.

### Culture and economic development

Spilling and van der Ros (1988) argue that knowledge of culture and traditions can be important in order to understand the economic development in a region. The culture may state the premises, decide the factors of motivation or build a barrier against development. They use the furniture industry at Sunnmøre (a region incorporating Stordal) as an example of economic development which was not supposed to happen according to economic theory. This industry has developed far from markets and raw materials, but the initiative has been present. In this region it is argued that there exists a cultural tradition in being independent, taking initiative and having the courage to take financial risks.

It is often difficult to distinguish between myths and reality, and we do not want to speculate about 'the Sunnmørian spirit' here. Nevertheless, let us give an example of what people from Sunnmøre say about themselves: 'We are inventive, modest, willing to learn, and blessed with a certain drive. All this has given us a platform on which to build a thriving industry. We are a population eager for development and improvement.' What they, among other things, see as a danger to themselves is, in addition to long distances and high transport costs, 'an unwillingness to share with others and the strong patriotism' (from Amdam, 1988). This is also a reputation which holds a certain foothold in Norwegian popular opinion, thus potentially inspiring its further development.

Such cultural traits are also supported by our research experiences. For instance, for research purposes we contacted the various enterprises in order to obtain evidence about how many workers held the combination of furniture factory work and farming. The head of the marketing department at one of the factories answered: 'With today's razor-sharp demands on efficiency I wonder whether we at all should waste our time in finding out!' That was a discreet way of saying that we should look for that information elsewhere. It also alludes to the nature of the working moral as well.

Whilst our investigations support the view that a culture of initiative and hard work have been a real foundation stone for factory development in Stordal, they do not explain why furniture production specifically developed. The people of Stordal may not themselves be able to answer that question. One of our informants argues that there might be something in the fact that just one person started producing furniture, then the others saw this was successful and wanted to try it as well. This is nevertheless hazardous, given both the competition in starting the same trade as the neighbour, combined with the unamenable geography and natural conditions.

Many of the furniture factories were built in several stages, reflecting a cautious and pragmatic expansion. In spite of fluctuations in the market and the volatilities of production, there have been no serious closures since the mid 1970s. One factory went bankrupt around 1980, but this is explained by poor management and a desire for rapid economic growth. The incident only serves as an example of how vulnerable such enterprises are. Some of the workers were absorbed by the other factories. Those who were not properly established in the community moved out, and others were unemployed for a long time.

In the initial stages of development of the furniture industry, the management applied a strategy for separating 'good' labour from 'bad', and introduced a trial period when employing new workers. This allowed them to closely assess capabilities and flexibility of labour. If the person was energetic and showed a willingness to work he was given the job. The workers readily accepted this sort of control and monitoring, and they looked upon it as an opportunity to go on to something else if it turned out that they did not satisfy the management. This positive attitude is an example of the respect they had for the founders and how they trusted their qualified judgement. Above all, it shows how the best labour was socially sorted and disciplined.

One may ask whether the competition in being the greatest and best is a motivating force in small-scale industrial development. Even if the success of the enterprises may largely be due to their own efforts, the municipality has supported it through the provision of industrial estates and (indirectly) by building houses. Such local state support is reinforced by the local media, linking the success of the labour process to notions of cultural and community solidarity. The local newspapers write about 'fantastic production', 'record-breaking sales', 'a lot of overtime, but good spirits in the sewing department' and 'increase in efficiency well received by workers', and contribute in their own way towards creating an attitude of 'bearing the brunt together'.

## *The rural wage labourer: cooperation across social classes?*

Højrup (1983) argues that in the rural world of ideas, crises are tackled with more work and less spending (p. 88). If this 'rural world of ideas' is compared to the reality of farmers and other self-employed, this is a strategy of survival that seems both logical and reasonable.

A similar strategy as the one we find in Højrup's 'the rural world of ideas' is adopted by the *workers* at the furniture factories in Stordal. When there is a lot of work, large orders or crisis in production, the workers show great willingness to do their bit, in order to help the enterprises. Earlier on they would even do that without wages. Such an effort shown by the workers increases production without employing more people.

A female worker told us about solidarity among the workers and cooperation between workers and management. She argued that today the various factories appear to cooperate, even if it has not always been like that. At times they have been competing for labour and wages. Earlier the employers also could demand that their employees work overtime. Later on this changed, and the workers were more free to decide their overtime themselves.

One of our informants, who is not closely connected with the furniture factories, argued that the discussions about cooperation between furniture factories is not entirely true to the facts. If they cooperate on the level of wages, they may compete in other fields. This is for example evident when considering firm expansion. 'If one factory-owner is building, all are building', goes the refrain.

There is then, perhaps more cooperation and unity between owners and workers in enterprises in smaller rural communities than in their urban counterparts. The workers know their boss as neighbour or fellow villager. They know each other's families, and they are conscious of the fact that they are all members of the same rural community. People meet and know about each other from various occasions and in different situations. At smaller enterprises the owners may also know the workers' situations more intimately. The owner and employer might work in production together for short periods. One may be a part-time farmer whilst the other may only seek wage labour in the summer periods.

In the 'jubilee book' for one of the factories (Tenfjord, 1987) a worker and former Mayor of the municipality says:

> I never experienced any disputes...The good relationship between management and employees, where all are inspired to do their share and social antagonism barely exists, is typical of the Stordal enterprises in general (1987, p. 40).

Another says:

> The workers are our most valuable asset. It is evident that the factory would not have been what it is today without the hard and good work of the employees. The workers and leaders work together in order to bring the factory to the top within furniture production...cooperation is the key to the enormous success, cooperation on all levels, cooperation between management and workers, designers and agents (manager, 1987, pp. 43–4).

It is necessary to undertake more detailed research concerning the labour conditions inside the furniture factories. Earlier working-life research and history, suggests that the manufacturing industry and the solidaristic and paternalistic rhetoric may hide many conflicts, both among employees in general, among employees on various levels in the organisation, and between management and employees (e.g. Lysgaard, 1985). What is presented as cooperation may conceal antagonistic interests.

### Workers' solidarity with the locality and their employers

In the jubilee book mentioned above, one of the veteran workers argues that during the earliest period, when the manufacturing production had just begun, the workers would have their pay withheld. Such a sacrifice was seen as necessary should the factory and jobs survive, and engendered little protest. The veteran argues: 'We who worked in the production, felt that we did our best in keeping the enterprises of rural Norway alive' (p. 24). Is this story representative of most Norwegian enterprises, or is it something special to the Stordal locality? We may see this in relation to the fact that Stordal is a small rural community, where the manufacturing industry not only represents the property of the founder families, but also represents and contributes greatly to the identity of the local inhabitants as a social group. The furniture factories are not simply owned by people who think in terms of industrial growth and rising sales; whilst the workers stress how important these jobs are for the employment and settlement in the municipality. In this sense local sense of place and employment are highly reinforcing.

The rural wage-labourer may be more dependent upon the factory than the wage labourer in larger non-rural places. In Norwegian rural districts economic life is more vulnerable, and just *that* job in the community is often the only alternative to moving out. There is a high level of dependence on the 'job' as an economic means of survival as well as a source of rural identity. The established rural wage-labourer with his own enterprise (for instance his own farm), is the most immobile labourer. In that sense he will also be the labourer who is most likely to put up with hard times. It is said that people from Stordal keep together, especially if there is a threat of an external enemy. This external enemy may be the restructuring of production and markets which often leads to lost jobs, unemployment and being forced to move somewhere else.

*Community identity and the suppression of conflicts?*

From the discussion and empirical observations presented thus far, we can assess how conflicts are suppressed by community identity and the knowledge of being a full member of that community. It is strongly emphasised by respondents that the furniture industry is important to the *community*, to the jobs and to the settlement in the valley.

At the risk of idyllising the countryside (n.b. 'Gemeinschaft is by no means idyllic – it is authority, strength, paternalism, submission, revolt, as well')[2] we would like to summarise what has been said about Stordal so far.

The factories, represented by the workers, have several responsibilities. These concern:

   (i) increase sales and make a profit for the owners (though this is under-communicated);
   (ii) keep up a production which serves the community – concretised in jobs.

Also the wage-labourers with no enterprise of their own, or labourers who have no family ties to the management and owners of the enterprise, show their solidarity with the production (for instance by extra effort in busy periods or hard times). In this sense wage relations (or the cash nexus) to the factory are not as unambiguous as they may be in the large-scale industrial production of the more urban districts.

Solidarity with furniture production is more than an ideology or concept of labour related to a *self-employed life mode*. The ideology of the wage-labourers in Stordal (the rural wage-labourer with or without his own enterprise or business) is also adapted to, and created by, the particular rural community. Here they can find a common identity, and social control mechanisms belonging to that community (they meet and are members of many social networks outside the factory). Cooperation and solidarity with the factories may be explained in the same way: the rural wage-labourer has few or no other alternatives in the labour market. The wage-labourer who also owns his own enterprise, usually his small farm, is the less mobile, and he is most eager to keep the factory alive as a safe place of work. Hence, the common cultural identity and the solidarity with the enterprises is closely connected to geographical and social immobility.

More broadly we can propose that the wage-labourer ideology (as defined by life-mode analysis) is somewhat modified by the rural community, creating a sort of 'equality ideology' between the employees and the employers. Aspects of the self-employed life mode (as for instance, solidarity with the production) can also be mistaken for or combined with the fact that people are attached to the rural community in various ways. Other factors that may affect the employees' attitude is lack of alternatives in the employment market, a wish for industrial growth to secure the future, and a common 'village identity' which says that 'we are doing it together'.

## Community firms?

Does this suggest that the furniture firms of Stordal are not capitalist firms that seek profit but rather kinds of *community firms* where the owners try to fulfill certain kinds of public needs? Here we have an interesting case of comparison. One of the authors in the early 1980s conducted a rural development project in Budal, a community very similar to Stordal (Almås, 1988). Budal (population 545) had one furniture factory (A/L Budalsmøbler), producing the traditional 'Budal Chair'. The industrial production in Budal was founded upon a strong handicraft tradition, as in Stordal, but in contrast to Stordal the Budal factory was a cooperative firm, owned by local people. In many ways the Budal furniture firm had the same characteristics as those in Stordal. Most of the owner-workers were part-time farmers as well, and they worked more when sales were high. The wages were moderate as in Stordal, but at the end of the year the profit was divided into portions according to the amount of work. The head of the cooperative factory was moderately better paid than the other owner-workers, and the main goal of the factory was to provide work for the local people, and profit was supposed to be less important (Almås, 1984, pp. 2–6).

Even if the Budal factory could be called a *community firm*, and there are some similarities between the two business cultures, there are also some important differences. The Stordal firms compete with each other in many ways. When public and private institutions look for the best price and quality, they compete to place the best bid and henceforth get the order. They also compete for the frontstage building site, and none of them wants to move out to the new and less prestigious backstage sites.[3] The factory owners also compete for the best labour force, but not by raising the wages. Keeping wages down at a moderate level is an important area of cooperation between the owners. They also lobby the municipality to get the most favourable conditions for their industry, but then compare the decisions and negotiations to see that none of them gets a better deal. The main goal of the Stordal factory owners is also profit, as they could not survive for a long time as private owners without that profit. It is even doubtful if the cooperative firm in Budal would survive without that profit, especially if they moved out of their special market niche.

We suggest that the Stordal furniture firms are not community firms, as is the 'Budalsmøbler' mentioned above. The Stordal firms function as capitalist firms, but have a cheap and loyal labour force who identify with the community and their employers. These social conditions constitute their competitive advantage, together with the supportive relations with the local authorities and cheap capital from the regional funds. Whilst the owners make money, they do not seem to seek maximum profit and there is little conspicuous consumption. We might call their profit logic 'maximal local profit' as they do not go out of Stordal with their capital in order to seek profit elsewhere. They behave like Norwegian capitalists should in the country where the 'Law of Jante' stands above the ten commandments.[4]

## Conclusions: local labour conditions and European integration

A life-mode analysis contributes to an explanation of the behaviour of the working class in Stordal. Those who work at the furniture factories are in many ways attached to the *self-employed life mode*. Both through their recent history as farmers and as members of the 'gründer' families, many of the workers identify with their firm as much as with their role as wage workers. Belonging to a community totally dominated by agriculture up to the 1930s, we also find an agrarian cultural lag which influences people's life mode. The particular regional and rural context gives an additional explanation to how people act. In a rural community, with a population of 1025 and close-knit social networks, the local cultural context is very influential, and it keeps conventional working-class values at a (social) distance. Other factors like immobility and lack of alternatives in the employment market may also modify the wage-labourer ideology.

In addition, the flexibility and part-time adaptation of many families in Stordal, shows that they partly follow a Chayanovian logic which extends beyond agriculture. As long as they have to pay a large amount of money, for instance on their mortgage, both members of the family often work full time. But even if their income is below the industrial average, they may afford a higher standard of housing in Stordal than in the neighbouring town of Ålesund. Later in life, when the children have left home and their needs are reduced, the family income may be reduced according to Chayanovian logic. However, other factors may influence elder women to seek employment, such as the need for social contact and socially constructed needs.

Increasingly, the furniture firms must make a recognisable profit to survive. With the tough winds from the 1992 single market of the EC, they may have to cut costs and export more. This internationalisation could severely test the locally constructed life modes and delicately organised labour processes. In the introduction to the chapter we asked what are the firms' competitive advantages in the market. As we have seen above, loyal workers, low wages and a stable labour force are extremely valuable assets on the labour market and these are both socially and locally constructed. Concerning the market for capital, the present national rural development policies provide 15 per cent support on investments in the area of Stordal. Taking into consideration that the European Economic Space (EES) is to develop joint EC and EFTA bodies to survey the treaty, this EES-body is likely to have a stronger say in the distribution of regional support.[5] From the Cecchini report we know that especially small and medium-sized firms will meet stiffer competition and that, because of this, the unemployment rates will increase shortly after 1992 (Cecchini, 1988).

If the Sunnmøre region loses this competitive advantage of cheap capital from the regional funds, the Stordal entrepreneurs may have to act more like capital owners elsewhere. They may also be unable to renew their production equipment, once the present machines are outworn or outdated. Far from being community firms, they may have to adhere to the raw laws of capitalism. Some of the factories export half of their products already, but EES means more competition. Mergers, closures and dismissals may follow as a consequence of the adjustment to the single European market of 1993.

## Notes

1. Based on Christensen and Højrup, 1989; Højrup, 1983.
2. Otnes, 1991, p. 294.
3. All the furniture factories are placed close to the beach, overlooking the fjord. This location tells a lot of the owners' power and prestige, but also shows that furniture production and employment is more important than leisure and tourism.
4. The 'Law of Jante' was formulated by the Danish-Norwegian author Aksel Sandemose. In the small town of Jante the first rule is that you should not think you *are* somebody. Second rule is that you should not think that you can teach *us* something, and so it goes . . .
5. The EC law states two criteria, low level of income and high unemployment, in order to get support from national regional funds. Stordal has neither of the two, and even if EFTA countries in the EES negotiations have claimed a sparse population as an additional criterion, its status is as yet unclear.

## References

*Agricultural Censuses* 1949, 1959, 1969, 1979.

Almås, R. (1984) *Budal. Eksempel på lokal utvikling i eit avgrensa bygdesamfunn.* Report, Centre for Rural Research, University of Trondheim.

Almås, R. (1988) 'Evaluation of a participatory development project in three Norwegian rural communities', *Community Development Journal*, Vol. 23, No. 1.

Amdam, J. (1988) *Idèar for regional utvikling i Ålesundsregionen.* Arbeidsrapport nr. V 8805, Møreforsking.

*Annual Report* from Agricultural Office of Stordal, 1990.

Bodenstedt, A. (1990) 'Rural culture – a new concept', *Sociologia Ruralis*, Vol. XXX, No. 1, pp. 5–17.

*Bygdebladet*, local newspaper.

Bærenholdt, J. O. (1991) *Bygdeliv.* Forskningsrapport nr. 78, Institut for Geografi, Samfundsanalyse og Datalogi, Roskilde Universitetscenter.

Cecchini, P. (1988) *The European Challenge 1992 – the benefits of a single market.* Commission of the European Communities, Brussels.

Chayanov, A. V. (1966 (1925)) 'The theory of peasant economy', in D. Thorner *et al.* (eds) *A. V. Chayanov on the Theory of Peasant Economy.* Homewood, Ill., Richard D. Irwin.

Christensen, L. R. and Højrup, T. (1989) Strukturel livsformanalyse. *Nord Nytt*; 37, Nordisk tidsskrift for folkelivsforskning, 53–91, 152.

Denzin, N. K. (1978) *The Research Act: a theoretical introduction to sociological methods.* New York: McGraw-Hill.

Gullestad, M. (1990) 'Home-decoration as a popular culture. Constructing homes, genders and classes in Norway'. Paper to the first EASA conference, Coimbra, Portugal, 31 August to 2 September, 1990. To be published by Routledge in a collection of articles edited by Teresa del Valle.

Højrup, T. (1983) *Det glemte folk.* Livsformer og centraldirigering. Institut for europæisk folkelivsforskning/Statens byggeforskningsinstitut, Hørsholm.

Lysgaard, S. (1985) *Arbeiderkollektivet.* Universitetsforlaget A/S.

Marsden, T. K. (1991) 'Theoretical issues in the continuity of petty commodity production'. Chapter 1 in S. Whatmore, P. Lowe and T. Marsden (eds) *Rural Enterprise: shifting perspectives on small-scale production.* Critical Perspectives on Rural Change Vol. 3. London: Fulton.

Otnes, P. (1991) Renessanse for Gemeinschaft? Om nærmiljø, lokalsamfunn, nettverk, hverdagsliv. *Tidsskrift for samfunnsforskning*, årgang 32, 291–311.

Population Census, Central Bureau of Statistics.

Population and Housing Census, Central Bureau of Statistics.

Regional Statistics 4/90.

Reinhardt, N. and Barlett, P. (1989) 'The persistence of family farms in United States', *Sociologia Ruralis*, Vol. 24, Nos 3/4.

Spilling, O. R. and van der Ros, J. (1988) *Kultur og regional utvikling.* Rapport nr. 13, Østlandsforskning.

Tenfjord, Johan Kåre (1987) *Helland Møbler As 1947–1987.*

CHAPTER 6

# On the Margins: Uneven Development and Rural Restructuring in the Highlands of Scotland[1]

*Richard J. Smith*

> The Highlands [are] . . . a classic illustration of the inadequacy of any theory of economic growth which suggests that rational organisation and efficiently enforced property rights are by themselves adequate guarantees of long-term development. (Lenman, 1981, p.119)

> While it is always necessary to remember the peculiarities of the physical environment in the Highlands, the essential differences are those of social structure. (Collier, 1953, p.4).

## Introduction

Although Lenman was writing about the Highlands of Scotland in the eighteenth century, his words remain true about conditions in the Highlands today. And Collier, writing in the 1940s, reminds us that the key to understanding the Highlands is in the analysis of its social structure. The Highlands have been a 'problem' for several centuries, and the solutions (sic) to these problems have resulted in an often tragic history. The problem for the people does not lie in the lack of development, but in the forms of development which have resulted in the particular conditions that are found in the Highlands today: depopulation, low incomes and associated poverty, poor quality housing, unemployment and underdevelopment. The contemporary structure of rural life and economy in the Highlands is the outcome of the particular relationship with the capitalist world economy, rather than the lack of such a relationship. As Carter argues:

any view of the Highlands as an area 'that the various revolutions in agriculture, industry and technology have passed by' is patently mistaken. The Highlands today are not independent of such processes – they are the result of them. (Carter, 1974, p.302)

Yet at the heart of the rural society of the Highlands there remains a strength, and that is crofting. This particular structure of landholding and labour organisation was born out of the Highlands' history, giving the region its distinctive social and economic structure as well as cultural form. To understand the Highlands, the people and their potential as well as problems, one needs to understand crofting, both its history and the role it plays in contemporary Highlands life. There have been numerous attempts to define crofting. The most often stated definition is that it is a distinctive form of land tenure that is specific to the seven crofting counties: Argyll, Caithness, Inverness, Orkney, Ross and Cromarty, Shetland, and Sutherland (Figure 6.1). Collier identifies its common characteristic as 'the combination of smallholding with outside employment' (1953, p.25), with the smallholding being worked by family labour. It therefore holds some characteristics similar both to petty commodity production as well as those of peasant production (see over).

This chapter first surveys the historical process that has created the current social and economic structure of the Highlands, in particular how different types of development and the reaction to them have created this distinctive structure. It then looks, in some detail, at the position of crofting in contemporary Highlands life, drawing on a study of crofting in the northwest. The social life of 'peripheral' areas are too often regarded as fixed. This chapter shows that the nature of social formations in such rural areas are, and have been, in a process of constant restructuring, not the least aspect of which is the ever changing meanings and values that people place on their actions (Cohen, 1982, 1985, 1986, 1987; Long et al., 1986; Shields, 1991). Crofting has a variety of meanings for those that are involved in it. The chapter shows how particular forms of labour activity evolve as the cultural practices for individual and collective definition and identity, even though those practices are in continual processes of change. Crofting then, beyond the particular legal and institutional framework within which it exists, is a set of social practices which are an arena for interpretation and re-interpretation.

Given that crofting is a form of pluriactivity, the relationship between crofting and other aspects of the rural economy is crucial. This raises important issues concerning the nature of the rural labour process. In particular, it encompasses the variable relationship between non-capitalist forms of labour organisation, in this case crofting, and wage labour. It is argued here that crofting is a distinctive form of petty commodity production, and not a form of subsistence agriculture, as it is so often described. Crofting's history shows that it emerges in a relationship with capitalist product markets, mediated by powerful landlords. As such, crofting existed, and currently exists, within a capitalist social formation.

138

**Figure 6.1** Crofting lands

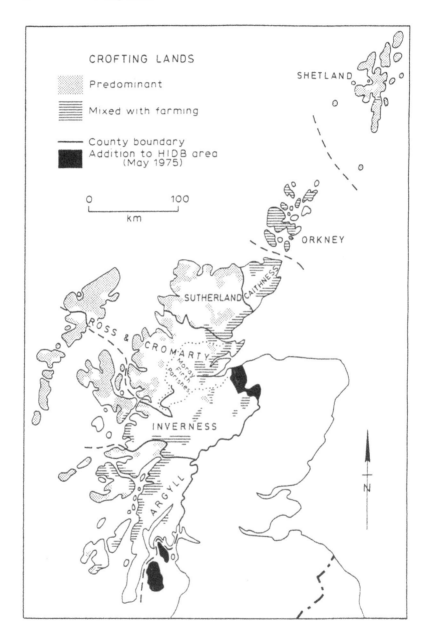

What is then important is the elaboration of this relationship, including the ways in which the state has regulated crofting.

Behind much of the history and contemporary conditions in the Highlands is the central role of land. The importance of crofting cannot be understood outside the history of the struggle by the Highland peasantry to gain control over the land from which they had been alienated. Similarly, the role and nature of landholding remains a central theme. In the past landowners, 'lairds' in Scotland, also held extensive direct power over the people who lived on that land. The transformation of the Highland landholding class, from 'pre-modern' clan chiefs to 'rational' capitalist developers of the clearances, and then to the sporting estate owners of today (changes which were also marked by significant replacement of personnel), is a fascinating history in itself. What is of importance here, however, is how the control of land was used to create a distinctive form of social organisation of production which remains crucial to our understanding of life in the rural parts of the Highlands today. This process occurred within the context of the creation of a distinctive place for the Highlands in the international division of labour within the world economy. This has been a process of peripheralisation with the economic relationship being one of unequal exchange leading to economic underdevelopment. Culturally this has led to the creation of the Highlands as a 'place on the margin' with an important, but now declining, role in the consumption culture of British elites. This dual relationship of economic and cultural marginality to mainstream British society has allowed crofters the 'space' to sustain their cultural distinctiveness.

### The Highlands of Scotland: historical preconditions

In the eighteenth century the Highlands were seen by contemporaries as being very different from the rest of Scottish and British society (Forbes, 1966, pp.xxxvii–xxxxix). The greatest problem for the state was controlling an unruly region (Mitchison, 1970). Nonetheless, the Highlands were increasingly being integrated into British society and economy. These processes led to the social disruption which culminated in the Stuart uprising of 1745, as sections of Highland society tried, in vain, to prevent the breaking up of the clan system (Smout, 1969). The political, social and legal conditions after the rebellion, which included the pacification of the region through military occupation, aided the economic integration into the wider economy. The history of the rest of the eighteenth century is one of the Highlands finding a position within both the British economy and the international division of labour, and a unique position within the culture of national elites.

In the eighteenth century the most important product in the Highlands was cattle, by which the peasantry mainly paid their rents. These were exported to markets beyond the Highlands. The price of these cattle rose by 300 per cent between the 1740s and the 1790s, which was a great impetus for closer economic ties (Smout, 1969, p.323). This initial increased integration did not transform the existing organisation of agricultural production (arable land held in runrig i.e. strip cultivation and communal grazing rights over the hill land) instead it appeared to strengthen it. However, it did intensify the process of change in internal clan social relationships, away from an attachment based on blood to that of landowner and tenant (Smout, 1969; Lenman, 1981). Towards the end of the eighteenth century there began a significant restructuring of the economy of the Highlands which led to the formation of the crofting system. Cattle became less important and two new commodities became central: kelp and sheep.

This transformation is what has become termed the 'clearances', a topic which still raises controversy within the Highlands. The lairds wished to maintain their tenants on their estates, but no longer in the hills tending their cattle and raising their crops. They were to be moved to the coasts and the emptied hinterland set aside for sheep grazing. At the coasts the tenantry were to be engaged in new economic activities, fishing or kelping. The finances of estates were to be placed on a firmer footing; the Highlands were to be improved, and improved to make a profit.

It was the rising demand for kelp (the alkaline ash residue from burnt seaweed, used in the manufacture of soap and glass) that was most striking. Prices rose from £2 a ton in 1750 to a peak of £20 a ton in 1810 (Gray, 1951, pp.197–8). Highland kelp was a substitute for Spanish barilla, supplies of which were halted during the 1790s and 1800s due to war. Its production increased significantly, and spread to encompass the Western Isles, the western mainland and the Northern Isles. Costs of production did not increase, but profits did, which were estimated to be by £16 per ton out of peak price of £20 (Gray, 1951, p.202). For the Hebrides alone it has been estimated that between 15,000 to 20,000 tons per year were exported at the turn of the nineteenth century, with profits in the region of £70,000 (Hunter, 1976, pp.16–17).

The lairds increased production of kelp by moving their tenants to the shore areas where the seaweed was readily available. The tenants were given a small plot of land, too small to grow enough food for a family, and unable to provide a surplus to pay rent. This ended the runrig structure of cultivation (Hunter, 1976, p.31). This structure of small family plots in townships and collective rights over hill land is the basis of crofting to this day. The tenants had to work, as wage labourers, at producing kelp to pay their rents (Hunter, 1976, p.18).[2] As Carter points out the kelpers stood in a dual relationship to the laird: 'as tenant to landlord and employee to employer' (Carter, 1974, p.300). This dual relationship highlights the role played by the ownership and control of land in the nature and route that development took in the Highlands. Land is the cement of this form of social organisation of production. It tied the tenant to the laird in a way that 'free labourers' were not tied to their employer. The position of the tenants as a peasantry reinforced their dependence as wage labourers and vice versa. This pernicious system was made all the more complete with the lack of alternative employment, or where the alternatives were even less enticing (such as the armed forces). With the reimportation of barilla, and the subsequent reductions in duties, the price of kelp fell to £10 a ton in 1815 and down to less than £4 a ton in 1828 (Hunter, 1976, pp.34–5). Withers shows that the substantial profits of the 1810s and early 1820s had become marginal and often losses by the 1830s (Withers, 1988, p.288, table 5.2). The economic underpinning of the system was removed. In these conditions labour control was tightened up, and the kelp estates became renowned for the poor conditions of life for the tenants and for being operated on a near 'feudal' basis (Carter, 1974, pp.300–1).

Kelp production is only one part of the picture, and in the history of the clearances it is the role of sheep that is more well known. It was not until the early nineteenth century that the lairds systematically reorganised their estates around the establishment of large tenant sheep farming,[3] many of the tenant farmers coming from outside the Highlands. Richards (1973) in his account of the Sutherland estate, provides us with a detailed study of the most important estate in the north of Scotland at a time of great social and economic change. Here, as elsewhere in the Highlands, the introduction of sheep was to place estate finances on a stronger footing. The establishment of sheep farms in the hinterlands was to be matched by the creation of coastal townships, with small plots for the tenants similar to those of the kelping areas, where the tenants were to make a living from agriculture, fishing or any other employment opportunities available. The diffusion of sheep farming was encouraged by the continued rise in prices for meat and wool. Livestock numbers rose significantly, for example in Sutherland there were an estimated 5,000 beasts in 1808 (Omand, 1982, p.246), but 168,170 in 1853 and over 240,000 in 1875 (Withers, 1988, p.246). Other areas show similar rates of growth. There were also marked rises in the rents for the tenanted farms: 30 to 50 per cent in Sutherland in the 1860s and 1870s alone; and between 50 and 100 per cent in Skye over the fifty years from 1830 (Withers, 1988). It was not until the decline of wool prices in the 1870s, and the competition from cheaper frozen mutton from Australia and New Zealand that sheep farming came under pressure, at which point the role of the Highlands in British society began to change.

The history of the Sutherland estate also shows the relationship between the Highland estates and the rest of the British economy. The marriage of Elizabeth Gordon, the Countess of Sutherland to George Leveson-Gower, later Marquis of Stafford, (reputedly the richest man in England) in 1785 was a union of Highland land with English capital, and it was this capital that was used to invest in the Sutherland economy. Devine (1989) has argued that there was an emergence of a new landed elite in the western Highlands and Islands in the first half of the nineteenth century. Ending any pretence of the clan basis for the laird tenant relationship. It also led to the penetration of Highland life by new capital. The dominant feature of nineteenth and twentieth-century rural Highland society is its attraction for the external industrial, commercial and financial elites.

By the later nineteenth century the Highlands became the main area for hunting estates in Britain and as such part of the consumption process rather than production sphere. This can clearly be seen in the rise in the number of deer forests. There were only 9 deer forests mentioned in the Old Statistical

Account of the 1780s. By 1884 there were 104 covering nearly 2,000,000 acres, and by 1912 there were 203 totalling over 3,250,000 acres, more than a third of the Highlands. The numbers being formed peaked in the 1870s and 1880s; with 62 in the fifteen years 1875 to 1890 (Bryden and Houston, 1976, pp.46-7; Withers, 1988, p.247).

This increase in popularity of the Highlands among the wealthy of Britain occurred when the monarchy established Balmoral as their main Scottish residence. Queen Victoria visited Scotland in 1842, only the second monarch to do so since 1707. The great improvement of communications, with the development of the railway system made the journey to the north quicker and in greater comfort. The monarchy then, as they still are today, provide the legitimacy for a particular form of rural lifestyle, and today they still stay at Balmoral from August to mid-October (Hayden, 1987, p.79), for the glorious twelfth and the grouse season. This period also saw the bastardisation or, indeed, 'Balmoralisation' of original Highland culture which through the romantic works of Scott and others presented the images and symbols of Highland culture and life in a 'tamed' form for a reconstructed Scottish and Highland identity (Jarvie, 1989; McCrone, 1989). By the late nineteenth century there was 'universal bourgeois admiration for Scots Highlanders' (Hobsbawm, 1990, p.41), a far cry from the fear of the savage of the early eighteenth century. A crucial element of this is that the images of the Highlands became to express distance more in forms of culture, and a culture that was 'romantic' to elites, than physical distance. The Highlands are a place separate in time more than space. It is no coincidence that most 'saleable' symbolism of the Highlands remain those of the '45 rebellion and of 'Brigadoon'.

### The making of the crofting community[4]

The social and economic changes of the late eighteenth and early nineteenth century lay the foundations of the crofting society, but it was not until the late nineteenth century that this structure was formalised in legislation. The key point here is the resistance of the Highlands tenantry against further erosion of their position. The social unrest and political manoeuvring that led to the passing of the Crofters Holding (Scotland) Act of 1886 is one of the most fascinating in Highland history.[5] The Act has taken on a high degree of mythological status in the region, and remains to this day one of the reasons why the Liberal Party, and its heirs the Liberal Democratic Party, is so immensely popular in the area.

The crofting legislation came out of the social agitation that has become termed the Land War, itself inspired by the success of events in Ireland and goaded by the depression in the economy which was the worst since the 1840s. Politically this took the form of the creation of the Highland Land Law Reform Association (HLLRA) in 1883. But this was of less importance than the action of crofters themselves, first in Skye, where in the Battle of the Braes, Glasgow police sent to maintain order were repulsed. This unrest soon spread to other islands (Hunter, 1976, pp.131-83). The government's response was the establishment of a Royal Commission (The Napier Commission).

The commissioners were generally sympathetic to the plight of the crofters, they included three who have been described as Celtic intellectuals, one of whom, Charles Fraser-Mackintosh, went on to become an MP for the Crofters Party (Smout, 1986, p.72). The commissioners sought for the crofters a collective arcadia (Smout, 1986, p.73). Gladstone was not prepared to go this far against the rights of the Highland lairds and reproduced in the 1886 Act the main elements of the 1881 Irish Land Act. This was supported by the HLLRA who seemed to desire little more than fair rents and security of tenure.

The Act gave the crofter the basic security of tenure, fair rent (with significant reductions in rent arrears) and, possibly, most important, the continuation of communal rights over the common grazing. A Crofters Commission was established to oversee the Act and look after the interests of the crofters. Whatever its limitations the Act remains a remarkable restriction on the rights of private property, and one of the earliest examples of land legislation as social policy. It is true that it does not interfere with landholding as a form of consumption, especially the sporting estates. It also gave the crofters no rights over taking in more land and land from which their forebears had been cleared. As such it tended to leave many grievances smouldering within Highland society.

It is impossible to discuss the emergence of the crofting community without dealing with the relationship between crofting and the wider economy. We have already seen that the main function of the Highlands had changed substantially. There was also a change in the kinds of work done by the peasantry. In the nineteenth century new forms of employment became important. The most significant of which was the development of an inshore fishing industry, a herring fishery being the most important (Gray, 1978). Besides this the Highlands became an important source of migrant labour (Smout, 1986, p.77-8), which included employment in: the merchant navy; the whaling industry; military service, the Highlands are renowned for its regiments; seasonal, and long-term employment, in the central belt of Scotland. For women particularly it has meant working in fish processing (as gutters, packers, etc.) or in domestic service both locally and away from home. The Highlands became increasingly a source of labour for industries and forms of employment which were either situated outside, or controlled from outside, the Highlands.

The well-being of crofting became closely tied to these forms of employment; for example, the collapse of the Scottish fishing industry, especially the herring fishery, in the period after the First World War, led to the decline and restructuring of the crofting economy. There was a sharp fall in total population and a rise in the proportion of elderly such that by 1931 the number of people over 65 was greater than the number of children (Smout, 1986, p.77). State support also became important, and in difficult times crofting has survived through state-created employment, for example, between 1897 and 1912 the highly congested districts boards not only provided work on public works to give employment but they also helped to support local fishing industry, the harris tweed industry and improve agriculture (Hunter, 1976, pp.184–5).

There have been numerous changes to the legislation that affect crofting, the most important of which has been the Land Settlement (Scotland) Act 1919 which was to create (in the crofting counties) new, larger crofts. This was to be done under the auspices of the Board of Agriculture, and what was seen as their slowness led to a revival of land raids in the 1920s (Smout, 1986, p.75). The Crofters (Scotland) Act 1955, re-established the Crofters Commission which had been abolished in 1911; and the Crofting Reform (Scotland) Act 1976, introduced the right of purchase of the croft by the crofter.

### The contemporary landed estate

> Land is the basic natural resource of the Highlands and any plan for economic and social development would be meaningless if proper use of land were not part of it. (Willie Ross, 1966 quoted in Hunter, 1979, p.58)

So stated Willie Ross, then Labour Secretary of State for Scotland when the Highlands and Islands Development Board (HIDB) was being established.[6] From its inception the HIDB recognised the central importance of land policy to the successful development of the Highlands, as its chairman wrote in 1976: 'a sound approach to land use can contribute more to the economic health of every part of the Highlands and Islands than any other single policy' (quoted in Hunter, 1979, p.49). The problem being identified here is the continued inequality in landholding in the Highlands, and therefore the power of a few individuals, families and companies, have over the fate of the region and the people. The Highlands have probably the most unequal distribution of land in Europe, the actual dimension of which is difficult to assess given the restrictions on access to information. Bryden and Houston in the early 1970s, calculated that there were 61 estates over 35.000 acres, but only 35 ownership units,[7] totalling some 2,457,000 acres, a third of all privately owned land in the Highlands. Some 8 units, in 26 estates, owned 883,000 acres, almost 10 per cent of the Highlands (Bryden and Houston, 1976, p.67). Given the scale and importance of private estates in the region, their role in the rural economy is crucial for the success or otherwise of any policy related to land use, and the possibility of restructuring employment.

Most Highland estates are owned by those who have strong economic links outside the Highlands; with many landowners having interests in finance, banking, insurance and manufacturing. More than half own land in other parts of Britain, typically in the south of England, the midlands or in lowland Scotland. Armstrong and Mather in their study of Highland estates concluded that:

> It seems clear that the principal motives for Highlands estate ownership are sport and family continuity. Family continuity is the most widely

quoted primary reason for land ownership and, as might be expected, is afforded greatest priority by proprietors of inherited estates with long family connections. Translated into decisions about land use, this thinking highlights survival as a primary objective. Decisions are likely to be fairly conservative and responsive to changing fiscal and other conditions rather than innovative or experimental. (1983)

These conservative views are reinforced by the fact that the owners do not see their estates as a source of income. A third of all estates are primarily orientated to sporting, and there is a sporting interest in virtually all of them.

MacGregor (1985) in his study of estates in Sutherland found that the three categories of estates – crofting, sporting and hill sheep farming – tend to overlap and are not mutually exclusive. Sporting was the dominant form, with 80 per cent of estate land in deer forest or grouse moor. The domination of sport for land use holds important effects for local employment and employment potential and in recent years estates have reduced the numbers employed. Between 1970 and 1980, there was a 34 per cent reduction in labour on the sporting estates, compared to an 18 per cent decline on the mixed use and sheep farming estates. Total estate employment is relatively small in the country, less than 109 full-time or full-time equivalents, of which the sporting estates accounted for 56 (all MacGregor, 1985).

In terms of employment, then, the large estate has become marginal, although in specific localities they remain of crucial importance, especially where estate employment on a seasonal or part-time basis can be organised around the needs of crofting and/or other economic activities. However, they remain important in their ability to delay and prevent development, and some estates have become notorious for their attempts to restrict development in their areas of control. This was a major problem facing the HIDB (Hunter, 1979, p.59) which held severely restricted powers to intervene on estate land.

## Contemporary developments in crofting agriculture

The Highlands have retained their position in the British agricultural division of labour as a supplier of livestock to be finished on lower ground, and for quality breeding stock, with 15 per cent of cattle and nearly a third of the Scottish sheep stock (Bryden and Houston, 1976, p.26). Only in the Moray Firth is there arable production of any importance. In most of the rest, hill farming and crofting agriculture predominates. Crofting agriculture is highly integrated into this structure. Indeed crofting agriculture has changed dramatically, it has become more specialised in sheep production (see below) with both cattle and subsistence agriculture declining significantly.

The general crofting policy in the post-war period has been to encourage the formation of viable economic agricultural units. The Crofters Commission and Department of Agriculture and Fisheries (DAFS) supported croft amalgamation to create larger units. A structure of grant aid was developed specifically for the crofting counties, which was established to increase agricultural output and improve the levels of technical efficiency on crofts. This was part of a general process where the state agencies operated on a distinction between agriculture and other economic activities. It was also a period where most aid for crofters was in the form of agricultural support. This tendency to concentrate on the agricultural aspect of crofting rather than its potential as a form of 'social cement' to hold population in marginal areas, encouraged the decline of population in rural areas. The alternative of a highly diversified structure such as in the Western Isles with weaving (in Harris) and fishing which can be combined with crofting have proved more successful in sustaining the rural population. Since the 1970s the policy has been to increase the numbers of breeding ewe flocks and the numbers of hill cows. This has been very successful in sheep production where the ewe subsidy and variable premium encourage an increase in numbers. However, the idea of supporting the number of livestock over quality may bring some problems to the Highlands as the current debate over the EC sheepmeat regime unfolds.

The distinctive land-use patterns and agricultural practices have changed dramatically. For example the keeping of cattle has declined to such an extent that few crofts now have any livestock except sheep, and the numbers continue to fall. Few crops are now grown and grass predominates in the arable land of the croft. Crofting has increasingly become a more specialised form of production with a near total concentration on sheep, although there are some local differences. This means that crofting agriculture is highly integrated into the markets for livestock, and the state regulation of agricultural production.

In recent years there have been some more targeted attempts to improve crofting: the Islands Development Programme (IDP), which covered the Western and Northern Isles; the Skye Development Programme (Skye DP), which was specifically directed at crofters in Skye; and the North West Development Programme (NWDP). All these programmes have been attempts to enhance the income from crofts by diversifying the economic activities on the croft and improving agricultural output. They all recognise the need to encourage the development of new income generating activities on the croft. This has mainly been in tourism, through the creation of bed and breakfast accommodation, or caravans/chalets/cottages on crofting land. It is seen that agriculture is likely to decline in importance in the future, and that new forms of economic activity will be able to replace crofting.

## Marginality, crofting and the labour process: an analysis

Crofting is a distinctive form of labour organisation in the Highlands, but this does not separate it from wider processes of social and economic restructuring. Crofting can be analysed at two levels: that of the internal social relations of production and the division of labour; and its external social and economic relations. This makes the discussion of petty commodity production relevant. Moreover, the economic reproduction of crofting cannot be separated from its cultural reproduction, given its central place in the development of Highland rural culture. Also, crofting is not seen, by those who undertake it, as a purely 'economic' activity (see below). In analytical terms crofting represents a rich case study of the relationships between marginality and restructuring. The study of crofting helps us to understand the mediating effects of both local conditions, including culture, and the state on the general restructuring process.

The key factor in the labour process in the crofting areas of the Highlands has been the control of land, i.e. the maintenance of the crofting system. Furthermore, since crofting has always existed within a structure of pluriactivity, the relationships between crofting and other forms of work need to be explained. In the past there was a complex household structure where different members of the household may at different times be involved in a wide range of off-croft economic activities.

There are obvious relationships to the literature on simple and petty commodity production. There is agreement with Friedmann's distinction between 'simple commodity producers' and the 'peasantry' (1980) and her position that agricultural households who rely on commodity relations for reproduction are simple commodity producers (1980, pp.162–3). Similarly, we can agree with Bernstein's identification that petty commodity production operates within the general conditions of commodity exchange and that its defining characteristic is the unity of family labour and capital (1988, p.262). It is clear that crofting is embedded within systems of commodity exchange, yet there remain elements that are reminiscent of peasant social structure. For example, there are still some communal aspects of crofting, although these have declined in the late twentieth century, especially the grazing rights over the common hill land and the basic organisation in townships. Collective gathering, dipping and other forms of work sharing are common. This tendency for there to be elements of both forms in any empirical situation is common (Long, 1984, pp.26–7, note 1).

The difficulty requiring clarification concerns the significance of the complex diversity of activities to these broader theoretical positions. Crofters are people who define themselves as crofters through the holding of land, they are engaged in a huge variety of economic relationships only one aspect of which is actually defined as agricultural production. Increasingly, other forms of labour on the croft are becoming more important. On the one hand, there is a deepening of the process of reproduction through commodification as more of the family labour becomes related to new forms of market relationships; on the other, it provides the resources to maintain a distinctive way of life. This is inherent ambiguity can also be clearly seen in the position of peasants in Third World countries (Long, 1984, pp.12–13). What this suggests is that the analysis of such complex forms should be seen not solely as the outcome of a particular logic of capital, or indeed the tendency to see petty commodity production as 'functional' for capital; but that these social economic structures have their own values and meanings (see below).

A further key aspect in petty commodity production is the role of land as an inhibitor to capital penetration, that it is in the nature of production on land, and not the structure of the unit of production. For example Goodman and Redclift argue that:

> The principal objective constraints to the imposition of a unified, specifically capitalist labour process, and hence to the capacity to revolutionise the means of production, are organic nature, land and space . . . the main obstacle to the full realisation of value through real subsumption is not the existence of family-owned farms per se, but the objective limits which nature and land present to expanded reproduction of agriculture; (1985, pp.240, 242)

It is certainly the case that agriculture, at all levels, has seen a substitution of capital for labour and therefore some increase in formal subsumption of production. Indeed this is as true, although not to the same absolute extent, for crofting as in any other form of agricultural production. There has been a shift away from the organisation of production using few inputs and using intensively family and self labour to produce a wide range of subsistence goods, to one of extensive sheep husbandry with an increasing proportion of bought-in inputs. Crofting has been part of the general process where capital extracts surplus value through this 'formal' subsumption rather than through transforming the labour process into that of capitalist social relations (Marsden, 1986). What crofting highlights, however, is not so much the problems capitalism has with 'organic nature'. We have seen how the Highlands were transformed to produce for the British economy. Rather, that the social organisation of production and agriculture is highly sensitive to the institutional structures that are embedded within.[8] Crofting represents one of the oldest examples of the relationship between the state as regulator, and petty commodity production. This is not to argue that the state is the sole reason for the survival of petty commodity producers, but that the particular form it takes exists within the institutional framework of legislation and regulation. This relationship can produce the 'niche' that enables petty commodity producers to survive in an otherwise hostile economic climate. There are some parallels here with the work of Sinclair (1984) on small-scale fishing in Newfoundland.

Goodman and Redclift recognise the importance of what they term, 'ideology and the labour process' (1985, p.242); they make the first steps towards an analysis of the position of the capitalist farming lobby in the west as being based on the successful mobilisation of significant non-capitalist aspects of rural/agricultural life. Therefore, this ideological level of rural life is critical to the understanding of the legitimation of state regulation and support for agriculture and rural society – although it is recognised that this is to the benefit of some more than others. This position needs to be developed. This process of ideological legitimation is not only important in relation to the state, it is also crucial in the creation of self identities (see below). Crofting, has its own ideological level, and the internalisation, or acceptance, of the crofters' own understanding of what should be their rights, has, in turn, greatly influenced the legal and institutional framework. This relationship was described by the Taylor Commission (1954) in the following terms:

Above all they have the feeling that the croft, its land and its houses, are their own. They have gathered its stones and reared its buildings and occupied it as their own all their days. They have received it from their ancestors who won it from the wilderness and they cherish the hope that they will transmit it to the generations to come. Whatever be the legal theory they feel it to be their own – and in this respect the provisions of the Crofters Act do no more than set the seal of Parliamentary approval on their own deepest convictions. (quoted in Hunter, 1976, pp.207–8)

It seems clear that this has only been possible because the Highlands were, and are, recognised as being on the margins of mainstream British society. It was inconceivable in the late nineteenth century that smallholders in other parts of Britain should be given the same rights as Highland crofters, but then they were unable to mobilise the necessary images that could legitimate such intervention. This marginalisation has allowed the necessary social space for the survival of a distinctive form of social organisation, a special regulated form of petty commodity production. Its reproduction is not only related to commodity markets for products but also employment opportunities. In addition, the role of the state as regulator or production and source of social and economic welfare is vital.

This theoretical discussion can be given more salience by examining contemporary conditions in the Highlands.[9] As outlined above crofting has always survived, indeed can only survive, in a set of dependent relations with other forms of employment or support, which requires examination of the internal divisions of labour within the family and household. Today there is less family labour on the croft. The changes in the demographic structure has meant that many crofter households consist of elderly individuals or couples without children. They are less able to sustain the labour-intensive work practices of the earlier period. Just as in the past the household relied on both female employment and on croft work, so the more recent diversification into tourism relies heavily on women. The idea that tourism is 'women's work' is common throughout Britain (see Bouquet, 1984). As early as the 1940s the potential of tourism as part of crofting life was being recognised (Collier, 1953, pp.159–62).[10] But the old forms of female employment have gone and the typical forms of contemporary employment, for men or women, make it more difficult to 'fit in' with the needs of the croft. This is part of the reason for the shift towards sheep and the decline of cattle. Sheep require less day-to-day care although there are intensive periods such as lambing. Some crofters have responded to this by deliberately following employment strategies such as self-employment or pluriactive employment so that they can maintain the croft.

These changing internal dynamics of crofting can be explained by a focus on some of the conditions found from empirical surveys in the northwest, First, a large proportion of the crofters are retired. In the original panel interviews 43 per cent were retired compared with 23 per cent 65 years or over for the area, although this includes ex-policemen and women still in their fifties. This is particularly due to the difficulties in acquiring crofts when people are young (the average age at the transfer of croft was 48 in 1987 (Crofters Commission Annual Reports)). People keep their crofts, working the land literally until they die. Among those employed there is a concentration in manual labour, two of whom are self-employed in the building trade. A further two are self-employed in the fishing industry, one as a fisherman, the other as a fish merchant. Only two have professional occupations, both non-locals; one of whom also operates a successful tourist business. Several work their crofts full-time, one of whom has amalgamated several crofts to effectively become a full-time farmer. Another has left his work in the building trade to spend most of his time on the croft. By examining these experiences one gains an insight of the variety of the positions that crofters are in vis à vis the rest of the local economy.

A significant number depend on transfer payments, a factor that has become well established since the 1930s. There is some dependence on state employment (only two in the panel). The conditions of crofting are highly localised. For example, in the Kinlochbervie area in the west, those crofters involved in the fishing industry see crofting as a form of security given the problems faced by the white-fish fishery. Here, younger crofters are developing and diversifying crofts. A crofter in Assynt, who is highly committed to crofting as part of his identification with local and Highland culture, is investing money from his employment to develop and diversify his croft. This will reduce his dependence on off-croft work (he is self-employed in the building trade), spending less time on such work. Another, in the north, has deliberately chosen to be self-employed in fish-farming so that he can take time off work at crucial points of the year, i.e. lambing. A significant difference was found between the north and the western areas. Crofters in the west are more willing to invest in diversifying into new areas, especially tourism, whilst crofters in the north emphasise agriculture as the most important aspect of crofting to them.

Crofting now exists in a complex articulation with the external public and private economy. This prevents us from seeing it as an insular form of production, but one in which the particular and distinctive as well as the more general relationship with external commodity markets need to be specified. Certainly as a form of agricultural production it has changed greatly but these relationships remain of importance to any analysis. Similarly the internal social relations of production have also changed, but they remain central to crofting. Crofting is a form of organisation of petty commodity production that is sustained by being embedded within other social, economic and legal/state relationships.

## Crofting: self and communal identity

To those active in crofting, it is a central part of their lives and therefore identities. This can be regarded as part of the ideological level of crofting (see above). It is all too easy to see crofting as just an economic activity. One of the main problems that crofting has faced, in the post war period, is the tendency of the state agencies to see their role in relation to crofting in economic, particularly agricultural, terms. Mewett in his study of crofting as a form of occupational pluralism, uses an economic model on the allocation of resources to sustain the crofting household. He regards the present continuation of crofting, where there is no direct imperative for crofting as a source of income for 'household maintenance', as an 'optimal strategy' in relation to the ewe subsidy (Mewett, 1977, p.46). This 'economic rationality' style of analysis is seriously limited. Few crofters organise their work in such a manner and the evidence suggests that croft work is far from being an efficient economic activity. Earnings from crofting vary, but it has been estimated (for 1988) that for a substantial number, as many as a quarter, the croft loses money, and even for crofts with up to 150 ewes the total net annual profit was only £439 (Crofters Union, 1989). Therefore returns to labour are at best marginal. From a sociological point the over emphasis on economic rationality fails to present what is important about crofting to those who actually croft. Two questions need to be answered. One is what does it mean to be a crofter? The second is, what role does crofting play in the creation of communal identity?

The following discussion gives an indication of the variety of meanings that being a crofter has for these people. The meaning of crofting is in a process of continual change, and therefore 'crofting' is a part of a discourse which allows it to be interpreted and reinterpreted, providing new meanings and importance in a changing world. In the marginal area of the northwest crofting has become the arena for community and self definition. There are similarities here with Long's aim:

> Our general research focus should be clear: we aim to develop types of analysis which give more serious weight to the ways in which the actions and strategies of farmers, petty commodity producers, and small scale entrepreneurs shape the impact and outcomes of capital intervention. (Long et al., 1986, p.7)

This highlights the role of actors as creative agents even within the context of peripheralisation and marginalisation.

Several different groups involved in crofting can be distinguished: the resident, the local who has become a crofter; the returnee, someone born locally who has now returned to work the croft; and the incomer, a non-local who has taken up crofting. Each group has some distinguishing aspects about them which makes their experiences of interest and value.

For the resident, crofting often appears the most natural of activities. Although, there are many locals who neither wish nor have the opportunity to take up crofting. Thus, the decision to become a crofter is a valuable one to study. Here the family is of crucial importance. A significant number succeeded the croft at a crucial point in the family's history, around a death or serious illness. To become a crofter is a direct continuation of the family and the land. This is expressed in the way people continue to discuss and represent those who formerly worked the land. In other cases the croft is worked closely with the parents, often with the retired father doing much of the daily routine whilst the son is at work.

There are some interesting differences between the northern parishes and the western ones in the emphasis that they place on certain features of crofting. In the north the agricultural aspects of crofting are the most important, and there is a general disdain towards tourism involving only non-locals. In the west there is a stronger belief in providing income and security from the diversified development of the croft. This does not mean that crofting is less important in the north; rather, that certain aspects within the distinctive history of that area have become emphasised over others. In the north there is a general feeling that the best of crofting has gone. It was the world of their parents who were the last true crofting generation. In discussion of this generation it was the hard work and the range of agricultural activities that were undertaken in the croft that was emphasised. Working the land has become the way of expressing a locality's distinctiveness, and tourism represents a dilution of that culture. In the north a defence of a primarily agricultural form of crofting has become a statement of the area's uniqueness.

In the west other economic activities are seen as the only way of sustaining crofting. The crofts are smaller, the land is poorer, and there is a much more developed tourist industry. Employment in fishing or fishfarming has brought relative prosperity in the 1980s. This economic growth has led to the formation of an important number of small businesses, and self-employment. However, there are some indicators that the structure of local communities have been eroded to such an extent that communal identity is weaker in the west than the north. For example the proportion of the housing stock which are holiday homes has reached over 30 per cent in some of the western parishes, and only 6 per cent in the north (Mackay, 1989, p.15).

The returnee is a common figure in crofting townships; these are usually people who left and who have now returned on retirement. It is a major task to take on a croft which may not have been worked for years. These crofts require substantial investment to improve the land, build up the stock, repair the buildings and fences. Of all the people involved in crofting these are the least likely to see any economic return on their labour. To these people, to work the croft seems as much a *duty* as a pleasure. Crofting brings them back into the world that they have left. They have the kinship links and the family history which helps to locate them in the social matrix. Crofting also helps to mark out the *boundaries* between the world that they had to live in for forty years or more, and brings them back to what they regard as having always been home. To come back and not work the croft is too much like coming back to die.

There are three kinds of incomers found among crofters: those who have retired to a croft; those who have come 'to get away from it all' and see crofting as an 'alternative way of life'; and those who have come because of their work and have decided to stay. For these becoming a crofter is part of that decision. These different groups bring different sets of values and meanings to the actions of crofting. Among those interviewed there were only people from the first and last group. For those retiring to a croft, they have become active crofters because it gives the opportunity to do something they have not done before, and because it helps in their integration into the local social world.

This is also true for those who have decided to stay in the area and become crofters, but it would be too simple to say that this was the sole, or indeed most important reason. A few see the croft as an important income source. It is no coincidence that the only crofters interviewed in the northern parishes that had substantial tourist facilities were incomers. Even to these the agricultural side of crofting was conducted as much for intrinsic satisfaction as for money. To others, becoming a crofter had been a slower and a more complex process. When asked why they had become involved in crofting, responses included lengthy descriptions of formative relationships that they had held with local crofters. Certain qualities associated with crofting were of particular importance. These qualities were expressed in their relationships with these people. To stay and become a crofter had become part of a local identification with the values of place *and* people.

In many ways the last group highlight the key interconnections. The identification of particular activities, a form of work, a combination of place, people and collective identity. The common analytical thread here is that crofting is a set of activities that give a sense of 'belonging'. Cohen, building on the work of Barth, argues that the sense of belonging becomes most marked at the boundaries, because it is here that social distinctions between groups need to be expressed (Cohen, 1985, p.12). The sense of belonging to a place, community, locality, is seen as an integral and essentially integrative part of social life. In this sense crofting provides a way to mark out the boundaries of local identity from that of the wider world. Concerning crofting in Whalsay, he writes that it:

> leads to view of crofting, however changed it may be, as an essential counterweight to, if not rejection of, the modern, market-oriented life to which Whalsay has become increasingly subjected since the war . . . In this version, to croft is to make a statement of commitment to the community and to the life it represents. (Cohen, 1987, p.109)

One aspect of this style of analysis that is particularly powerful is the way in which land, the croft, the past and culture are intertwined. A feature about crofting areas is the way in which the past lives on in the names that places are given, and the ways in which past crofters are talked about. This is not an empty land socially, and these names are not ghosts, the land is the history and the people. In Gaelic this is called 'duthchas', the idea of customary rights over land that provide legitimation to claims to land even after centuries of capitalist ownership (Withers, 1988, p.414). The croft belongs not only to the present but also the past and the future. This provides us with an important link between day-to-day social practices and the sociology of place. The sense of belonging is as much a feeling of belonging to a place as to a culture. There is no better way to belong to a place than to *work the land of that place*. it is not just a case of having a croft, it is the social significance of working the croft as well.

## Conclusion

Crofting represents a set of social practices that help form the distinctive local identities that constitute the major distinctive element of Highland culture. It has been argued here that these identities are not static. The social and economic position of areas and regions change and part of this concerns the perspectives that people have of their own work activities. Crofting has experienced periods of optimism and long periods of depression. Recently there has been much discussion within the crofters movement (particularly through the reactivated Crofters Union) about crofting being a model of development for other rural areas of Britain. Forty years ago there was a crofting 'problem' (Collier, 1953). Today crofting is seen as holding the potential for supporting populations in peripheral areas. It is a model that can be used elsewhere. The history of crofting indicates that such a structure can flourish where there is a strong local economy. This suggests that a crofting policy should not be simply seen as a purely agricultural policy.

The history of the Highlands, outlined above, shows the processes by which an area becomes marginalised in social and economic terms. The integration into the national economy is associated with the area becoming first a source of products and then increasingly as a source of manpower. Finally, it is a setting for conspicuous consumption by the wealthy. These economic relations have brought about social changes, the most important of which was the destruction of the clan system and the creation of the crofting community. Also they constructed new images and perceptions of the nature of Highland life. In the eighteenth century the Highlands was a wild area populated by savages that threatened national security, by the nineteenth century it had become a romantic place with the Highlanders being seen as the embodiment of values that were worthy of state protection. The marginality works in two ways: how the Highlands (and Highlanders) are seen and understood by those outside; and how the people perceive their own position. As Shields writes: 'Marginal places, those towns and regions which have been "left behind" in the modern race for progress, evoke both nostalgia and fascination' (1991, p.3).

How outsiders see and understand the Highlands has resulted in an image of the Highlands as a marginal place, far from the modern world. Also, Highlanders have constructed their own understanding of themselves as a people on the periphery.

If the history of the Highlands is one of a sustained process of marginalisation, which has resulted in the creation of distinctive social relations of production, then any contemporary social and economic policy must try and strengthen the positive elements of that social structure. At a time when the organisation of agricultural production more broadly is experiencing a period of dramatic restructuring; and when new ideas and policies are required, we could look at forms of rural life that have helped sustain the most marginal of areas through a difficult history. Perhaps they can help to reformulate new social and economic policies for the countryside in the post-productivist era. We may have much to learn from crofting.

**Notes**

1. The Highlands of Scotland is a huge region, it is half the area of Scotland, one-sixth of that of mainland Britain. I am only dealing with rural life and economy, it is a feature of the twentieth century for an increasing proportion of the population to be concentrated in urban areas, especially Inverness. This tends to hide the continued decline in rural population and the social and economic difficulties faced by isolated and fragile rural communities, which is clearly shown in the example of the northwest discussed in detail in the text. Although I do make points which are of relevance to all of the area, most of the discussion is about the crofting areas of the western part, i.e. the Western Isles and the west and northern part of the mainland. I concentrate on the northwest, not only because that is the area that I have done most of my field work, but also because less research has been done in that area than the Western Isles, which are usually seen as the main centre of crofting.

2. In other parts of Scotland a similar social organisation of production came out of the development of different industries. For example in Shetland, where the production of stockfish led to a structure of tenants in debt bondage to lairds because of small holdings from which tenants could neither grow enough to feed themselves nor pay the rent (Smith, 1989).

3. The first clearance to make way for sheep north of the great glen was in 1785 (Smout, 1969, p.334).

4. This title is taken from James Hunter's excellent account of the history of crofting (Hunter, 1976).

5. The Crofters Act is not universally acclaimed, in the 1960s some argued that it was the very structure of crofting, which was ossified by the Act of 1886, that was preventing the economic development of the Highlands (see Carter, 1974, p.293).

6. The Highlands and Islands Development (Scotland) Act of 1965 established the HIDB with a remit to improve the social and economic conditions in the crofting counties. At that time it was given more powers than any other development agency in Britain. It was set up to 'solve' the 'Highland problem', and it initially accepted the then orthodoxy in regional development of the necessity of creating an industrial base through attracting large-scale industrial plants, which were to act as growth points for the region (Carter, 1974, pp. 281–3). For a critical history of HIDB see Grassie (1983). The HIDB has now (1991) been replaced by Highland Enterprise (HE) and at the local level by Local Enterprise Companies (LECs). Besides the 'thatcherite' titles, it is not clear, as yet, what changes this will make to the development policy in the Highlands.

7. Where an 'ownership unit is defined as an estate or collection of estates owned by the same family or company' (Bryden and Houston, 1976, p.67).

8. The weak link in the analysis of agriculturalists in the class structure is a lack by commentators to elaborate on their specific relationship to the state, this is particularly glaring in the literature on small farmers (Newby *et al.*, 1980; Winter, 1984). Winter in his discussion on family farms in the class structure writes: 'Nevertheless there have been omissions . . . considerations of the ideological and political levels have been neglected, not least the role of the State in the survival of family farming' (1984, pp.123–4). Newby *et al.*, limit their discussion to the kind of political support that small farmers give (1980, pp.62–3). Given that agriculture is embedded within a structure that is penetrated at all levels by the state this is a major restriction on their work. Furthermore, the role of the state as the upholder of property is central to a sociological understanding of capitalist society. Given that the distinctiveness of agricultural production is its exploitation of land as a re-usable resource, and that it has been argued that this uniqueness means that agricultural production has not been penetrated by capital in the same way as other forms of production and thereby allowed the existence of petty commodity producers (Goodman and Redclift, 1985). The role of the state in maintaining the rights over land and therefore the perpetuation of this social structure must be given greater prominence (see Flynn *et al.*, 1990 for a discussion of some salient points).

9. This section and the rest of the chapter is based on research carried out by the author in 1989 and 1990 on crofting in the northwest of the Highland mainland. This was part of the monitoring of the North West Development Programme (NWDP) carried out in collaboration with Dr Mark Shucksmith, Dept of Land Economy, University of Aberdeen, and funded by the HIDB and Scottish Development Agency (SDA); and of an interim assessment report of the programme with Dr Shucksmith, and Dr J. Bryden of the Arkleton Trust, also funded by the HIDB.

   The research consisted of in-depth interviews with 23 crofting households (the panel) which were interviewed in twice, and approximately a further 30 interviews, in less depth, with crofters and others living in the area, and a postal survey of 110 households within the NWDP. Some of this work has been published as internal reports (Smith and Shucksmith, 1989; Bryden *et al.*, 1990).

10. Collier (1953, pp.159–62) believed that bed and breakfast style accommodation was potentially the most beneficial form of tourist activity for crofting families, but was greatly underdeveloped with the exception of Skye.

## References

Armstrong, A. and Mather, A. (1983) *Land Ownership and Land Use in the Scottish Highlands*. Aberdeen: O'Dell Memorial Monograph 13.

Bechofer, F. and Elliott, B. (eds) (1980) *The Petite Bourgeoisie*. London: Macmillan.

Bernstein, B. (1988) 'Capitalism and petty-bourgeois production: class relations and divisions of labour', in *Journal of Peasant Studies* Vol. 15, No. 2.

Bouquet, M. (1984) 'Women's work in rural south-west England', in N. Long (ed) *Family and Work in Rural Societies*. London: Tavistock.

Bradley, T. and Lowe, P. (eds) (1984) Locality and Rurality (Norwich: Geo Books).

Bryden, J. and Houston, G. (1976) *Agrarian Change in the Scottish Highlands*. London: Martin Robertson.

Bryden, J., Shucksmith, M. and Smith, R.J. (1990) *Interim Impact Assessment of the North West Development Programme*. Report for the HIDB (HIDB unpublished report).

Callander, R. (1987) *A Pattern of Landownership in Scotland*. Finzean: Haughend.

Carter, I. (1974) 'The Highlands of Scotland as an underdeveloped region', E. Dekadt and G. Williams (eds) *Sociology and Development*. London: Tavistock, pp.279–311.

Cohen, A. (1982) *Belonging: identity and social organisation in British rural cultures*. Manchester: MUP.

Cohen, A. (1985) *The Symbolic Construction of Community*. London: Tavistock.

Cohen, A. (1986) *Symbolising Boundaries: identity and diversity in British cultures*. Manchester: MUP.

Cohen, A. (1987) *Whalsay: symbol, segment and boundary in a Shetland Island community*. Manchester: MUP.

Collier, A. (1953) *The Crofting Problem*. Cambridge: CUP.

Crofters Union (1989) A Survey of Crofting Incomes. Unpublished report.

Darling, F. (1945) *Crofting Agriculture*. Edinburgh: Oliver & Boyd.

Devine, T.M. (ed) (1989) *Improvement and Enlightenment*. Edinburgh: John Donald.

Devine, T.M. (1989) 'The emergence of the new elite in the Western Highlands and Islands, 1800–60', T.M. Devine (ed) (1989) *Improvement and Enlightenment*. Edinburgh: John Donald.

Devine, T.M. and Mitchison, R. (eds) (1988) *People and Society in Scotland*. Edinburgh: John Donald.

Flynn, A., Lowe, P. and Cox, G. (1990) *The Rural Land Development Process* (ESRC Countryside Change Initiative Working Paper 6).

Forbes, D. (1966) 'Introduction', in A. Ferguson *An Essay on the History of Civil Society*. Edinburgh: EUP.

Friedmann, H. (1980) 'Household production and the national economy: concepts for the analysis of agrarian formations', in *Journal of Peasant Studies*, Vol. 7, No. 2.

Giddens, A. and Mackenzie, G. (eds) *Social Class and the Division of Labour*. Cambridge: CUP.

Goodman, D. and Redclift, M. (1985) 'Capitalism, petty commodity production and the farm enterprise' *Sociologia Ruralis*, Vol. XXV.

Grassie, J. (1983) *Highland Experiment*. Aberdeen: AUP.

Gray, M. (1951) 'The kelp industry in the Highlands and Islands' in *Economic History Review* second series, Vol. 4, No. 2.

Gray, M. (1957) *The Highland Economy*. Edinburgh: Oliver & Boyd.

Gray, M. (1978) *The Fishing Industries of Scotland, 1790–1914: a study in regional adaption* Oxford: OUP.

Hayden, I. (1986) *Symbol and Privilege*. Tucson: University of Arizona Press.

Highland Regional Council (1983) Statistical Area 10: The North West of Sutherland (HRC).

Highland Regional Council (1987) North West of Sutherland: Local Plan.

Highland Regional Council (various dates) Economic Review.

Highlands and Islands Development Board (1988) North West Development Programme (leaflet).

Hobsbawm, E. (1990) *Nations and Nationalism since 1780*. Cambridge: CUP – Canto edition.

Hunter, J. (1976) *The Making of the Crofting Community*. Edinburgh: John Donald.

Hunter, J. (1979) 'The crofter, the laird and the agrarian socialist: the Highland land question in the 1970s' in N. Drucker and H. Drucker (eds) *The Scottish Government Yearbook*. Edinburgh: Paul Harris.

Jarvie, G. (1989) 'Culture, social development and the Scottish Highland gatherings', in D. McCrone *et al.* (eds) (1989) *The Making of Scotland: nation, culture and social change*. Edinburgh: EUP.

Lenman, B. (1977) *An Economic History of Modern Scotland*. London: Batsford.

Lenman, B. (1981) *Integration, Enlightenment, and Industrialization: Scotland 1746–1832*. London: Arnold.

Long, N. (ed) (1984) *Family and Work in Rural Societies*. London: Tavistock.

Long, N., Box, C., Curtin, C. and Van der Ploeg, J.D. (eds) (1986) *The Commoditization Debate: labour, process, strategy and social network*. Dept of Sociology: Wageningen.

McCrone, D. (1989) 'Representing Scotland: culture and nationalism', D. McCrone, S. Kendrick and P. Straw (eds) (1989) *The Making of Scotland: nation, culture and social change*. Edinburgh: EUP.

McCrone, D., Kendrick, S. and Straw, P. (eds) (1989) *The Making of Scotland: nation, culture and change*. Edinburgh: EUP.

MacGregor, B. (1985) 'Land development and employment creation on the landed estates in the northern Highlands', *Planning Outlook*, Vol. 28, No. 2.

Macinnes, A. (1988) 'Scottish gaeldom: the first phase of clearance', T.M. Devine and R. Mitchison (eds) (1988) *People and Society in Scotland*. Edinburgh: John Donald.

Mackay Consultants (1989) *North West Demographic Survey*. Report for HIDB.

Marsden, T.K., Whatmore, S., Munton, R. and Little, J. (1986) 'Towards a political economy of agriculture: a British perspective', *International Journal of Urban and Regional Research*, Vol. 10, No. 4, pp.498–522.

Massey, D. (1984) *Spatial Divisions of Labour*. London: Macmillan.

Mather, A. (1978) *State-aided Land Settlement in Scotland*. Aberdeen: O'Dell Memorial Monograph.

Mewett, P. (1977) 'Occupational Pluralism in Crofting', *Scottish Journal of Sociology*, No. 2.

Mewett, P. (1982a) 'Associational categories and the social location of relationships in a Lewis crofting community', in A. Cohen (ed) *Belonging: identity and social organisation in British rural cultures*. Manchester: MUP.

Mewett, P. (1982b) 'Exiles, nicknames, social identities and the production of local consciousness in a Lewis crofting community', in A. Cohen (ed) *Belonging: identity and social organisation in British rural cultures*. Manchester: MUP.

Mewett, P. (1986) 'Boundaries and discourse in a Lewis crofting community' in A. Cohen (ed) *Symbolising Boundaries: identity and diversity in British cultures*. Manchester: MUP.

Mitchison, R. (1983) *Lordship to Patronage: Scotland 1603-1745*. London: Arnold.

Omand, D. (ed) (1982) *The Sutherland Book*. Northern Times, Golspie.

Newby, H., Rose, D., Saunders, P. and Bell, C. (1980) 'Farming for survival: the small farmer in contemporary rural class structure', in F. Bechofer and B. Elliott (eds) *The Petite Bourgeoisie*. London: Macmillan.

Phillipson, N. T. and Mitchison, R. (eds) (1970) *Scotland in the Age of Improvement*. Edinburgh: EUP.

Richards, E. (1973) *The Leviathan of Wealth*. London: RKP.

Richards, E. (1985) *A History of the Highland Clearances*. Vol. 2. London: Croom Helm.

Shields, R. (1991) *Places on the Margin*. London: RKP.

Sinclair, P. (1984) 'Fishers of northwest Newfoundland: domestic commodity producers in advanced capitalism', in *Journal of Canadian Studies* Vol. 19, No. 1.

Smith, R. J. (1989) 'Shetland in the world economy: a sociological perspective', in D. McCrone, *et al.* (eds) *The Making of Scotland: nation, culture and social change*. Edinburgh: EUP.

Smith, R. J. and Shucksmith, M. (1989) *The North West Development Programme. Context One: The Changing Agricultural Structure*. (Dept. of Land Economy: University of Aberdeen. Report for HIDB.)

Smout, T. C. (1969) *A History of the Scottish People: 1560-1830*. London: Collins.

Smout, T. C. (1970) 'The Landowner and the Planned Village in Scotland, 1730-1830', in N. T. Phillipson and R. Mitchison (eds) (1970) *Scotland in the Age of Improvement*. Edinburgh: EUP.

Smout, T. C. (1986) *A Century of the Scottish People: 1830-1950*. London: Collins.

Winter, M. (1984) 'Agrarian class structure and family farming', in T. Bradley and P. Lowe (eds) *Locality and Rurality*. Norwich: Geo Books.

Withers, C. (1988) *Gaelic Scotland: the transformation of a culture region*. London: Routledge.

# CHAPTER 7

# *Representing the Region: Welsh Farmers and the British State*

*Jonathon Murdoch*

The terms 'locality' and 'region' have recently become central to geographical analysis. In the British literature it is locality that has moved centre stage during the 1980s (see Cooke, 1986, 1989), reflecting perhaps a weak regional structure in the UK. Whilst there has been some recognition of the existence of a 'new regional geography' (Sayer, 1989) this has more often than not covered locality studies also. Some authors have even detected a weakening of regional structures in favour of more localised patterns of change (see Urry, 1984).

What distinguished this spatial 'turn' from previous geographical work was its theoretical underpinnings, derived from a variety of sources within both Marxist and humanist geography (Gilbert, 1988). Particularly influential amongst Anglo-Saxon geographers has been the structurationist approach, characterised most notably by the work of Giddens (for a comprehensive account see Giddens, 1984). In developing the theory of structuration Giddens introduced the concept of 'locale' to refer 'to the use of space to provide the settings of interaction, the settings of interaction in turn being essential to specifying its contextuality' (1984, p. 118). While the introduction of this term shows that Giddens is alert to the importance of space as a 'setting' it would appear, as Cooke (1989) has pointed out, that the spatial is 'passive' in, rather than 'constitutive' of, social interaction.

This 'passive' notion of space seems to be only too prevalent in past work on localities and regions. Whilst the theoretical tools are available to define a more constitutive spatial context they do not seem to have been fully developed within existing empirical work. According to Murphy:

160

> most empirical studies – including those that espouse a commitment to geographically informed social theory – continue to pose questions about developments in particular regions without exploring the nature and significance of the regions they choose for study. (1991, p. 24)

The region becomes, therefore, merely a 'backdrop' for a discussion of social change with little attention given to how regions themselves are constituted and how this constitution is implicated in dynamic social processes.

In what follows a brief review of these theoretical tools will be given which allows us to assess the significance of the term 'region' and which locates it within the emerging literature concerning the social construction of space. A case study of regional development will then be presented. This concerns the attempt by Welsh farming unions to represent Welsh agriculture within the British state. This is presented as one facet in the forging of a regional identity, one which became institutionalised within the state structure.[1]

### The constitution of regions: towards a reconception

Murphy argues that:

> the nature, extent and character of the regions in our empirical studies must become a part of our conceptualization of the social processes that take place in those regions. This in turn requires a social theory in which regional settings are not treated simply as abstractions or as a priori spatial givens, but instead are seen as the results of the social processes that reflect and shape particular ideas about how the world is or should be organised. (1991, p. 24)

Whilst much of the discussion around the social constitution of space has focused on the status of the term locality (see Duncan and Savage, 1991 for an overview), within the European context, 'region' has been more central to a theoretically informed geography (Gilbert, 1988; Trigilia, 1991). A particularly useful contribution has been made by Paasi (1986, 1991) who provides a broad analytical framework for the investigation of regional development. We will consider this in some detail.

Paasi agrees that little attention has been paid to the historical constitution of regions and he outlines a series of stages through which regions may pass as they emerge and become institutionalised. He identifies four stages: the constitution of territorial shape; the definition of symbolic shape; the establishment of regional institutions; and consolidation within the regional system and social consciousness of society (1991, p. 243). These stages should not be seen as sequential; they may be the establishment of regional institutions; and consolidation within the regional system and social consciousness of society (1991, p.243). These stages may be partly simultaneous or ordered in different ways.

First, the development of territorial shape refers:

> to the localisation of social practices (for example, economy, politics,

and administration) through which the regional transformation takes place and a region achieves its boundaries and will be identified as a distinct unit in the spatial structure. (1991, p. 244)

The other stages will be founded upon this basis.

Second, the symbolic shape is formed:

which establishes specific structures of the territorial symbols for a region... the symbolic sphere caries with it history and traditions and promotes the reproduction of social consciousness. (1991, p. 245)

This symbolic shape comes to embody the system of practices undertaken on behalf of the region and in turn shapes the nature of such practices. The symbols of the region can come to express group solidarity across a range of fields (political, economic and cultural) and may legitimise the practices within such fields. The state is central here for it is the site wherein 'the economic, political, and administrative prerequisites for the constitution of regions within regional transformation will be created' (1991, p.245).

The third stage is characterised by the emergence of institutions. These are more permanent expressions of the region as they represent standardised modes of behaviour serving to formalise relationships and practices within the spheres of politics, culture and the economy.

This is the field of group formation in which the 'supraindividual' logic of regional history is realised: individuals are socialised into varying regional community memberships, or in fact certain historically given (ideal) communities and identities are ascribed to individuals in various social practices... It is through these 'memberships' that the perpetual production and reproduction of social consciousness takes place at various social scales. (1991, p. 246)

Fourth, as a result of these (institutionalised) practices the region attains an established place in the spatial structure and social consciousness of society. The region is thus a social entity of historical duration located at a particular scale of social life. It is produced and reproduced in the multitude of social practices which express collective social life on the basis of this regional representation. Paasi sees such practices as a 'structure of expectations' which form a 'frame' (somewhat akin to Raymond Williams's 'structure of feeling' or Bourdieu's 'habitus'):

This frame is quite permanent and is represented in the form of time-space-specific, region bounded, institutionally embedded schemes of perception, conception and action which can comprise real and imagined, and mythical features of the region. (1991, p. 249)

The region in this formulation is not a mere backdrop but is an intimate part of the social processes which constitute it. This is not a mere geographic entity; instead it represents the binding together of territory (in both its natural and symbolic aspects – if these can be separated) and the social practices which give meaning to that territory.

These regional practices assert the value of space; mixing social and natural features in the definition of what constitutes the specificity of their territory. Whilst we are here concerned with the constitution of regions we should be clear that the processes of territorial identity apply to all spatial scales, from the local to the national. In fact nationalism is often the means by which regional identities are strengthened: ' "nationalism" as ideology and movement may be viewed as the dominant mode of politicizing space by treating it as a distinctive and historic territory' (Williams and Smith, 1983, p. 504).

This building of a regional identity may be an expression of a collective identity and can be conceptualised as 'an instrument for implanting a sense of national solidarity and consciousness, and of homogenizing and levelling heterogeneous and stratified populations' (Williams and Smith, 1983, p. 510), but we should be wary of ascribing this collective consciousness to all groups within a given territory. This is because the constitution of the region may have been undertaken by a variety of social actors with a variety of aims; these may not include all the potential actors in that territory; and many actors may choose to identify with collectives at different scales (local, national or even transnational).

In analysing the constitution of regions we must follow the process of institution-building. As Paasi puts it we must:

> problematise the production and reproduction of space and collective representations: how this takes place through various institutional practices, how the material and 'mental' spatial fix will be created through these practices, how various social groupings emerge, etc. (1991, p. 244)

In the rest of this chapter we will demonstrate this process of 'region-building' as we follow a group of actors in their attempts to construct a Welsh identity within the sphere of agricultural policy-making. As we shall see, in this area of its activity the British state chose largely to ignore the existence of Wales as a region with its own separate identity. But through the actions of regional representatives the state was forced into such a recognition. In such ways regions are reconstituted and reproduced.

### Forging a regional identity: agricultural interest groups and the policy process in Wales

*Territorial shape*

Paasi describes the first stage in the historical development of a region as the establishment of 'territorial shape' through the localisation of social practices such as economic, political and administrative practices, including labour processes and work identities. Urry (1984) suggests that, economically, regions no longer betray any structured unity. As far as Wales is concerned such a unity is hard to discern in the recent past. As Williams says:

Anyone rash enough to write about the Welsh econumy in modern times is immediately brought up against what can only be descibed as a fundamental problem. Namely, that there must be serious doubts as to whether there has been in modern times, any such thing as 'The Welsh Economy'. Certainly it seems permanently to have been the case that the economic links of the various parts of Wales run east–west to England rather than north–south to other parts of Wales. (1983, p. 35)

Welsh agriculture is similarly difficult to characterise in any coherent way. The pattern of farming in Wales has traditionally varied according to terrain and the proximity of markets: northwest Wales has concentrated on butter and cheese manufacture for the nearby urban markets (mainly in England); in the mountain areas of north and central Wales sheep provided the main source of income; whilst in the lowlands of the southeast there has been an emphasis on arable crops and livestock fattening together with the traditional manufacture of butter and cheese (Howell, 1977).

By the turn of the twentieth century Welsh agriculture could still be described as semi-subsistence farming (Ashby and Evans, 1944). Moreover, the structure of landholding remained fairly static. Around 90 per cent of rural land was in the possession of landowners and the average size of farm stood at less than 50 acres (Davies, 1974). Socially the rural areas were marked by an acute cleavage between the 'gentry' and the 'peasantry'. This cleavage was most acutely manifested in the cultural distance between the Welsh-speaking, nonconformist peasantry and the Anglicised landowning class, leading to a profound political tension between the two. According to Adamson, nonconformist religion provided the 'ideological framework for tenant solidarity (underpinning) a common consciousness on the part of the tenantry' (1984, p. 212). This accentuated the linguistic and political gulf between landlord and tenant. Welsh national identity was utilised by the peasantry in this struggle against an English landowning class, in due course becoming channelled into the political struggles between the Liberals and the Tories (Morgan, 1963).

Despite the wholesale antipathy felt in rural areas towards this landowning class, landowners only began to divest themselves of their holdings in any quantity in the years following the First World War. Between 1918 and 1922 every major Welsh landowner placed at least part of his estate on the market (see Davies, 1974 for the details of this process). Many tenant farmers took advantage of this spate of selling to buy their farms, albeit with hefty mortgages. Consequently, the area farmed by owner-occupiers increased to 36 per cent between 1919 and 1922 (Howell, 1977, p.58).

With the onset of depression during the 1920s and 1930s the level of debt associated with landownership made life very difficult for many farmers. By 1941 owner occupation was virtually unchanged at 37 per cent (Williams, 1985). Nevertheless by this time 'the transition from subsistence farming to production for the market was virtually complete' (Ashby and Evans, 1944, p. 17). Farming had become more specialised, more mechanised (albeit within the limits of a continuous shortage of capital) and more integrated into the UK national economy, both for sale of output and purchase of inputs. Another consequence of this process was the virtual elimination of wage labour from the Welsh countryside, whilst the number of independent farmers stayed almost constant, 'leading to the further simplification of the agricultural class structure into a mass of family farmers' (Day *et al.*, 1989).

Administratively there was some recognition of Welsh identity. Under the Board of Agriculture (responsible for agriculture before the establishment of the Ministry of Agriculture (MAFF) in 1920) Wales was given recognition by the creation of a Welsh branch in 1912. This was consolidated in the new Ministry and the Welsh department was responsible for advising the Ministry on Welsh problems. Its work consisted chiefly of monitoring and the payment of various grants (Ashby and Evans, 1944, p. 151). This role was not greatly expanded during the inter-war period. Although the Ministry began to move towards the formulation of a more recognisable agricultural policy this hardly impacted upon the Welsh office.

By the Second World War, therefore, the region as a locally bounded set of social practices, was more evident in some spheres than others. Economically the region's agriculture was more closely tied into the UK economy. Administratively there was some recognition of 'Wales' but this fell far short of any autonomous decision-making powers. However, the struggles over landed property rights and the new structure of landownership which followed from the 'flight of the landowners' had strengthened the symbolic shape of the region within rural society (Day, 1984). Welsh farmers, although indebted, at least had control over a larger proportion of 'their' land.

*Institution-building*

After 1939 there was an almost continual expansion of state involvement in agriculture (Tracy, 1982). The outbreak of war necessitated a speedy increase in food production and the post-war food shortages ensured the state's continued involvement. The establishment of the national institutional structure, the annual price review, and the incorporation of the National Farmers Union into the decision-making process has been well documented (Allen, 1959; Beresford, 1975; Bowers, 1985; Cox *et al.*, 1986a, 1986b; Grant, 1983; Self and Storing, 1958). The regional structure through which the state implemented its agricultural policies has been much less considered. It is at this level, however, that the struggle to institutionalise 'Wales' initially took place.

The post-war growth in state intervention in agriculture was paralleled by a growth in the administrative structure of the Ministry. By the early 1950s MAFF had established an extensive local structure and had increased in size by six times between 1939 and 1951 (Ryan Committee, 1951). The position of Wales within the structure was little different to any of the English regions. The Welsh Department still functioned to report to the Ministry on the effect of its policies upon Welsh agriculture. There seemed little chance of the Welsh Department gaining any more autonomy over policy. This became clear in the late 1950s when the Arton Wilson Committee investigated the structure of the expanded Ministry of Agriculture, Fisheries and Food (MAFF).

The Committee's examination of the MAFF's administrative structure led them to conclude that the Ministry was composed of a 'patchwork of organisations, often uncoordinated and working within 22 different sets of boundaries' (1956, para.1). The Committee, therefore, recommended the creation of a regional structure headed by regional controllers to coordinate the Ministry's spread of operations. In reference to Wales, however, the Committee argued that 'Wales is not a region but a nation' (1956, para.424):

> we strongly recommend that there should be the greatest possible degree of devolution of authority to the Welsh Secretary, over and above the duties and powers we have proposed for Regional Controllers in England. (para.426)

These proposals were echoed in the Council for Wales Third Memorandum of 1957. This was wide-ranging survey of state administration in Wales. As far as agriculture was concerned the Committee argued that the administrative arrangements could not:

> effectively deal with the problems and needs in Wales ... A policy formulated by the Ministry in London can at best only deal with those aspects of agriculture common to both England and Wales ... the paramount need is that the machinery of administration in Wales should be designed so that Welsh problems ... are given particular attention by someone whose primary concern is Wales. Hence there is a very strong case for a transfer from the Minister of Agriculture ... to a Secretary of State for Wales of Ministerial responsibility for all the formers functions in regard to Wales. (para.202)

This proposal formed part of a general call for political and administrative devolution across a range of government departments, investing in a new Welsh Secretary of State policy-making powers independent of the central state. Unsurprisingly, the Report was almost completely ignored and subsequently the entire Council for Wales resigned (Osmond, 1977, p. 101).

The significance of these events for the conduct of agricultural policy was highlighted by another development at this time; the establishment of a Welsh farmers union.

The primary interest group representing farmers was the NFU. Although the Union had been established in eastern England in 1908, it had spread into Wales by the First World War. In 1927 the NFU published its first Welsh-language document in an attempt to reassure Welsh farmers that their identity would be preserved in an English *and* Welsh union. However, the overall thrust of this document was that the interests of Welsh farmers would be best secured by joining with their English colleagues to further the interests of the industry as a whole (NFU, 1927).

Through the 1930s the NFU made slow but steady progress in its acquisition of Welsh members but it was not until the Second World War, and the Union's consolidation of its position in government, that it could push ahead in a more widespread recruitment drive. This continued in the post-war period and by 1955 the NFU's Welsh membership stood at 32,000 (out of a total number of 48,000 Welsh farmers) (*Farmers Weekly*, 9 December 1955).

The NFU attempted to consolidate its broad coalition of large and small, arable and livestock, farmers within a centralised framework complemented by 'special interest' committees. By the early 1950s this structure was showing signs of stress, particularly in Wales. There were undercurrents of dissatisfaction in many of the NFU's Welsh branches, particularly in west Wales, with the under-representation of Wales within the Union. For a variety of reasons (see Murdoch, 1988 for details) these undercurrents burst forth in late 1955 when a group of NFU members in Carmarthen (south Wales) decided to form a breakaway union – the Farmers Union of Wales (FUW).

The initial reaction of the NFU to this development was to ignore it. However, as the FUW established itself and attempted to recruit NFU members, the friction between the unions increased. A Welsh secretary of the NFU called the 'splinter move' an 'act of treachery' and a national NFU official asserted 'it is far better to have these people forced into the open rather than have a small number of "quislings" hidden among us' (Murdoch, 1988).

Despite the attempt to portray the breakaway union as a small band of separatists, the FUW gradually consolidated its position. By 1959 the *Financial Times* could report that:

> the FUW is a force to be reckoned with. After three years it has an income of £34,000 . . . its membership, though undisclosed, is probably not less than 10,000 . . . drawn off perhaps a quarter of the NFU's 30,000 subscribers . . . There is clearly mass support for a farmers' organisation for Wales independent of the NFU. (29 May 1959)

The FUW had achieved this position by concentrating its policy proposals on the *small farmer*. It presented the interests of Welsh farmers as inextricably linked to the interests of small farmers and argued that a union such as the NFU, dominated by large farmers, could not adequately represent Welsh agricultural interests. The FUW did not play the nationalist card. Whilst most nationalist sympathisers welcomed the formation of an organisation representing Welsh farmers, the FUW itself played down any overt associations with the nationalist cause. The union's aim was recognition by the British state; a perception of the union as a nationalist organisation would have made the achievement of such recognition a more formidable task. For these reasons, the FUW, like the NFU, stressed it was a non-political organisation with no ties to any political party.

The FUW's aim was clear; a seat at the Annual Price Review. It realised that until it had a seat at the pricing policy negotiations it could not hope to adequately represent, or even claim to represent, Welsh farmers. The NFU's aim was equally clear; to keep the FUW out of such negotiations in order to maintain its position as the only representative of *all* farmers. As a centralised union with strong links to the central state, the NFU was against any autonomy for Wales in the political process. The Union argued against devolution on the rather vague grounds that it would 'harm Welsh agriculture' (Wormell, 1978, p. 279). For the FUW, on the other hand, the principles upon which it was founded predisposed it to seek the maximum amount of devolution to Wales. It had set out to secure for Welsh farmers 'equal status, equal representation, and equal responsibility to those of their fellow farmers in England, Scotland and Ulster' and although a Welsh seat at the price review was the main aim, the shift of policy-making powers to Wales could only increase the union's chances of gaining state recognition.

The election of a Labour government in 1964 led to the establishment of a new government post; Secretary of State for Wales. However, although the new government's manifesto had envisaged the Welsh minister taking responsibility for a wide range of functions, including agriculture, no commitment was initially made as to when he might acquire such functions. This had to be 'painfully extracted' from a 'reluctant Whitehall' (Rowlands, 1972, p. 334). The first major change in agricultural policy administration came in 1969 when the Secretary of State was permitted to share, with the Minister of Agriculture, some responsibility for agriculture in Wales. These responsibilities included: the administration of grant and subsidy schemes; a seat at the Annual Price Review; and the ability to make appointments to Welsh committees. Without doubt the most important of these new functions was the Welsh Secretary's seat at the Annual Price Review, which meant for the first time a voice at these negotiations speaking specifically for Wales. However, this was tempered by the disclosure that no Welsh Office staff had any responsibility for agriculture; the Secretary of State relied almost entirely on the MAFF for 'guidance' (Hansard, Vol.796, col.5).

One reason why it was so difficult for the Welsh Office to acquire any responsibility for agriculture can be traced to the history of agricultural administration:

> Where there was no tradition of a unified administration covering England and Wales – as in the case of health insurance, housing and local government – it was a relatively easy task to set up self-contained government departments ... But in those spheres of government activity, such as agriculture ... where there was no established tradition of jointly administering English and Welsh affairs, it was much more difficult – not least because of the attitude of civil servants themselves who objected to the concept of 'area' administration because it conflicted with their functional view of things. (Randall, 1972, p.360).

Furthermore, this unified system across England and Wales resulted in 'great political pressure towards conformity' (Randall, 1972, p. 361). This tradition of a centrally formulated agricultural policy, uniformly implemented across England and Wales bred resistance to the devolution process. The more the MAFF gave to the Welsh Office in terms of policy-making autonomy the harder 'political uniformity' would be to achieve.

Despite the resistance, during the early 1970s the Welsh Office acquired more functions, including health services and education. In 1973 the Kilbrandon Commission on the Constitution reported in favour of elected Assemblies for Wales and Scotland and the 1974 Labour government's dependence on Plaid Cymru and the Scottish Nationalist Party for a parliamentary majority ensured that the devolution issue remained at the centre of the political stage.

Contemporaneous with these developments was the entrance of the UK to the EC and thus the shift of agricultural policy formation from London to Brussels. The coalescence of these political changes meant that by 1978 (the end of the transition period of Britain's EEC membership and immediately prior to a referendum on devolution in Wales and Scotland) the MAFF was prepared to cede another measure of responsibility for Welsh agriculture to the Welsh Office. The Secretary of State took over the 670 staff in the Ministry's Welsh Department at Aberystwyth and the five Division Offices in Wales.

Given the extent to which Wales was now recognised within the agricultural policy process, it seemed anomalous to keep the FUW outside the policy community. Despite the NFU's opposition, MAFF decided, after conducting an audit of the Union's membership, to grant the FUW recognition on 1 April 1978. The FUW had thus gained its long-sought seat at the Annual Price Review and was granted consultative status, along with the NFU's Welsh Council, at the new Welsh Office Agricultural Department (WOAD).

### Consolidating the region: beyond marginality?

The establishment of an institutional framework concerned with Welsh agriculture would seem to represent a full recognition of the distinctiveness of the region. However, it is worth counselling caution at this point. Vielle, for instance, writing on peripheral areas, says 'the State, symbol of independence, is the real instrument of dependence' (1988, p. 60). The existence of this framework may stand for a new form of regional authority within the state or may indicate the institutionalisation of marginality. In order to understand which of these scenarios is most appropriate to the Welsh region we will explore in more detail the nature of the institutional relationships which have existed since 1978. We look first at the WOAD and its relationship to the central state institutions, particularly MAFF. Second, we examine in more detail the relationships between the farmer unions and the state agencies.

The Welsh Office Agricultural Department (WOAD)

Clearly, the establishment of the WOAD amounted to some measure of devolution to Wales. This should not be overestimated, however. According to a senior civil servant in the department, the Secretary of State for Wales 'exercises this authority jointly with the Minister of Agriculture and the other Agricultural Ministers' (Committee for Welsh Affairs, 1981, para.9).

UK agricultural policy has to meet the various needs of the country as a whole. There is, therefore, no policy which could be considered specifically Welsh. What the WOAD attempts to do is ensure that Welsh interests, as it defines them, are adequately catered for within this general policy. How the department undertakes this task was explained by the Assistant Secretary in charge of the Policy and Commodities Division:

> Towards the end of the summer . . . we decide what the main outline or condition of the industry is. We then work gradually towards meeting the unions discuss with them how they see the industry. Eventually, after a number of meetings between ourselves and the unions . . . and meetings with the other agricultural departments and the other UK unions, we evolve the annual review. (Committee for Welsh Affairs, 1981, para.61)

The Annual Review remains the focal point of policy formulation within the UK. However, decisions on levels of price support now take place in Brussels. It is at the Annual Price Review that the UK's negotiating position in Europe is formulated. The Secretary of State for Wales plays no part in the Brussels negotiations. As explained by a WOAD official, this is because:

> the English agricultural industry is the largest sector of the agricultural industry in the UK: it has more farmers, more money, capability, etc. Because of that, the Minister of Agriculture has the lead in Brussels. The other Ministers do not have that representational responsibility. He speaks for the UK. (Interview)

Furthermore, WOAD officials are not necessarily present at the Brussels negotiations (Committee for Welsh Affairs, 1981, para.14).

Other aspects of policy formulation also rest more fully within the MAFF. European Community (EC) Directives, for instance, have to be transformed into domestic regulations. The staff in the WOAD is small in comparison with the numbers in the MAFF (in the mid 1980s the figures were 670 compared to 12,500 – Greenwood and Wilson, 1984, p. 15) so the drafting of domestic regulations is done by the Ministry in London. The next stage, as a WOAD official explained, is that:

> they (MAFF) would come to the other agricultural departments and say 'these are the things we have in mind, what do you think?' We have the opportunity to comment on and suggest alternatives to the policy they had. Once the four Agriculture Departments had their ideas . . . they would then go out to the industry and say 'what do you think of this' . . . The regulations should then be agreed, referred back to the European Commission and laid before Parliament. (Interview)

Once again the lead comes from the MAFF; the WOAD merely have the opportunity, along with the other Agriculture Departments and the unions to put their views into the drafting process.

Despite the WOAD's acquisition of administrative powers from the MAFF there is very little room for the development of a specifically Welsh policy. This has resulted in some scepticism as to just how much autonomy from MAFF the WOAD actually enjoys. As a union official, with experience of negotiations in both Wales and London, put it:

> it's often said that WOAD is just a postbox to the MAFF. Certain functions were devolved but they were largely administrative functions like the processing of claims and feeding-up-the-ladder type functions where WOAD takes commodity matters and puts the Welsh view to the MAFF; they do not put it in Brussels and MAFF then have to regard Scottish Office input and take a UK line. (Interview)

The WOAD input cannot be dismissed as merely 'token', yet given the size and resources of the departmental interests which may be ranged against it, it is hard to see that much could be gained unilaterally by the department.

WOAD personnel are aware of these limitations and as far as possible try to minimise the scope of conflicts with the other agricultural departments, particularly the MAFF. As a WOAD official put it:

> the government is a government and the Ministers are anxious to work together – unilateral movement can lead to dissension and is not going to be welcomed by many. A policy has evolved of everybody keeping in step. People are anxious to work together. (Interview)

It is, therefore, difficult to know how effective the WOAD is within the policy process. WOAD officials believe they are successful in getting their departmental view across. In the words of one:

> whilst the Ministry of Agriculture has at the end of the day prime responsibility for formulating policy . . . nevertheless we would expect, and have always had, a capability for inputting our own views and ensuring, so far as we can, they are heard and not only heard but implemented. (Interview)

None of this would seem to contradict Kellas and Madgewick, who have argued that the Welsh and Scottish Offices:

> are small and peripheral parts of a large and complex system . . . For most of the time the two offices are engaged in the humdrum business of implementing policies decided elsewhere and introducing modest variations where they can to suit the conditions, needs and idiosyncracies of the other two countries. (1982, p. 29)

However, we should not assume that this situation is necessarily fixed. A WOAD official commenting on the MAFF/WOAD relationship said:

> it's changing all the time because you're getting different people there and different people have different concepts about what the collaboration is. We started off with the desire of working very closely together because we were operating the same schemes in the same countries in the same sort of way. We were also closely connected with MAFF because until 1978 this office was a MAFF office. Change occurs

all the time, people here change and in MAFF there are changes. It is easy to discount personalities and to discount the growing awareness that Welsh agriculture is very different to the English scene. (Interview)

This statement implies that the institutionalisation of Welsh 'difference' guarantees its eventual acceptance within the state. The role of WOAD officials is to highlight and accentuate this difference inside a policy process which, by custom and practice, has always sought to minimise it.

The unions

Although the WOAD has struggled to impose itself on the agricultural policy process it has been able to draw upon non-governmental resources in Wales in an attempt to bolster its standing. The role of the farming unions, in particular, has been crucial in allowing the WOAD to develop its position. 'No bureau can survive unless it is continually able to demonstrate that its services are worthwhile to some group with influence over sufficient resources to keep it alive' (Downs, quoted in Jordan and Richardson, 1987, p. 169).

In Wales there are two such groups; the NFU and FUW. However, the levels of resources available to each are by no means commensurate; despite the granting of equal status with the NFU, the FUW clearly cannot match the NFU's scale of activity or proximity to the MAFF. This is understood by the FUW. As one official explained:

our status with them is not equal, no doubt about that. First, sheer scale of operation and money; more, better paid staff... The way in which we're viewed by the establishment is different to the way they regard the NFU. It would be a cliché to talk about 'the old school tie' and the 'farmers club' and so on but it's true to a large extent. The NFU has got that sort of influence in those sort of circles. In the main, although we have it, it's not on the same scale; the degree of infiltration just isn't the same by any means ... they usually win the day and I guess the reason is they're there, they've got this amazing presence as an organisation and they are the NFU – the National Farmers Union – they have an air of national credibility. (Interview)

At the regional level the situation is somewhat different. Within the NFU responsibility for dealing with the WOAD was devolved to the Welsh Council.

The NFU's Welsh Council numbers about 50 delegates drawn from the Welsh county branches. The Chairman and Vice-Chairman (elected by the council bi-annually) negotiate with the WOAD. The Chairman is also a member of the NFU's national office holders committees and is part of the joint NFU negotiating team at the Price Review.

Though the Welsh Council enjoys good access at the WOAD its input to the NFU's national policy is more difficult to determine. Some members regard it as no more than 'a powerless talking shop'. Clearly the Council has to work within the constraints of the NFU's centrally formulated national policies and has very limited scope within which to develop specifically Welsh policy proposals.

It is possible to distinguish in the relationship between the WOAD and the two Welsh unions a resemblance to that presiding at the centre between MAFF and the NFU. However, this example of interest intermediation involves two, entirely separate, groups, negotiating on an equal basis. Furthermore, because the WOAD itself has no policy-making autonomy there are further dimensions to this relationship: the role of the WOAD in UK policy formulation and the access of the unions at the centre.

Because the policy is negotiated ultimately at the UK level, the unions in Wales have no opportunity to formulate specifically Welsh policies with WOAD officials: they can only try to ensure a Welsh input into the national policy. An ex-chairman of the NFU Welsh Council pointed out that:

> any policy that originates in Wales, if it is to get anywhere, the UK unions have to agree to it and then go jointly to Whitehall really before it gets into the policy. (Interview)

It is accepted practice that, although they can consult with the MAFF, the Welsh union go first to the WOAD. As the previous respondent put it 'etiquette would rule out going straight to the Minister'. Therefore, both unions have, through necessity, built up some working relationships with the WOAD. From this, both 'sides' attempt to gain mutual advantage.

For the unions, the main advantage of WOAD is easier access to the policy process. According to an FUW staff member:

> its a damn sight better in simple personnel terms, which are a major part of politics, to have people on your doorstep rather than five hours travel away. We get to know the people in the Welsh Office here and they tend to bat our wicket for us because they live out here in the sticks as well ... they feel that people in London are so far away from it that they don't know what the real world's all about ... they get fired with the same kinds of notions and emotions that we're basically all about ... They are there to lobby for us on the inside. (Interview)

A similar view of the WOAD/union relationships is shared by WOAD officials. As one said:

> they (the unions) see their role now as an interpreter of government policies and interest in what farming is all about and what farming ought to be doing; equally they see their role as the mouthpiece of farmers' interests and bringing the attention of government to the particular problems facing the farming community ... We want them on our side when implementing policies ... basically, we've got the same objectives as they have – promoting the interests of the farming community. (Interview)

These comments indicate a common perception on the part of both the unions and the WOAD on the role of each. The unions help the WOAD to shape its 'departmental view' which is then brought to bear on the national policy process. This 'departmental view', in turn, shapes the kinds of policy proposals that the unions know are achievable and, therefore, constrains the demands they make. However, it is important to bear in mind that it is the unions' leadership which is incorporated at this level. As an ex-President of the FUW put it:

> the relationship between myself as leader of the FUW with the government is hellishly important. The closer you can get to the official thinking the better it is. We were telling them things in private that we would not dare say in public because the leader of the organisation has to look further ahead than the rank-of-file. (Interview)

The incorporation of the union leadership in this way can lead to tensions with the unions' members in situations where the policy outcomes do not fully address the grievances of farmers. At times this has led to outbreaks of conflict which the unions have been powerless to contain (for instance, over the imposition of milk quotas). Perhaps more significantly, the incorporation of the unions into these kinds of policy communities shapes the demands they make on the state. The FUW provides a good example here.

The FUW began its life proposing a policy which would enable the small farmer to survive under a regime which disproportionately rewarded large farmers. The Union condemned 'any legislation which forces a farmer through economic pressure to give up his farm' (FUW, 1958). Small farmers were leaving the industry, the FUW argued, not because they were inefficient but because their initial disadvantages were being further emphasised by production and size-based grants and subsidies, making the pressures upon them unbearable. Farming should be efficient, the union argued.

> but the standard of measuring efficiency must be laid on the foundation of the family farm and not on the basis of tycoonery where capital has been accumulated from sources outside agriculture. To be big and to be efficient are not synonymous. (President of the FUW quoted in *Cambrian News* [a local newspaper in mid-Wales] 5 June 1964)

This concern for the family farm and the ethic of family continuity led into a wider concern for the Welsh rural areas:

> As more and more families and young people leave the rural areas the increasing number of old people remaining there have to be cared for by a gradually shrinking predominantly middle-aged productive population. Such an imbalance in population age groups adversely affects the rural economy, so that great injections of state financial assistance are needed to maintain essential services and to encourage new industries. An impoverished area, having poor lines of communication and low amenities, cannot attract new industrial development, such as is needed to draw in more people to work and live in the area and which could be more expensive to establish than it would cost to prevent deterioration of the position in the first place. (FUW, 1975, p. 30)

In these ways the concerns of the FUW were quite distinct from those of the NFU. The NFU, as a centrist, England *and* Wales organisation, found regional and wider concerns difficult to integrate into its espousal of a uniform productivist agricultural policy. Equally, as the representative of the whole farming community the NFU could not clearly identify and concentrate upon the concerns of small farmers. By contrast, the FUW could highlight all these regional and local concerns and build them into the centre of its policy demands.

In recent years, however, the distance between the FUW and the NFU has narrowed considerably. Notwithstanding the assertion of an FUW official that 'we have always been a radical organisation . . . we were a splinter and yet we've got a certain amount of establishment kudos . . . we're able to balance off a fairly difficult tightrope act' (Interview), both unions work within the policy parameters of the state. As a result, the FUW became less concerned with the overall direction and wider effects of agricultural policy and became more closely involved in negotiating over the levels of support, prices, headage payments, etc. 'Insider' status entailed the organisation following the practices of consultation and negotiation which the existing policy procedures demanded. The price the FUW paid was the ability to stand outside the policy process and to challenge the whole thrust of the policy. Concern over the exodus of small farmers and the plight of the wider rural community had necessarily to give way to much narrower negotiations concerned with technical 'fine tuning' of the policy.

In general, this was the main function of incorporation. The unions could present a set of demands to which WOAD policy makers, themselves constrained by national policy makers, could respond. Whilst they gained ready access to the institutions of policy-making the unions had to be prepared to 'speak the same language' as the policy makers.

This is a familiar practice within the British state:

> there is a natural tendency for the political system in Britain to encourage the formation of stable policy communities, one of the primary purposes of which is to achieve a negotiated and stable policy environment. The underlying value is that, whenever possible, outcomes should be negotiated between policy professionals with each participant fully aware of the needs and desires of fellow members of the policy community. This is not to suggest that there is an absence of conflict, but that conflict is, by agreement, kept within manageable bounds, if only by concentrating on issues which are susceptible to bargaining. (Jordan and Richardson, 1987, p. 181)

The WOAD, the NFU and the FUW form such a community. Union leaders and state officials define what is possible and what is necessary for Welsh agriculture. But the policy community can only be maintained if all its members speak the same language, see the world in compatible ways, and agree on the necessary solutions. The normal practice is for policy issues to be resolved by its union leadership behind closed doors with state representatives. Here the minimum of publicity is sought whilst the 'elite' negotiates over the details of the policy.

However, the indications are that this situation will no longer be so cosy. EC milk quotas marked a turning point in this respect. The crisis of agricultural policy (persistent surpluses and an ever expanding agricultural budget) forced radical action to curb expenditure. Despite NFU opposition to quotas, and deep FUW misgivings, they were able to do nothing to change the policy. Moreover, the introduction of quotas was met with outright opposition and direct action by farmer's action groups in Wales, further highlighting the impotency of the unions. Milk quotas would seem to be just the beginning. The whole approach to EC agricultural policy from the UK government's position is characterised by a desire to 'get back to the market', in effect to rein in state expenditure.

This crisis poses two problems for the unions. First, declining membership. Where farm incomes are falling, farmers may be more unwilling to pay union subscription fees. The NFU has already been forced, through a shortage of cash, into a major reorganisation, cutting the size of its headquarters council from 150 to 100, and pruning its committee structure down by a third. It seems probable that the FUW will have to follow suit. Second, with all sectors of agriculture beginning to feel the squeeze the traditional conflicts been 'corn' and 'horn', and between large and small farmers are becoming increasingly unmanageable. The NFU already faces dissatisfaction over its small farms policy and the thorny question of splinter groups in its ranks reappeared (*Farmers Guardian*, 29 January 1988). How well the union will be able to manage these conflicts remains to be seen, but the likelihood is that as the squeeze continues such outbreaks will become more frequent. This may, of course, open the way to the establishment of a united Welsh union and a decline in political centralisation.

On this second problem the FUW is in a slightly different position. The spread of its membership across sectors is much narrower, embracing mainly milk, sheep and beef farmers. Whilst there will undoubtedly be some tension here it is unlikely to place the FUW in too compromised a position. Furthermore, the FUW can more readily appeal to the socio-structural attributes of its membership. As one official explained:

> instead of saying he's a sheep farmer and he's a dairy farmer and, they have conflicting interests, we say 'look boys, we're all small farmers or we're all family farmers and our interests structurally and regionally are the same'. If the worst comes to the worst we can back it up with the nationalist argument that we're Welsh farmers. So we've always had a safety valve for that sort of tension. (Interview)

Traditionally, the strategy of the unions has been almost solely concerned with getting inside the policy process to ensure that their demands were fully integrated into the policy. This mode of operation may have run its course. The external pressures bearing upon the agricultural policy-making institutions suggest crucial changes in the whole direction of former power policy are underway. Although the unions may be able to gain limited modifications in these policies they will not be able to prevent them coming into force, as the introduction of milk quotas showed. It seems therefore that the unions are locked into a mode of representation from which they cannot escape but which ultimately may render them impotent. Their incorporation may serve merely to legitimise policies which weaken and marginalise Welsh farmers. As one of the leaders of the action group at the forefront of opposition to milk quotas commented in reference to agricultural policy reform:

> all this kind of thing is a convenient blind alley, it can fit into the overal plan to get those of us who are left down here to be a' 'reservation', a nice sort of tourist attraction. It's precisely because of that that we're carrying the battle on. We want to maintain a thriving broad based agricultural industry here in Wales. There's a damn sight more at stake than a few farmers going bust ... You cut back the agricultural industry and you've literally destroyed whole communities in Wales. (Interview)

### Conclusion: institutional practice and regional development

The struggle to represent Wales within the British state has made some headway in the agricultural policy sphere. However, Welsh agriculture has come under the aegis of a centrally formulated policy, first in London and latterly in Brussels, which has done little to accommodate regional differentiation. The political pressure for more autonomy led to the creation of an independent Welsh farmers union and a Welsh agricultural department.

The WOAD and the unions together establish a view of Welsh agricultural needs. This has not, however, resulted in the formulation of a specifically Welsh agricultural policy, tailored to the particular needs of the region's farmers, but in a list of demands to be negotiated at the centre. The WOAD stands at the interface between the central state and Welsh agricultural interest groups. It acts not only as the voice of the centre in Wales but also as the voice of Wales at the centre. It has sustained this dual role by carefully managing the kinds of demands being made upon it from within the region; the incorporations of the unions and their willingness to share a common perception of regional 'needs' allows this management process to proceed.

For the unions, their incorporation into the policy process is double-edged. When the policy outcomes are relatively benign in their effects then they are able to manage their dual role as the voice of the region with that of 'partners of the state'. Where policy outcomes are deeply unpopular, as during a period of decline in the agriculture sector, the unions find themselves in a compromised position. Despite such tensions, however, incorporation is addictive; groups accorded such status are unwilling to give it up even though the times change.

What this analysis points towards is the importance of an institutional analysis of regional development. Regions are represented by groups of actors working within sets of social relations. We can agree with Paasi that the state is central to the forging of the economic, political and administrative shape of the region. As we have seen above, social and political practices outside the state forced it to accommodate regional aspirations. However, these aspirations were then brought within the state's institutional framework and translated into policy-relevant demands which could be accommodated within the existing set of institutional practices. The articulation of quite different representations of the region became more difficult in a situation where, superficially at least, the state had gone some way towards accommodating regional demands.

This is one facet of regional development. Through the practices of representatives – of farmers, of the state, of rural communities, etc. – the region takes shape. However, what the above case study shows is that not all these practices have equal status. The institutional framework is an accommodation of regional aspirations within a centralised, spatially indifferent state structure. An analysis of such frameworks can show these 'allocate influence [and] . . . impose certain perceptions, responsibilities and interest on the actors [and] simultaneously limit their use of that influence' (Hall, 1986, p.265). These representatives, therefore, do not simply represent the region: they are forced to calculate, negotiate and compromise on what the region might be and what the region might need. These calculations, negotiations and compromises take place within institutional structures which reach into the region from the centre. These structures are designed to transplant regional representations back to the centre where they can be translated into 'manageable' demands, to be accommodated within the existing procedures of governance.

The regional shape, the 'material and "mental" spatial fix', in Paasi's words, is the outcome of complex social practices across the different fields of social life, not least concerning small-scale agriculture and its associated organisations. We can no longer portray the region as merely a 'backdrop' to these social practices. However, we must further problematise everything done in the name of the region. We must closely examine how the region or locality is represented, the sets of social relations surrounding these representations, and the circumstances of those ostensibly being represented.

### Notes

1. This chapter is based upon research conducted in Wales between 1984 and 1988. The author is grateful to the Economic and Social Research Council for funding this work and to Graham Day for his support and encouragement.

### References

Adamson, D. (1984) 'Social class and ethnicity in nineteenth century Wales', *Sociologica Ruralis*, Vol.23, Nos.3/4, pp.202–16.

Allen, G. (1959) 'The NFU as a pressure group', *Contemporary Review*, May/June, pp.265–332.

Arton Wilson Committee (1956) *Report of the Committee to Review the Provincial and Local Organisation and Procedures of the MAFF*. London, HMSO.

Ashby, A. and Evans, H. (1944) *The Agriculture of Wales and Monmouthshire*. Cardiff, University of Wales Press.

Beresford, T. (1975) *We Plough the Fields*. Harmondsworth, Penguin.

Bowers, J. (1985) 'British agricultural policy since the Second World War', *Agricultural History Review*, Vol.33, No.1, pp.66–77.

Committee for Welsh Affairs (1981) Minutes of Evidence, Wednesday 29 April, Welsh Office Agriculture Department, London, HMSO.

Cooke, P. (1986) *Global Restructuring, Local Response*. London, Economic and Social Research Council.

Cooke, P. (1989) 'Locality, economic restructuring and world development', in P. Cooke (ed) *Localities*. London, Allen and Unwin.

Council for Wales (1957) Third memorandum, Cmd 53, London, HMSO.

Cox, G., Lowe, P. and Winter, M. (1986a) 'The state and the farmer: perspectives on agricultural policy', in G. Cox, P. Lowe and M. Winter (eds) *Agriculture: people and policies*. London, Allen and Unwin.

Cox, G., Lowe, P. and Winter, M. (1986b) 'From state direction to self regulation: the historical development of corporatism in British agriculture', *Policy and Politics*, Vol.14, No.4, pp.475–90.

Day, G. (1984) 'Development and national consciousness: the Welsh case', in H. Vermeulen and J. Boissevin (eds) *Ethnic Challange: the politics of ethnicity in Europe*, Gottingen, Edition Herodot.

Day, G., Rees, G. and Murdoch, J. (1989) 'Social change, rural localities and the state: the restructuring in rural Wales', *Journal of Rural Studies*, Vol.5, No.3, pp.227–44.

Duncan, S. and Savage, M. (1991) 'Commentary', *Environment and Planning A* Vol.23, pp.155–64.

FUW (1958) A Statement of Policy for the Farmers of Wales, Aberystwyth, FUW.

FUW (1975) Price Review Memorandum, Aberystwyth, FUW.

Giddens, A. (1984) *The Constitution of Society*. Cambridge, Polity.

Gilbert, A. (1988) 'The new regional geography in English and French and French-speaking countries', in *Progress in Human Geography*, Vol.12, pp.208–28.

Grant, W. (1983) 'The NFU: the classic case of incorporation', in D. Marsh (ed) *Pressure Politics*. London, Junction.

Greenwood, J. and Wilson, D. (1984) *Public Administration in Britain*. Hemel Hempstead, Allen and Unwin.

Hall, P. (1986) *Governing the Economy: the politics of state intervention in Britain and France*. Cambridge, Polity.

Howell, D. (1977) *Land and People in Nineteenth Century Wales*. London, Routledge and Kegan Paul.

Jordan, A. and Richardson, J. (1987) *Government and Pressure Groups in Britain*. Oxford, Clarendon.

Kellas, J. and Madgewick, P. (1982) 'Territorial ministers: the Scottish and Welsh Offices, in P. Madgewick and P. Rose (eds) *The Territorial Dimension in UK Politics*. London, Macmillan.

Morgan, K. (1963) *Wales in British Politics, 1868–1922*. Cardiff, University of Wales Press.

Murdoch, J. (1988) 'State and agriculture in rural Wales', unpublished Ph.D thesis, University College of Wales, Aberystwyth.

Murphy, A. (1991) 'Regions as social constructs: the gap between theory and practice', *Progress in Human Geography*, Vol.15, No.1, pp.22–35.

NFU (1927) Undeb Cenedlaethol yr Amaethwyr, London, NFU.

Osmond, J. (1977) *Creative Conflict*. Llandysul, Gower.

Paasi, A. (1986) 'The institutionalisation of regions: a theoretical framework for understanding the emergence of regions and the constitution of regional identity', *Fennia*, Vol.164, pp.105–46.

Paasi, A. (1991) 'Deconstructing regions: notes on the scales of spatial life', *Environment and Planning A*, Vol.23, pp.239–56.

Randall, P. (1972) 'Wales in the structure of central government', *Public Administration*, Vol.50, pp.353–73.

Rowlands, E. (1972) 'The politics of regional administration: the establishment of the Welsh Office', *Public Administration*, Vol.50, pp.333–53.

Ryan Committee (1951) Report of the Committee Appointed to Review the Organisation of the Ministry of Agriculture, Fisheries and Food, London, HMSO.

Sayer, A. (1989) 'The 'new' regional geography and problems of narrative', *Environment and Planning D*, Vol.7, pp.253–76.

Self, P. and Storing, M. (1958) 'Farmers and the state', *Political Quarterly*, Vol.29, pp.17–27.

Tracy, M. (1982) *Agriculture in Western Europe: challenge and responses 1880–1980*. St Albans, Granada.

Triglia, C. (1991) 'The paradox of the region: economic regulation and the representation of interests', *Economy and Society*, Vol.30, No.3, pp.306–27.

Urry, J. (1984) 'Capitalist restructuring, recomposition and the regions', in T. Bradley and P. Lowe (eds) *Locality and Rurality: economy and society in rural regions*. Norwich, Geo Books.

Vielle, P. (1988) 'The state of the periphery and its heritage', *Economy and Society*, Vol.17, No.1, pp.55–90.

Williams, L.J. (1983) 'The economic structure of Wales since 1859', in G. Williams (ed) *Crisis of Economy and Ideology: essays on Welsh society, 1840–1980*. Bangor, BSA.

Williams, L.J. (1985) *Welsh Historical Statistics* (two volumes). Cardiff, Welsh Office.

Williams, C. and Smith, A. (1983) 'The national construction of social space, *Progress in Human Geography*, Vol.7, pp.502–18.

Wormell, P. (1978) *Anatomy of Agriculture*. London, Harrap.

# Index

For Product Safety Concerns and Information please contact our EU
representative  GPSR@taylorandfrancis.com
Taylor & Francis Verlag GmbH, Kaufingerstraße 24, 80331 München, Germany